ANARCHY WORKS

Examples of Anarchist Ideas in Practice

DETRITUS BOOKS
olympia, wa

ORIGINALLY PUBLISHED BY ARDENT PRESS IN 2010

This edition published in the USA by Detritus Books, 2025.

This work is licensed under the Creative Commons Attribution-NonCommercial-ShareAlike 4.0 International (CC BY-NC-SA 4.0) creativecommons.org

DETRITUS BOOKS
PO BOX 6171
OLYMPIA, WA 98507
detritusbooks.com

Detritus Books ISBN: 978-1-948501-34-7

Distributed by AK Press

Printed in Canada

10 9 8 7 6 5 4 3 2 1

No more talk about the old days, it's time for something great.

I want you to get out and make it work...

—Thom Yorke

Dedicated to the wonderful people of RuinAmalia, La Revoltosa, and the Kyiv infoshop, for making anarchy work.

ALTHOUGH THIS BOOK STARTED OUT AS AN INDIVIDUAL PROJECT, in the end a great many people, most of whom prefer to remain anonymous, helped make it possible through proofreading, fact-checking, recommending sources, editing, and more. To acknowledge only a small part of this help, the author would like to thank John, Jose, Vila Kula, aaaa!, L, J, and G for providing computer access throughout a year of moves, evictions, crashes, viruses, and so forth. Thanks to Jessie Dodson and Katie Clark for helping with the research on another project, that I ended up using for this book. Also thanks to C and E, for lending their passwords for free access to the databases of scholarly articles available to university students but not to the rest of us.

> There are hidden stories all around us,
> growing in abandoned villages in the mountains
> or vacant lots in the city,
> petrifying beneath our feet in the remains
> of societies like nothing we've known,
> whispering to us that things could be different.
> But the politician you know is lying to you,

the manager who hires and fires you,
the landlord who evicts you,
the president of the bank that owns your house,
the professor who grades your papers,
the cop who rolls your street,
the reporter who informs you,
the doctor who medicates you,
the husband who beats you,
the mother who spanks you,
the soldier who kills for you,
and the social worker who fits your past and future into
 a folder in a filing cabinet
all ask
"WHAT WOULD YOU DO WITHOUT US?
It would be anarchy."

And the daughter who runs away from home,
the bus driver on the picket line,
the veteran who threw back his medal but holds on to
 his rifle,
the boy saved from suicide by the love of his friends,
the maid who must bow to those who can't even cook
 for themselves,
the immigrant hiking across a desert to find her family
 on the other side,
the kid on his way to prison because he burned down a
 shopping mall they were building over his childhood
 dreams,
the neighbor who cleans up the syringes from the vacant
 lot, hoping someone will turn it into a garden,
the hitchhiker on the open road,
the college dropout who gave up on career and health
 insurance and sometimes even food so he could write
 revolutionary poetry for the world,
maybe all of us can feel it:
our bosses and tormentors are afraid of what they would
 do without us,
and their threat is a promise—
the best parts of our lives are anarchy already.

INTRODUCTION

Anarchy would never work | 9
What exactly is anarchism? | 14
A note on inspiration | 22
The tricky topic of representation | 35

1. HUMAN NATURE

Aren't people naturally selfish? | 3
Aren't people naturally competitive? | 8
Haven't humans always been patriarchal? | 33
Aren't people naturally warlike? | 38
Aren't domination and authority natural? | 43
A broader sense of self | 54

2. DECISIONS

How will decisions be made? | 59
How will decisions be enforced? | 75
Who will settle disputes? | 79
Meeting in the streets | 81

3. ECONOMY

Without wages, what is the incentive to work? | 85
Don't people need bosses and experts? | 90
Who will take out the trash? | 98
Who will take care of the elderly and disabled? | 99
How will people get healthcare? | 101
What about education? | 103
What about technology? | 108
How will exchange work? | 114
What about people who still want a consumerist lifestyle? | 116
What about building and organizing large, spread-out infrastructure? | 118

How will cities work? | 123
What about drought, famine, or other catastrophes? | 131
Meeting our needs without keeping count | 133

4. ENVIRONMENT

What's to stop someone from destroying the environment? | 139
What about global environmental problems, like climate change? | 148
The only way to save the planet | 152

5. CRIME

Who will protect us without police? | 157
What about gangs and bullies? | 169
What's to stop someone from killing people? | 171
What about rape, domestic violence, and other forms of social harm? | 173
Beyond individual justice | 179

6. REVOLUTION

How could people organized horizontally possibly overcome the state? | 187
How do we know revolutionaries won't become new authorities? | 205
How will communities decide to organize themselves at first? | 218
How will reparations for past oppressions be worked out? | 223
How will a common, anti-authoritarian, ecological ethos come about? | 225
A revolution that is many revolutions | 236

7. NEIGHBORING SOCIETIES

Could an anarchist society defend itself from an authoritarian neighbor? | 241
What will we do about societies that remain very patriarchal, or racist? | 247
What will prevent constant warfare and feuding? | 249
Networks not borders | 255

8. THE FUTURE

Won't the state just re-emerge over time? | 259
What about other problems we can't foresee? | 263
Making anarchy work | 264

IT WORKS WHEN WE MAKE IT WORK

267

BIBLIOGRAPHY

271

INTRODUCTION

Anarchy Would Never Work

ANARCHISM IS THE BOLDEST OF REVOLUTIONARY SOCIAL MOVEments to emerge from the struggle against capitalism—it aims for a world free from all forms of domination and exploitation. But at its heart is a simple and convincing proposition: people know how to live their own lives and organize themselves better than any expert could. Others cynically claim that people do not know what is in their best interests, that they need a government to protect them, that the ascension of some political party could somehow secure the interests of all members of society. Anarchists counter that decision-making should not be centralized in the hands of any government, but instead power should be decentralized: that is to say, each person should be the center of society, and all should be free to build the networks and associations they need to meet their needs in common with others.

The education we receive in state-run schools teaches us to doubt our ability to organize ourselves. This leads many to conclude anarchy is impractical and utopian: it would never work. On the contrary, anarchist practice already has a long record, and has often worked quite well. The official history books tell a selective story, glossing over the fact that all the components of an anarchist society have existed at various times, and innumerable stateless societies have thrived for millennia.

How would an anarchist society compare to statist and capitalist societies? It is apparent that hierarchical societies work well according to certain criteria. They tend to be extremely effective at conquering their neighbors and securing vast fortunes for their rulers. On the other hand, as climate change, food and water shortages, market instability, and other global crises intensify, hierarchical models are not proving to be particularly sustainable. The histories in this book show that an anarchist society can do much better at enabling all its members to meet their needs and desires.

The many stories, past and present, that demonstrate how anarchy works have been suppressed and distorted because of the revolutionary conclusions we might draw from them. We can live in a society with no bosses, masters, politicians, or bureaucrats; a society with no judges, no police, and no criminals, no rich or poor; a society free of sexism, homophobia, and transphobia; a society in which the wounds from centuries of enslavement, colonialism, and genocide are finally allowed to heal. The only things stopping us are the prisons, programming, and paychecks of the powerful, as well as our own lack of faith in ourselves.

Of course, anarchists do not have to be practical to a fault. If we ever win the freedom to run our own lives, we'll probably come up with entirely new approaches to organization that improve on these tried and true forms. So let these stories be a starting point, and a challenge.

What exactly is anarchism?

VOLUMES HAVE BEEN WRITTEN IN ANSWER TO THIS QUESTION, AND millions of people have dedicated their lives to creating, expanding, defining, and fighting for anarchy. There are countless paths to anarchism and countless beginnings: workers in 19th century Europe fighting against capitalism and believing in themselves instead of the ideologies of authoritarian political parties; indigenous peoples fighting colonization and reclaiming their traditional, horizontal cultures; high school students waking up to the depth of their alienation and unhappiness; mystics from China one thousand years ago or from Europe five hundred years ago, Daoists or Anabaptists, fighting against government and organized religion; women rebelling against the authoritarianism and sexism of the Left. There is no Central Committee giving out membership cards, and no standard doctrine. Anarchy means different things to different people. However, here are some basic principles most anarchists agree on.

AUTONOMY AND HORIZONTALITY: All people deserve the freedom to define and organize themselves on their own terms. Decision-making structures should be horizontal rather than vertical, so no one dominates anyone else; they should foster power to act freely rather than power over others. Anarchism opposes all coercive hierarchies, including capitalism, the state, white supremacy, and patriarchy.

MUTUAL AID: People should help one another voluntarily; bonds of solidarity and generosity form a stronger social glue than the fear inspired by laws, borders, prisons, and armies. Mutual aid is neither a form of charity nor of zero-sum exchange; both giver and receiver are equal and interchangeable. Since neither holds power over the other, they increase their collective power by creating opportunities to work together.

VOLUNTARY ASSOCIATION: People should be free to cooperate with whomever they want, however they see fit; likewise, they should be free to refuse any relationship or arrangement they do not judge to be in their interest. Everyone should be able to move freely, both physically and socially. Anarchists oppose borders of all kinds and involuntary categorization by citizenship, gender, or race.

DIRECT ACTION: It is more empowering and effective to accomplish goals directly than to rely on authorities or representatives. Free people do not request the changes they want to see in the world; they make those changes.

REVOLUTION: Today's entrenched systems of repression cannot be reformed away. Those who hold power in a hierarchical system are the ones who institute reforms, and they generally do so in ways that preserve or even amplify their power. Systems like capitalism and white supremacy are forms of warfare waged by elites; anarchist revolution means fighting to overthrow these elites in order to create a free society.

SELF-LIBERATION: "The liberation of the workers is the duty of the workers themselves," as the old slogan goes. This applies to other groups as well: people must be at the forefront of their own liberation. Freedom cannot be given; it must be taken.

A note on inspiration

PLURALISM AND FREEDOM ARE NOT COMPATIBLE WITH ORTHODOX ideologies. The historical examples of anarchy do not have to be explicitly anarchist. Most of the societies and organizations that have successfully lived free of government have not called themselves "anarchist"; that term originated in Europe in the 19th century, and anarchism as a self-conscious social movement is not nearly as universal as the desire for freedom.

It is presumptuous to assign the label "anarchist" to people who have not chosen it; instead, we can use a range of other terms to describe examples of anarchy in practice. "Anarchy" is a social situation free of government and coercive hierarchies held together by self-organized horizontal relationships; "anarchists" are people who identify themselves with the social movement or philosophy of anarchism. Anti-authoritarians are people who expressly want to live in a society without coercive hierarchies, but do not, to the best of our knowledge, identify as anarchists—either because the term was not available to them or because they do not see the specifically anarchist movement as relevant to their world. After all, the anarchist movement as such emerged from Europe and it inherited a worldview in accordance with this background; meanwhile there are many other struggles against authority that spring from different worldviews and have no need to call themselves "anarchist." A society that exists without a state, but does not identify itself as anarchist, is "stateless"; if that society is not stateless by chance, but consciously works to prevent the emergence of hierarchies and identifies with its egalitarian characteristics, one might describe it as "anarchistic."[1]

The examples in this book have been selected from a wide range of times and places—about ninety altogether. Thirty are explicitly anarchist; the rest are all stateless, autonomous, or consciously anti-authoritarian. More than half of the examples are from present-day Western society, a third are drawn from stateless societies that provide a view of the breadth of human possibility outside of Western civilization, and the remaining few are classical historical examples. Some of these, such as the Spanish Civil War, are cited multiple times because they are well documented and offer a wealth of information. The number of examples included makes it impossible to explore each one in the detail it deserves. Ideally the reader will be inspired to pursue these questions herself, distilling further practical lessons from the attempts of those who came before.

It will become apparent throughout this book that anarchy exists in conflict with the state and capitalism. Many of the examples given here were ultimately crushed by police or conquering armies, and it is in large part due to this systematic repression of alternatives that there have not been more examples of anarchy working. This bloody history implies that, to be thoroughgoing and successful, an anarchist revolution would have to be global. Capitalism is a global system, constantly expanding and colonizing every autonomous society it encounters. In the long run, no one community or country can remain anarchist while the rest of the world is capitalist. An anti-capitalist revolution must destroy

1   Sam Mbah and I.E. Igariway write that before colonial contact nearly all traditional African societies were "anarchies," and they make a strong argument to this effect. The same could also be said of other continents. But as the author does not come from any of these societies, and since Western culture traditionally believes it has the right to represent other societies in self-serving ways, it is best to avoid such broad characterizations, while still endeavoring to learn from these examples.

capitalism totally, or else be destroyed. This does not mean that anarchism must be a single global system. Many different forms of anarchist society could coexist, and these in turn could coexist with societies that were not anarchist, so long as the latter were not confrontationally authoritarian or oppressive. The following pages will show the great diversity of forms anarchy and autonomy can take.

The examples in this book show anarchy working for a period of time, or succeeding in a specific way. Until capitalism is abolished, all such examples will necessarily be partial. These examples are instructive in their weaknesses as well as their strengths. In addition to providing a picture of people creating communities and meeting their needs without bosses, they raise the question of what went wrong and how we could do better next time.

To this end, here are some recurring themes that may be beneficial to reflect on in the course of reading this book:

ISOLATION: Many anarchist projects work quite well, but only make an impact in the lives of a tiny number of people. What engenders this isolation? What tends to contribute to it, and what can offset it?

ALLIANCES: In a number of examples, anarchists and other anti-authoritarians were betrayed by supposed allies who sabotaged the possibility of liberation in order to gain power for themselves. Why did anarchists choose these alliances, and what can we learn about what kind of alliances to make today?

REPRESSION: Autonomous communities and revolutionary activities have been stopped cold by police repression or military invasion time after time. People are intimidated, arrested, tortured, and killed, and the survivors must go into hiding or drop out of the struggle; communities that had once provided support withdraw in order to protect themselves. What actions, strategies, and forms of organization best equip people to survive repression? How can those on the outside provide effective solidarity?

COLLABORATION: Some social movements or radical projects choose to participate in or accommodate themselves to aspects of the present system in order to overcome isolation, be accessible to a greater range of people, or avoid repression. What are the advantages and pitfalls of this approach? Are there ways to overcome isolation or avoid repression without it?

TEMPORARY GAIN: Many of the examples in this book no longer exist. Of course, anarchists are not trying to create permanent institutions that take on lives of their own; specific organizations should come to an end when they are no longer helpful. Realizing that, how can we make the most of bubbles of autonomy while they last, and how can they continue to inform us after they have ceased to be? How can a series of temporary spaces and events be linked to create a continuity of struggle and community?

The tricky topic of representation

IN AS MANY CASES AS WAS POSSIBLE, WE SOUGHT DIRECT FEEDBACK from people with personal experience in the struggles and communities described in this book. With some examples this was impossible, due to unnavigable chasms of distance or time. In these cases we had to rely exclusively on written representations, generally recorded by outside observers. But representation is not at all a neutral process, and outside observers project their own values and experiences onto what they are observing. Of course, representation is an inevitable activity in human discourse, and moreover outside observers can contribute new and useful perspectives.

However, our world is not that simple. As European civilization spread and dominated the rest of the planet, the observers it sent out were generally the surveyors, missionaries, writers, and scientists of the ruling order. On a world scale, this civilization is the only one with the right to interpret itself and all other cultures. Western systems of thought were forcibly spread around the world. Colonized societies were cut up and exploited as slave labor, economic resources, and ideological capital. Non-Western peoples were represented back to the West in ways that would confirm the Western worldview and sense of superiority, and justify the ongoing imperial project as necessary for the good of the peoples being forcibly civilized.

As anarchists trying to abolish the power structure responsible for colonialism and many other wrongs, we want to approach these other cultures in good faith, in order to learn from them, but if we're not careful we could easily fall into the accustomed eurocentric pattern of manipulating and exploiting these other cultures for our own ideological capital. In cases where we could find no one from the community in question to review and criticize our own interpretations, we have tried to situate the storyteller in the telling, to subvert his or her objectivity and invisibility, to deliberately challenge the validity of our own information, and to propose representations that are flexible and humble. We don't know exactly how to accomplish this balancing act, but our hope is to learn while trying.

Some indigenous people whom we consider comrades in the struggle against authority feel that white people have no right to represent indigenous cultures, and this position is especially justified given that for five hundred years, Euro/American representations of indigenous peoples have been self-serving, exploitative, and connected to ongoing processes of genocide and colonization. On the other hand, part of our goal in publishing this book has been to challenge the historical eurocentrism of the anarchist movement and encourage ourselves to be open to other cultures. We could not do this by only presenting stories of statelessness from our own culture. The author and most of the people working on this book in an editorial capacity are white, and it is no surprise that what we write reflects our backgrounds. In fact, the central question this book seeks to address, whether anarchy could work, seems itself to be eurocentric. Only a people who have obliterated the memory of their own stateless past could ask themselves whether they need the state. We recognize that not everyone shares this historical blindspot and that what we publish here may not be useful for people from other backgrounds. But we hope that by telling stories of the cultures and struggles of other societies, we can help correct the eurocentrism endemic to some of our communities and become better allies, and better listeners, whenever people from other cultures choose to tell us their own stories.

Someone who read over this text pointed out to us that reciprocity is a fundamental value of indigenous worldviews. The question he posed to us was, if anarchists who are mostly Euro/American are going to take lessons from indigenous or other communities, cultures, and nations, what will we offer in return? I hope that wherever possible, we offer solidarity—widening the struggle and supporting other peoples who struggle against authority without calling themselves anarchists. After all, if we are inspired by certain other societies, shouldn't we do more to recognize and aid their ongoing struggles?

Linda Tuhiwai Smith's book *Decolonizing Methodologies: Research and Indigenous Peoples* (London: Zed Books, 1999) offers an important perspective on some of these themes.

Recommended Reading

- Errico Malatesta, *At the Cafe: Conversations on Anarchism*. London: Freedom Press, 2005.
- The Dark Star Collective, *Quiet Rumours: An Anarcha-Feminist Reader*. Oakland: AK Press, 2002.
- CrimethInc., *Days of War, Nights of Love*. CrimethInc. 2002.
- Daniel Guerin, *Anarchism: From Theory to Practice*. New York: Monthly Review, 1996.
- bell hooks, *Ain't I a Woman? Black women and feminism*. Boston: South End Press, 1981.
- Mitchell Verter and Chaz Bufe, eds. *Dreams of Freedom: A Ricardo Flores Magon Reader*. Oakland: AK Press, 2005.
- Vine Deloria, Jr. *Custer Died for Your Sins: an Indian Manifesto*. New York: Macmillan, 1969.
- Ward Churchill, *From a Native Son: Selected Essays on Indigenism 1985–1995*, Cambridge: South End Press, 1999; or his interview on Indigenism and Anarchism in the journal *Upping the Anti*.

1. HUMAN NATURE

ANARCHISM CHALLENGES THE TYPICAL WESTERN CONCEPTION of human nature by envisioning societies built on cooperation, mutual aid, and solidarity between people, rather than competition and survival of the fittest.

Aren't people naturally selfish?

EVERYBODY HAS A SENSE OF SELF-INTEREST, AND THE CAPABILITY to act in a selfish way at other people's expense. But everyone also has a sense of the needs of those around them, and we are all capable of generous and selfless actions. Human survival depends on generosity. The next time someone tells you a communal, anarchistic society could not work because people are naturally selfish, tell him he should withhold food from his children pending payment, do nothing to help his parents have a dignified retirement, never donate to charities, and never help his neighbors or be kind to strangers unless he receives compensation. Would he be able to lead a fulfilling existence, taking the capitalist philosophy to its logical conclusions? Of course not. Even after hundreds of years of being suppressed, sharing and generosity remain vital to human existence. You don't have to look to radical social movements to find examples of this. The United States may be, on a structural level, the most selfish nation in the world—it is the richest of "developed" countries, but has among the lowest life expectancies because the political culture would sooner let poor people die than give them healthcare and welfare. But even in the US it's easy to find institutional examples of sharing that form an important part of the society. Libraries offer an interconnected network of millions of free books. PTA potlucks and neighborhood barbecues bring people together to share food and enjoy each other's company. What examples of sharing might develop outside the restrictive bounds of state and capital?

Currency-based economies have only existed a few thousand years, and capitalism has only been around a few hundred years. The latter has proven to work quite miserably, leading to the greatest inequalities of wealth, the largest mass starvations, and the worst distribution systems in world history—though hats off, it's produced a lot of wonderful gadgets. It might surprise people to learn how common other types of economies have been in earlier times, and how much they differed from capitalism.

One economy developed over and over by humans on every continent has been the gift economy. In this system, if people have more than they need of anything, they give it away. They don't assign value, they don't count debts. Everything you don't use personally can be given as a gift to someone else, and by giving more gifts you inspire more generosity and strengthen the friendships that keep you swimming in gifts too. Many gift economies lasted for thousands of years, and proved much more effective at enabling all of the participants to meet their needs. Capitalism may have drastically increased productivity, but to what end? On one side of your typical capitalist city someone is starving to death while on the other side someone is eating caviar.

Western economists and political scientists initially assumed that many of these gift economies were actually barter economies: proto-capitalist exchange systems lacking an efficient currency: "I'll give you one sheep for twenty loaves of bread." In general, this is not how these societies described themselves. Later, anthropologists who went to live in such societies and were able to shed their cultural biases showed people in Europe that many of these were indeed gift economies, in which people intentionally kept no tally of who owed what to whom so as to foster a society of generosity and sharing.

What these anthropologists may not have known is that gift economies have never been totally suppressed in the West; in fact they surfaced frequently within rebellious movements. Anarchists in the US today also exemplify the desire for relationships based on generosity and the guarantee that everyone's needs will be met. In a number of towns and cities, anarchists hold Really Really Free Markets—essentially, flea markets without prices. People bring goods they have made or things they don't need anymore and give them away for free to passersby or other participants. Or, they share useful skills with one another. In one free market in North Carolina, every month:

> two hundred or more people from all walks of life gather at the commons in the center of our town. They bring everything from jewelry to firewood to give away, and take whatever they want. There are booths offering bicycle repair, hairstyling, even tarot readings. People leave with full-size bed frames and old computers; if they don't have a vehicle to transport them, volunteer drivers are available. No money changes hands, no one haggles over the comparative worth of items or services, nobody is ashamed about being in need. Contrary to government ordinances, no fee is paid for the use of this public space, nor is anyone "in charge." Sometimes a marching band appears; sometimes a puppetry troupe performs, or people line up to take a swing at a piñata. Games and conversations take place around the periphery, and everyone has a plate of warm food and a bag of free groceries. Banners hang from branches and rafters proclaiming "FOR THE COMMONS, NOT LANDLORDS OR BUREAUCRACY" and "NI JEFES, NI FRONTERAS" and a king-size blanket is spread with radical reading material, but these aren't essential to the event—this is a social institution, not a demonstration.
>
> Thanks to our monthly 'Free Markets, everyone in our town has a working reference point for anarchist economics. Life is a little easier for those of us with low or no

income, and relationships develop in a space in which social class and financial means are at least temporarily irrelevant.[2]

The traditional society of the Semai, in Malaya, is based on gift-giving rather than bartering. We could not find any accounts of their society recorded by the Semai themselves, but they explained how it worked to Robert Dentan, a Western anthropologist who lived with them for a time. Dentan writes that the "system by which the Semai distribute food and services is one of the most significant ways in which members of a community are knit together... Semai economic exchanges are more like Christmas exchanges than like commercial exchanges."[3] It was considered "punan," or taboo, for members of Semai society to calculate the value of gifts given or received. Other commonly held rules of etiquette included the duty to share whatever they had that they did not immediately need, and the duty to share with guests and anyone who asked. It was punan not to share or to refuse a request, but also to ask for more than someone could give.

Many other societies have also distributed and exchanged surpluses as gifts. Aside from the social cohesion and joy that is gained from sharing with your community without greedily keeping accounts, a gift economy can also be justified in terms of personal interests. Often, a person cannot consume what they produce all by themselves. The meat from a day's hunt will go bad before you can eat it all. A tool, like a saw, will lay unused most of the time if it is the property of a single person. It makes more sense to give away most of the meat or share your saw with your neighbors, because you are ensuring that in the future they will give extra food to you and share their tools with you—thus ensuring that you have access to more food and a wider range of tools, and you and your neighbors become richer without having to exploit anybody.

---

2   "The Really Really Free Market: Instituting the Gift Economy," *Rolling Thunder*, No. 4 Spring 2007, p. 34.
3   Robert K. Dentan, *The Semai: A Nonviolent People of Malaya*. New York: Holt, Rinehart and Winston, 1979, p. 48.

From what we know, however, members of gift economies would probably not justify their actions with arguments of calculated self-interest, but with moral reasoning, explaining sharing as the right thing to do. After all, an economic surplus is the result of a certain way of looking at the world: it is a social choice and not a material certainty. Societies must choose, over time, to work more than they need to, to quantify value, or to only consume the minimum required for their survival and to surrender all the rest of their produce to a common storehouse controlled by a class of leaders. Even if a hunting party or a group of gatherers gets lucky and brings home a huge amount of food, there is no surplus if they consider it normal to share it with everyone else, glut themselves with a big feast, or invite a neighboring community to party until all the food is eaten. It's certainly more fun that way than measuring out pounds of food and calculating what percentage we earned.

As for loafers, even if people do not calculate the value of gifts and keep a balance sheet, they will notice if someone consistently refuses to share or contribute to the group, violating the customs of the society and the sense of mutual aid. Gradually, such people will damage their relationships, and miss out on some of the nicer benefits of living in a society. It seems that in all known gift economies, even the laziest of people were never refused food—in stark contrast to capitalism—but feeding a few loafers is an insignificant drain on a society's resources, especially when compared to pampering the voracious elite of our society. And losing this tiny amount of resources is far preferable to losing our compassion and letting people starve to death. In more extreme cases, if members of such a society were more aggressively parasitic, attempting to monopolize resources or force other people to work for them—in other words, acting like capitalists—they could be ostracized and even expelled from the society.

Some stateless societies have chiefs who play ritual roles, often related to giving gifts and spreading resources. In fact, the term "chief" can be deceptive because there have been so many different human societies that have had what the West classifies as "chiefs," and in each society the role entailed something a little different. In many societies chiefs held no coercive power: their responsibility was to mediate disputes or conduct rituals, and they were expected to be more generous than anyone else. Ultimately they worked harder and had less personal wealth than others. One study found that a common reason for the people to depose or expel a chief was if the chief was not considered generous enough.[4]

Aren't people naturally competitive?

IN WESTERN SOCIETY, COMPETITION IS SO NORMALIZED IT'S NO wonder we consider it the natural mode of human relations. From youth, we're taught that we have to be better than everyone else to be worth anything ourselves. Corporations justify firing workers, depriving them of sustenance and healthcare, so the company can "stay competitive." Fortunately, it does not have to be this way. Industrial capitalism is only one of thousands of forms of social organization humans have developed, and with any luck it won't be the last. Obviously, humans are capable of competitive behavior, but it's not hard to see how much our society encourages this and suppresses cooperative behavior. Countless societies throughout the world have developed cooperative forms of living that contrast greatly with the norms at work under capitalism. By now, nearly all of these societies have been integrated into the capitalist system through colonialism, slavery, warfare, or habitat destruction, but a number of accounts remain to document the great diversity of societies that have existed.

The Mbuti hunter-gatherers of the Ituri Forest in central Africa have traditionally lived without government. Accounts by ancient historians suggest the forest-dwellers have lived as stateless hunter-gatherers during the time of the Egyptian pharoahs, and according to the Mbuti themselves they have always lived that way. Contrary to common portrayals by outsiders, groups like the Mbuti are not isolated or primordial. In fact they have frequent interactions with the sedentary Bantu peoples surrounding

---

4 Christopher Boehm, "Egalitarian Behavior and Reverse Dominance Hierarchy," *Current Anthropology*, Vol. 34, No. 3, June 1993.

the forest, and they have had plenty of opportunities to see what supposedly advanced societies are like. Going back at least hundreds of years, Mbuti have developed relationships of exchange and gift-giving with neighboring farmers, while retaining their identity as "the children of the forest."

Today several thousand Mbuti still live in the Ituri Forest and negotiate dynamic relationships with the changing world of the villagers, while fighting to preserve their traditional way of life. Many other Mbuti live in settlements along the new roads. Coltan mining for cell phones is a chief financial incentive for the civil war and the habitat destruction that is ravaging the region and killing hundreds of thousands of inhabitants. The governments of Congo, Rwanda, and Uganda all want to control this billion dollar industry, that produces primarily for the US and Europe, while miners seeking employment come from all over Africa to set up camp in the region. The deforestation, population boom, and increase in hunting to provide bush meat for the soldiers and miners have depleted local wildlife. Lacking food and competing for territorial control, soldiers and miners have taken to carrying out atrocities, including cannibalism, against the Mbuti. Some Mbuti are currently demanding an international tribunal against cannibalism and other violations.

Europeans travelling through central Africa during their colonization of that continent imposed their own moral framework on the Mbuti. Because they only encountered the Mbuti in the villages of the Bantu farmers surrounding the Ituri forest, they assumed the Mbuti were a primitive servant class. In the 1950s, the Mbuti invited Western anthropologist Colin Turnbull to live with them in the forest. They tolerated his rude and ignorant questions, and took the time to teach him about their culture. The stories he recounts describe a society far outside of what a Western worldview considers possible. Around the time that anthropologists, and subsequently, Western anarchists, began to argue about what the Mbuti "meant" for their respective theories, global economic institutions were elaborating a process of genocide that threatens to destroy the Mbuti as a people. Notwithstanding, various Western writers have already idealized or degraded the Mbuti to produce arguments for or against primitivism, veganism, feminism, and other political agendas.

Therefore, perhaps the most important lesson to take from the story of the Mbuti is not that anarchy—a cooperative, free, and relatively healthy society—is possible, but that free societies are not possible so long as governments try to crush any pocket of independence, corporations fund genocide in order to manufacture cell phones, and supposedly sympathetic people are more interested in writing ethnographies than fighting back.

In Turnbull's perspective, the Mbuti were resolutely egalitarian, and many of the ways they organized their society reduced competition and promoted cooperation between members. Gathering food was a community affair, and when they hunted often the whole band turned out. One half would beat the bush in the direction of the other half, who waited with nets to snare any animals that had been flushed out. A successful hunt was the result of everyone working together effectively, and the whole community shared in the catch.

Mbuti children were given a high degree of autonomy, and spent much of their days in a wing of the camp that was off-limits to adults. One game they frequently played involved a group of small children climbing up a young tree until their combined weight bent the tree towards the earth. Ideally, the children would let go all at once, and the supple tree would shoot upright. But if one child was not in synch and let go too late, the child would be launched through the trees and given a good scare. Such games teach group harmony over individual performance, and provide an early form of socialization into a culture of voluntary cooperation. The war games and individualized competition that characterize play in Western society provide a notably different form of socialization.

The Mbuti also discouraged competition or even excessive distinction between genders. They did not use gendered pronouns or familial words—e.g., instead of "son" they say "child," "sibling" instead of "sister"—except in the case of parents, in which there is a functional difference between one who gives birth or provides milk and one who provides other forms of care. An important ritual game played by adult Mbuti worked to undermine gender competition. As Turnbull describes it, the game began like a tug-of-war match, with the women pulling one end of a long rope or vine and the men pulling the other. But as soon as one side started to win, someone from that team would run to the other side, also symbolically changing their gender and becoming a member of the other group. By the end, the participants collapsed in a heap laughing, all having changed their genders multiple times. Neither side "won," but that seemed to be the point. Group harmony was restored.

The Mbuti traditionally viewed conflict or "noise" as a common problem and a threat to the harmony of the group. If the disputants could not resolve things on their own or with the help of friends, the entire band would hold an important ritual that often lasted all night long. Everyone gathered together to discuss, and if the problem still could not be solved, the youth, who often played the role of justice-seekers within their society, would sneak into the night and begin rampaging around the camp, blowing a horn that made a sound like an elephant, symbolizing how the problem threatened the existence of the whole band. For a particularly serious dispute that had disrupted the group's harmony, the youth might give extra expression to their frustration by crashing through camp itself, kicking out fires and knocking down houses. Meanwhile, the adults would sing a two-part harmony, building up a sense of cooperation and togetherness.

The Mbuti also underwent a sort of fission and fusion throughout the year. Often motivated by interpersonal conflicts, the band would break up into smaller, more intimate groups. People had the option to take space from one another rather than being forced by the larger community to suppress their problems. After travelling and living separately for a time, the smaller groups joined together again, once there had been time for conflicts to cool down. Eventually the whole band was reunited, and the process started over. It seems the Mbuti synchronized this social fluctuation with their economic activities, so their period of living together as an entire band coincided with the season in which the specific forms of gathering and hunting require the cooperation of a larger group. The period of small, disparate groups coincided with the time of the year when the foods were in season that were best harvested by small groups spread throughout the whole forest, and the period when the whole band came together corresponded with the season in which hunting and gathering activities were better accomplished by big groups working together.

Unfortunately for us, neither the economic, political, or social structures of Western society are conducive to cooperation. When our jobs and social status depend on outperforming our peers, with the "losers" being fired or ostracized without regard to how it hurts their dignity or their ability to feed themselves, it's not surprising that competitive behaviors come to outnumber cooperative behaviors. But the ability to live cooperatively is not lost to people who live under the destructive influences of state and capitalism. Social cooperation is not restricted to societies like the Mbuti who inhabit one of the few remaining pockets of autonomy in the world. Living cooperatively is a possibility for all of us right now.

Earlier this decade, in one of the most individualistic and competitive societies in human history, state authority collapsed for a time in one city. Yet in this period of catastrophe, with hundreds of people dying and resources necessary for survival sorely limited, strangers came together to assist one another in a spirit of mutual aid. The city in question is New Orleans, after Hurricane Katrina struck in 2005. Initially, the corporate media spread racist stories of savagery committed by the mostly black survivors, and police and national guard troops performing heroic rescues while fighting off roving bands of looters. It was later admitted that these stories were false. In fact, the vast majority of rescues were carried out not by police and professionals, but by common New Orleans residents, often in defiance of the orders of authorities.[5] The police, meanwhile, were murdering people who were salvaging drinking

---

5 Amy Goodman, "Louisiana Official: Federal Gov't Abandoned New Orleans," *Democracy Now*, September 7, 2005. *Fox News*, *CNN*, and *The New York Times* all falsely reported murders and roving gangs of rapists in the Superdome, where refugees gathered during the storm. (Aaron Kinney, "Hurricane Horror Stories," Salon.com)

water, diapers, and other living supplies from abandoned grocery stores, supplies that would otherwise have been ultimately thrown away because contamination from floodwaters had made them unsalable.

New Orleans is not atypical: everyone can learn cooperative behaviors when they have the need or desire to do so. Sociological studies have found that in nearly all natural disasters, cooperation and solidarity among people increase, and it is common people, not governments, who voluntarily do most of the work carrying out rescues and protecting one another throughout the crisis.[6]

Haven't humans always been patriarchal?

ONE OF THE MOST ANCIENT FORMS OF OPPRESSION AND HIERARCHY is patriarchy: the division of humans into two rigid gender roles and the domination of men over women. But patriarchy is not natural or universal. Many societies have had more than two gender categories, and have allowed their members to change gender. Some even created respected spiritual roles for those who did not fit into either of the primary genders. The majority of prehistoric art depicts people who are either of no determinate gender or people with ambiguous, exaggerated combinations of masculine and feminine traits. In such societies, gender was fluid. It was something of a historic coup to enforce the notion of two fixed, idealized genders that we now consider natural. Speaking in strictly physical terms, many perfectly healthy people are born intersexed, with male and female physiological characteristics, showing that these categories exist on a fluid continuum. It makes no sense to make people who do not fit easily into one category feel as though they are unnatural.

Even in our patriarchal society, in which everyone is conditioned to believe that patriarchy is natural, there has always been

---

6 Jesse Walker ("Nightmare in New Orleans: Do disasters destroy social cooperation?" *Reason Online*, September 7, 2005) cites the studies of sociologist E.L. Quarantelli, who has found that "After the cataclysm, social bonds will strengthen, volunteerism will explode, violence will be rare…"

resistance. Much current resistance by queer people and transgender people takes a horizontal form. One organization in New York City, called FIERCE!, includes a wide spectrum of people excluded and oppressed by patriarchy: transgender, lesbian, gay, bisexual, two-spirit (an honored category in many Native American societies for people who are not identified as strictly men or women), queer, and questioning (people who have not made up their minds about their sexuality or gender identity, or who do not feel comfortable in any category). FIERCE! was founded in 2000, mostly by youth of color, and with anarchist participation. They uphold a horizontal ethic of "organizing by us, for us," and they actively link resistance to patriarchy, transphobia, and homophobia with resistance to capitalism and racism. Their actions have included protesting police brutality against transgender and queer youth; education through documentary films, zines, and the internet; and organizing for fair healthcare and against gentrification, particularly where the latter threatens to destroy important cultural and social spaces for queer youth.

At the time of this writing they are particularly active in a campaign to stop the gentrification of the Christopher Street Pier, which has been one of the only safe public spaces for homeless and low-income queer youth of color to meet and build community. Since 2001, the city has been trying to develop the Pier, and police harassment and arrests have multiplied. The FIERCE! campaign has helped provide a rallying point for those who want to save the space, and changed the public debate so that other voices are heard besides those of the government and business owners. Our society's attitudes about gender and sexuality have changed radically in the past centuries, largely because of groups like this taking direct action to create what is said to be impossible.

Resistance to patriarchy goes back as far as we care to look. In the "good old days" when these gender roles were supposedly unchallenged and accepted as natural, we can find stories of utopia, that upset the assumption that patriarchy is natural, and the notion that civilized progress is bringing us steadily from our brutal origins towards more enlightened sensibilities. In fact the idea of total freedom has always played a role in human history.

In the 1600s, Europeans were streaming to North America for a variety of reasons, building new colonies that exhibited a wide range of characteristics. They included plantation economies based on slave labor, penal colonies, trading networks that sought to compel the indigenous inhabitants to produce large quantities of animal skins, and fundamentalist religious utopias based on the total genocide of the native population. But just as the plantation colonies had their slave rebellions, the religious colonies had their heretics. One noteworthy heretic was Anne Hutchinson. An anabaptist who came to New England to escape religious persecution in the old world, she began to hold women's meetings in her house, discussion groups based on free interpretation of the Bible. As the popularity of these meetings spread, men began to participate as well. Anne won popular support for her well argued ideas, which opposed the slavery of Africans and Native Americans, criticized the church, and insisted that being born a woman was a blessing and not a curse.

The religious leaders of the Massachusetts Bay Colony put her on trial for blasphemy, but at trial she stood by her ideas. She was heckled and called an instrument of the devil, and one minister said, "You have stepped out of your place, you have rather been a husband than a wife, a preacher than a hearer, and a magistrate than a subject." Upon her expulsion Anne Hutchinson organized a group, in 1637, to form a settlement named Pocasset. They intentionally settled near to where Roger Williams, a progressive theologian, had founded Providence Plantations, a settlement based on the idea of total equality and freedom of conscience for all inhabitants, and friendly relations with the indigenous neighbors. These settlements were to become, respectively, Portsmouth and Providence, Rhode Island. Early on they joined to form the Rhode Island Colony. Both settlements allegedly maintained friendly relations with the neighboring indigenous nation, the Narragansett; Roger Williams' settlement was gifted the land they built on, whereas Hutchinson's group negotiated an exchange to buy land.

Initially, Pocasset was organized through elected councils and the people refused to have a governor. The settlement recognized equality between the sexes and trial by jury; abolished capital punishment, witchtrials, imprisonment for debt, and slavery; and granted total religious freedom. The second synagogue in North America was built in the Rhode Island colony. In 1651 one member of Hutchinson's group seized power and got the government of England to bestow him governorship over the colony, but after two years the other people in the settlement kicked him out in a mini-revolution. After this incident, Anne Hutchinson realized that her religious beliefs opposed "magistracy," or governmental authority, and in her later years she was said to have developed a political-religious philosophy very similar to individualist anarchism. One might say that Hutchinson and her colleagues were ahead of their times, but in every period of history there have been stories of people creating utopias, women asserting their equality, laypeople negating the religious leaders' monopoly on truth.

Outside of Western civilization we can find many examples of non-patriarchal societies. Some stateless societies intentionally preserve gender fluidity, like the Mbuti described previously. Many societies accept fixed genders and division of roles between men and women, but seek to preserve equality between these roles. Several of these societies allow transgender expressions—individuals changing their gender or adopting a unique gender identity. In hunter-gatherer societies "a sharp and hard division of labor between the sexes is not universal... [and in the case of one particular society] virtually every subsistence activity can be, and often is, performed by either men or women".[7]

The Igbo of western Africa had separate spheres of activity for men and women. Women were responsible for certain economic tasks and men for others, and each group held power autonomously over their sphere. These spheres designated who produced which goods, domesticated which animals, and took which responsibilities in the garden and market. If a man interfered in the women's sphere of activity or abused his wife, the women had

---

7 Roger M. Keesing, Andrew J. Strathern, *Cultural Anthropology: A Contemporary Perspective,* 3rd Edition, New York: Harcourt Brace & Company, 1998, p.83.

a ritual of collective solidarity that preserved the balance and punished the offender, called "sitting on a man." All the women would assemble outside the man's house, yelling at him and insulting him in order to cause him shame. If he did not come out to apologize the mob of women might destroy the fence around his house and his outlying storage buildings. If his offense were grievous enough, the women might even storm into his house, drag him out, and beat him up. When the British colonized the Igbo, they recognized men's institutions and economic roles, but ignored or were blind to the corresponding women's sphere of social life. When Igbo women responded to British indecency with the traditional practice of "sitting on a man," the British, possibly mistaking it for a women's insurrection, opened fire, putting an end to the gender-balancing ritual and cementing the institution of patriarchy in the society they had colonized.[8]

The Haudennosaunne, called the Iroquois by Europeans, are a matrilineal egalitarian society of eastern North America. They traditionally use several means to balance gender relations. Whereas European civilization utilizes gender division to socialize people into rigid roles and to oppress women, queer, and transgendered people, the gendered division of labor and social roles among the Haudennosaunne functions to preserve a balance, assigning each group autonomous niches and powers, and allowing a greater degree of movement between genders than is considered possible in Western society. For hundreds of years the Haudennosaunne have coordinated between multiple nations using a federative structure, and at each level of organization there were women's councils and men's councils. At what might be called the national level, which concerned itself with matters of war and peace, the men's council made the decisions, though the women held a veto power. At the local level, women held more influence. The basic socio-economic unit, the longhouse, was considered to belong to the women, and men had no council at this level. When a man

---

[8] Judith Van Allen " "Sitting On a Man": Colonialism and the Lost Political Institutions of Igbo Women." *Canadian Journal of African Studies.* Vol. ii, 1972, pp. 211–219.

married a woman, he moved into her house. Any man who did not behave could ultimately be kicked out of the longhouse by the women.

Western society typically sees the "higher" levels of organization as being more important and powerful—even the language we use reflects this; but because the Haudennosaunne were egalitarian and decentralized, the lower or local levels of organization where the women had more influence were more important to daily life. In fact when there was no feud between the different nations the highest council might go a long time without meeting at all. However, their's was not a "matriarchal" society: men were not exploited or devalued the way women are in patriarchal societies. Rather, each group had a measure of autonomy and means for preserving a balance. Despite centuries of colonization by a patriarchal culture, many groups of Haudennosaunne retain their traditional gender relations and still stand out in sharp contrast to the gender-oppressive culture of Canada and the United States.

Aren't people naturally warlike?

POLITICAL PHILOSOPHERS LIKE THOMAS HOBBES AND PSYCHOLOgists like Sigmund Freud assumed that civilization and government have a moderating effect on what they saw as people's warlike and brutal instincts. Pop-culture representations of human origins, like the first scenes of the film *2001: A Space Odyssey* or the illustrations in children's books of hyper-masculine cavemen battling mammoths and sabertooth tigers, provide a picture that can be as convincing as memory: early humans had to fight one another and even battle nature to survive. But if early human life had been as bloody and warlike as our mythology has depicted it, humans would simply have died out. Any species with a reproductive cycle of 15–20 years that usually only produce one offspring at a time simply cannot survive if their chance for dying in any given year is more than a couple percent. It would have been mathematically impossible for *Homo sapiens* to have survived that imaginary battle against nature and against one another.

Anarchists have long alleged that war is a product of the state. Some anthropological research has produced accounts of peaceful stateless societies, and of warfare among other stateless societies that was little more than a rough sport with few casualties[9]. Naturally, the state has found its defenders, who have set out to prove that war is indeed inevitable and thus not the fault of specific oppressive social structures. In one monumental study, *War Before Civilization,* Lawrence Keeley showed that of an extensive sample of stateless societies, a large number had engaged in aggressive warfare, and a great majority had engaged at the very least in defensive warfare. Only a tiny minority had never encountered war, and a few fled their homelands to avoid war. Keeley was endeavoring to show that people are warlike, even though his results demonstrated that people could choose from a wide range of behaviors including being warlike, avoiding war but still defending against aggression, not knowing war at all, and disliking war so much they would flee their homeland rather than fight. Contrary to his title, Keeley was documenting war *after* civilization, not "before." A major part of his data on non-Western societies came from the explorers, missionaries, soldiers, traders, and anthropologists who rode the waves of colonization around the world, bringing land conflicts and ethnic rivalries to previously unimaginable scales through mass enslavement, genocide, invasion, evangelism, and the introduction of new weapons, diseases, and addictive substances. Needless to say, the civilizing influence of the colonizers generated warfare at the margins.

---

9   Johan M.G. van der Dennen, "Ritualized 'Primitive' Warfare and Rituals in War: Phenocopy, Homology, or...?"
    http://rechten.eldoc.ub.rug.nl/FILES/root/Algemeen/overigepublicaties/2005enouder/RITUAL/RITUAL.pdf   Among other examples, van der Dennen cites the New Guinea highlanders, among whom warring bands would face off, yell insults, and shoot arrows that did not have feathers, and thus could not be aimed, while another band on the sidelines would yell that it was wrong for brothers to fight, and attempt to calm the situation before blood was shed. The original source for this account is Rappaport, R.A. (1968), *Pigs for the Ancestors: Ritual in the Ecology of a New Guinea People.* New Haven: Yale University Press.

Keeley's study characterizes as warlike societies that had been peaceful for a hundred years but were chased off their land and, given the options of starving to death or invading their neighbors' territory for space to live, chose the latter. The fact that under these conditions of global colonialism, genocide, and enslavement any societies remained peaceful at all proves that if people really want to, they can be peaceful even in the worst of circumstances. Not to say that in such circumstances there is anything wrong with fighting back against aggression!

War may be the result of natural human behavior, but so is peace. Violence certainly existed before the state, but the state developed warfare and domination to unprecedented levels. As social critic Randolph Bourne pointed out, «war is the health of the State.» Proponents of the State can hardly disagree. Political theorist and Prussian general Baron von Clausewitz expressed the same sentiment when he said, «war is politics by other means.» It is no mistake that the institutions of power in our civilization—media, academia, government, religions—have exaggerated the prevalence of war and understated the possibility for peace. These institutions are invested in ongoing wars and occupations; they profit from them, and attempts to create a more peaceful society threaten their existence.

One such attempt is the Faslane Peace Camp, a land occupation outside Scotland's Faslane Naval Base, which houses Trident nuclear missiles. The Peace Camp is a popular expression of the desire for a peaceful society, organized on anarchist and socialist lines. Faslane Peace Camp has been continuously occupied since June 1982 and is now well established, with hot water and bathroom facilities, a communal kitchen and living room, and twelve caravans housing permanent residents and space for visitors. The Peace Camp serves as a base area for protests in which people block the roads, shut down the gates, and even penetrate the base itself to carry out sabotage. Galvanized by the Peace Camp, there is widespread popular opposition to the naval base, and some of Scotland's political parties have called for the base to be closed down. In September 1981, a group of Welsh women formed a similar camp, the Greenham Common Women's Peace Camp, outside an RAF base housing cruise missiles in Berkshire, England. The women were forcibly evicted in 1984 but immediately reoccupied the site, and in 1991 the last missiles were removed. The camp remained until 2000, when the women won permission to set up a commemorative memorial.

These peace camps bear some similarity to the Life and Labor Commune, the largest of the Tolstoyan communes. It was an agricultural commune established near Moscow in 1921 by people following the pacifist and anarchist teachings of Leo Tolstoy. Its members, nearly one thousand at their peak, were at odds with the Soviet government on account of refusing to perform military service. For this reason, the commune was finally shut down by the authorities in 1930; but during its existence, the participants created a large self-organized community in peace and resistance.

The Catholic Worker movement began in the United States in 1933 as a response to the Great Depression, but today many of the 185 Catholic Worker communities throughout North America and Europe focus on opposing the militarism of the government and creating the foundations of a peaceful society. Inseparable from their opposition to war is their commitment to social justice, which manifests in the soup kitchens, shelters, and other service projects to help the poor that form a part of every Catholic Worker house. Although Christian, the Catholic Workers generally criticize church hierarchy and promote tolerance of other religions. They are also anti-capitalist, preaching voluntary poverty and "distributist communitarianism; self-sufficien[cy] through farming, crafting, and appropriate technology; a radically new society where people will rely on the fruits of their own toil and labor; associations of mutuality, and a sense of fairness to resolve conflicts."[10] Some Catholic Workers even call themselves Christian Anarchists. Catholic Worker communities, which function as communes or aid centers for the poor, often provide a base for protests and direct actions against the military. Catholic Workers have entered military bases to sabotage weaponry, though

---

10 "The Aims and Means of the Catholic Worker," *The Catholic Worker*, May 2008.

they waited for the police afterwards, intentionally going to jail as a further act of protest. Some of their communities also shelter victims of war, such as torture survivors fleeing the results of US imperialism in other countries.

How peaceful a society could we create if we overcame the belligerence of governments and fostered new norms in our culture? The Semai, agriculturalists in Malaya, offer one indication. Their murder rate is only 0.56/100,000 per year, compared with 0.86 in Norway, 6.26 in the US, and 20.20 in Russia.[11] This may be related to their childrearing strategy: traditionally the Semai do not hit their children, and respect for their children's autonomy is a normalized value in their society. One of the few occasions in which Semai adults will typically intervene is when children lose their tempers or fight one another, in which case nearby adults will snatch up the children and take them to their respective houses. The major forces that uphold Semai peacefulness seem to be an emphasis on learning self-control and the great importance accorded to public opinion in a cooperative society.

According to Robert Dentan, a Western anthropologist who lived with them, "little violence occurs within Semai society. Violence, in fact, seems to terrify the Semai. A Semai does not meet force with force, but with passivity or flight. Yet, he has no institutionalized way of preventing violence—no social controls, no police or courts. Somehow a Semai learns automatically always to keep tight rein over his aggressive impulses."[12] The first time the Semai participated in a war was when the British conscripted them to fight against the Communist insurgency in the early

---

11 Graham Kemp and Douglas P. Fry (eds.), *Keeping the Peace: Conflict Resolution and Peaceful Societies around the World*, New York: Routledge, 2004. Semai murder rate, p. 191, other murder rates p. 149. The low Norwegian murder rate shows that industrial societies can also be peaceful. It should be noted that Norway has one of the lowest wealth gaps of any capitalist country, and also a low reliance on police and prisons. The majority of civil disputes and many criminal cases in Norway are settled through mediation (p. 163).

12 Robert K. Dentan, *The Semai: A Nonviolent People of Malaya*. New York: Holt, Rinehart and Winston, 1979, p. 59.

1950s. Clearly, warfare is not an inevitability and certainly not a human need: rather, it is a consequence of political, social, and economic arrangements, and these arrangements are ours to shape.

Aren't domination and authority natural?

NOWADAYS, IT IS HARDER TO MAKE IDEOLOGICAL JUSTIFICATIONS for the state. A massive body of research demonstrates that many human societies have been staunchly egalitarian, and that even within capitalism many people continue to form egalitarian networks and communities. In order to reconcile this with their view that evolution is a matter of fierce competition, some scientists have postulated a "human egalitarian syndrome," theorizing that humans evolved to live in close-knit, homogenous groups, in which the passing on of members' genes was not assured by the survival of the individual but by the survival of the group.

According to this theory, cooperation and egalitarianism prevailed within these groups because it was in everyone's genetic self-interest that the group survived. Genetic competition occurred between different groups, and the groups that did the best job of taking care of their members were the ones to pass on their genes. Direct genetic competition between individuals was superseded by competition between different groups employing different social strategies, and humans evolved a whole host of social skills that allowed for greater cooperation. This would explain why, for most of human existence, we have lived in societies with little or no hierarchy, until certain technological developments allowed some societies to stratify and dominate their neighbors.

This is not to say that domination and authority were unnatural, and that technology was a forbidden fruit that corrupted an otherwise innocent humanity. In fact, some hunter-gatherer societies were so patriarchal they used gang rape as a form of punishment against women, and some societies with agriculture and metal tools have been fiercely egalitarian. Some of the peoples in North America's Pacific Northwest were sedentary hunter-gatherers and they had a heavily stratified society with a slave class. And at the far end of the technological spectrum, nomadic hunter-gatherer groups in Australia were dominated by male elders. Older men could have multiple wives, younger men had none, and women were evidently doled out like social property.[13]

Humans are capable of both authoritarian and anti-authoritarian behavior. Horizontal societies that were not intentionally anti-authoritarian could easily have developed coercive hierarchies when new technologies made that possible, and even without a lot of technology they could make life hell for groups considered inferior. It seems that the most common forms of inequality among otherwise egalitarian societies were gender and age discrimination, which could accustom a society to inequality and create the prototype for a power structure—rule by male elders. This structure could become more powerful over time with the development of metal tools and weapons, surpluses, cities, and the like.

The point, though, is that these forms of inequality were not inevitable. Societies that frowned on authoritarian behaviors consciously avoided the rise of hierarchy. In fact, many societies have given up centralized organization or technologies that allow for domination. This shows that history is not a one-way track. For example, the Moroccan Imazighen, or Berbers, did not form centralized political systems over the past several centuries, even while other societies around them did. "Establishing a dynasty is next to impossible," wrote one commentator, "due to the fact that the chief is faced with constant revolt which ultimately becomes successful and returns the system to the old decentralized anarchic order."[14]

What is the factor that allows societies to avoid domination and coercive authority? A study by Christopher Boehm, surveying dozens of egalitarian societies on all continents, including peoples who lived as foragers, horticulturalists, agriculturalists, and pastoralists, found that the common factor is a conscious desire to remain egalitarian: an anti-authoritarian culture. "The primary

13 Dmitri M. Bondarenko and Andrey V. Korotayev, *Civilizational Models of Politogenesis*, Moscow: Russian Academy of Sciences, 2000.
14 Harold Barclay, *People Without Government: An Anthropology of Anarchy*, London: Kahn and Averill, 1982, p. 98.

and most immediate cause of egalitarian behavior is a moralistic determination on the part of a local group's main political actors that no one of its members should be allowed to dominate the others."[15] Rather than culture being determined by material conditions, it seems that culture shapes the social structures that reproduce a people's material conditions.

In certain situations some form of leadership is inevitable, as some people have more skills or a more charismatic personality. Consciously egalitarian societies respond to these situations by not institutionalizing the position of leader, by not affording a leader any special privileges, or by fostering a culture that makes it shameful for that person to flaunt his or her leadership or try to gain power over others. Furthermore, leadership positions change from one situation to another, depending on the skills needed for the task at hand. The leaders during a hunt are different from the leaders during house-building or ceremonies. If a person in a leadership role tries to gain more power or dominate his or her peers, the rest of the group employs "intentional leveling mechanisms": behaviors intended to bring the leader back down to earth. For example, among many anti-authoritarian hunter-gatherer societies, the most skillful hunter in a band faces criticism and ridicule if he is seen to brag and use his talents to boost his ego rather than for the benefit of the whole group.

If these social pressures do not work, the sanctions escalate, and in many egalitarian societies in the final instance they will kick out or kill a leader who is incurably authoritarian, long before that leader is able to assume coercive powers. These "reverse dominance hierarchies," in which the leaders must obey popular will because they are powerless to maintain their positions of leadership without support, have appeared in many different societies and functioned over long periods of time. Some of the egalitarian societies documented in Boehm's survey have a chief or a shaman who plays a ritual role or acts as an impartial mediator in disputes; others appoint a leader in times of trouble, or have a peace chief

---

15 Christopher Boehm, "Egalitarian Behavior and Reverse Dominance Hierarchy," *Current Anthropology*, Vol. 34, No. 3, June 1993.

and a war chief. But these positions of leadership are not coercive, and over hundreds of years have not developed into authoritarian roles. Often the people who fill these roles see them as a temporary social responsibility, which they wish to hand off swiftly because of the higher level of criticism and responsibility they face while occupying them.

European civilization has historically demonstrated a much higher tolerance for authoritarianism than the egalitarian societies described in the survey. Yet as the political and economic systems that would become the modern state and capitalism were developing in Europe, there were a number of rebellions that demonstrate that even here authority was an imposition. One of the greatest of these rebellions was the Peasants War. In 1524 and 1525, as many as 300,000 peasant insurgents, joined by townsfolk and some lesser nobility, rose up against the property owners and church hierarchy in a war that left about 100,000 people dead throughout Bavaria, Saxony, Thüringen, Schwaben, Alsace, as well as parts of what are now Switzerland and Austria. The princes and clergy of the Holy Roman Empire had been steadily increasing taxes to pay for rising administrative and military costs, as government became more top-heavy. The artesans and workers of the towns were affected by these taxes, but the peasants received the heaviest burden. To increase their power and their revenue, princes forced free peasants into serfdom, and resurrected Roman Civil law, which instituted private ownership of land, something of a step backwards from the feudal system in which the land was a trust between peasant and lord that involved rights and obligations.

Meanwhile, elements of the old feudal hierarchy, such as the knighthood and the clergy, were becoming obsolete, and conflicted with other elements of the ruling class. The new burgher mercantile class, as well as many progressive princes, opposed the privileges of the clergy and the conservative structure of the Catholic church. A new, less centralized structure that could base power in councils in the towns and cities, such as the system proposed by Martin Luther, would allow the new political class to ascend.

In the years immediately prior to the War, a number of Anabaptist prophets began travelling around the region espousing revolutionary ideas against political authority, church doctrine, and even against the reforms of Martin Luther. These people included Thomas Dreschel, Nicolas Storch, Mark Thomas Stübner, and most famously, Thomas Müntzer. Some of them argued for total religious freedom, the end of non-voluntary baptism, and the abolition of government on earth. Needless to say they were persecuted by Catholic authorities and by supporters of Luther and banned from many cities, but they continued to travel around Bohemia, Bavaria, and Switzerland, winning supporters and stoking peasant rebelliousness.

In 1524, peasants and urban workers met in the Schwarzwald region of Germany and drafted the 12 Articles of the Black Forest, and the movement they created quickly spread. The articles, with Biblical references used as justification, called for the abolition of serfdom and the freedom of all people; the municipal power for people to elect and remove preachers; the abolition of taxes on cattle and inheritance; a prohibition on the privilege of the nobility to arbitrarily raise taxes; free access to water, hunting, fishing, and the forests; and the restoration of communal lands expropriated by the nobility. Another text printed and circulated in massive quantity by the insurgents was the Bundesordnung, the federal order, which expounded a model social order based on federated municipalities. Less literate elements of the movement were even more radical, as judged by their actions and the folklore they left behind; their goal was to wipe the nobility off the face of the earth and institute a mysticist utopia then and there.

Social tension increased throughout the year, as authorities tried to prevent outright rebellion by suppressing rural gatherings such as popular festivals and weddings. In August 1524, the situation finally errupted at Stühlingen in the Black Forest region. A countess demanded that the peasants render her a special harvest on a church holiday. Instead the peasants refused to pay all taxes and formed an army of 1200 people, under the leadership of a former mercenary, Hans Müller. They marched to the town of Waldshut and were joined by the townspeople, and then marched on the castle at Stühlingen and besieged it. Realizing they needed some kind of military structure, they decided to elect their own captains, sergeants, and corporals. In September they defended themselves from a Hapsburg army in an indecisive battle, and subsequently refused to lay down their arms and beg pardon when entreated to do so. That autumn peasant strikes, refusals to pay tithes, and rebellions broke out throughout the region, as peasants extended their politics from individual complaints to a unified rejection of the feudal system as a whole.

With the spring thaw of 1525, fighting resumed with a ferocity. The peasant armies seized cities and executed large numbers of clergy and nobility. But in February the Schwabian League, an alliance of nobility and clergy in the region, achieved a victory in Italy, where they had been fighting on behalf of Charles V, and were able to bring their troops home and devote them to crushing the peasants. Meanwhile Martin Luther, the burghers, and the progressive princes withdrew all their support and called for the annihilation of the revolutionary peasants; they wanted to reform the system, not to destroy it, and the uprising had already sufficiently destabilized the power structure. Finally on May 15, 1525, the main peasant army was decisively defeated at Frankenhausen; Müntzer and other influential leaders were seized and executed, and the rebellion was put down. However, over the following years the Anabaptist movement spread throughout Germany, Switzerland, and the Netherlands, and peasant revolts continued to break out, in the hopes that one day the church and the state would be destroyed for good.

Capitalism and modern democratic states succeeded in establishing themselves over the following centuries, but they have been forever haunted by the specter of rebellion from below. Within statist societies, the ability to organize without hierarchies still exists today, and the possibility remains to create anti-authoritarian cultures that can bring any would-be leaders back down to earth. Appropriately, much of the resistance against global authority is organized horizontally. The worldwide anti-globalization movement arose largely from the resistance of the Zapatistas in Mexico, autonomists and anarchists in Europe, farmers and workers in Korea, and popular rebellions against financial institutions like the IMF, occurring across the world from South Africa to

India. The Zapatistas and autonomists especially are marked by their anti-authoritarian cultures, a marked break from the hierarchy of Marxist-Leninists who had dominated international struggles in previous generations.

The anti-globalization movement proved itself to be a global force in June, 1999, when hundreds of thousands of people in cities from London, England to Port Harcourt, Nigeria took the streets for the J18 Carnival Against Capitalism; in November later that year, participants in the same movement shocked the world by shutting down the summit of the World Trade Organization in Seattle.

The most remarkable thing about this global resistance is that it was created horizontally, by diverse organizations and affinity groups pioneering new forms of consensus. This movement had no leaders and fomented constant opposition to all forms of authority that developed within its ranks. Those who attempted to put themselves permanently in the role of chief or spokesperson were ostracized—or even treated to a pie in the face, as high profile organizer Medea Benjamin was at the US Social Forum in 2007.

Lacking leadership, short on formal organization, and constantly critiquing internal power dynamics and studying more egalitarian ways of organizing, anti-globalization activists went on to achieve further tactical victories. In Prague in September 2000, 15,000 protestors overcame the massive police presence and broke up the last day of the summit of the International Monetary Fund. In Quebec City in April, 2001, protestors breached the security fence around a summit planning the Free Trade Area of the Americas; police responded by filling the city with so much teargas that it even entered the building where the talks were taking place. Consequently many city residents came to favor the protestors. Police had to step up repression to contain the growing anti-globalization movement; they arrested 600 protestors and injured three with gunfire at the European Union summit in Sweden in 2001, and a month later they murdered anarchist Carlo Giuliani at the G8 summit in Genoa, where 150,000 people had gathered to protest the conference of the eight most powerful world governments.

The Dissent! Network arose out of the European anti-globalization movement to organize major protests against the G8 summit in Scotland in 2005. The Network also organized major protest camps and blockade actions against the G8 summit in Germany in 2007, and helped with the mobilizations against the G8 summit in Japan in 2008. Without a central leadership or hierarchy, the network facilitated communication between groups located in different cities and countries, and organized major meetings to discuss and decide on strategies for upcoming actions against the G8. The strategies were intended to enable diverse approaches, so many affinity groups could organize mutually supportive actions within a common framework rather than carrying out the orders of a central organization. For example, a blockade plan might designate one road leading to the summit site as a zone for people who prefer peaceful or theatrical tactics, while another entrance might be designated for people who wish to construct barricades and are willing to defend themselves against the police. These strategy meetings drew people from a dozen countries and included translations in multiple languages. Afterwards, fliers, announcements, position papers, and critiques were translated and uploaded to a website. The anarchist forms of coordination used by the protestors repeatedly proved effective at countering and sometimes even outmaneuvering the police and corporate media, which enjoyed teams of thousands of paid professionals, advanced communications and surveillance infrastructure including police infiltrators in the protest organization, and resources far beyond what was available to the movement.

The anti-globalization movement can be contrasted with the anti-war movement that arose in response to the so-called War on Terror. After September 11, 2001, world leaders sought to undercut the growing anti-capitalist movement by identifying terrorism as enemy number one, thus reframing the narrative of global conflict. Following the collapse of the Soviet Bloc and the end of the Cold War, they needed a new war and a new opposition. People had to view their options as a choice between hierarchical powers—statist democracy or fundamentalist terrorists—rather than between domination and freedom. In the conservative environment that followed September 11, the anti-war movement quickly came to be dominated by reformist and hierarchically-organized groups. Although the movement kicked off with the most widely attended day of protest in human history on February 15, 2003, the organizers deliberately channeled the energy of the participants into rigidly controlled rituals that did not challenge the war machine. Within two years, the anti-war movement had completely squandered the momentum built up during the anti-globalization era.

The anti-war movement could not stop the occupation of Iraq, or even sustain itself, because people are neither empowered nor fulfilled by passively participating in symbolic spectacles. In contrast, the effectiveness of decentralized networks can be seen in the many victories of the anti-globalization movement: the summits shut down, the collapse of the WTO and FTAA, the dramatic scaling back of the IMF and World Bank.[16] This non-hierarchical movement demonstrated that people desire to free themselves from domination, and that they have the ability to cooperate in an anti-authoritarian manner even in large groups of strangers from different nations and cultures.

So from scientific studies of human history to protesters making history today, the evidence overwhelmingly contradicts the statist account of human nature. Rather than coming from a brutally authoritarian ancestry and later subsuming these instincts into a competitive system based on obedience to authority, humankind has not had one single trajectory. Our beginnings seem to have been characterized by a range between strict egalitarianism and small-scale hierarchy with a relatively equal distribution of wealth. When coercive hierarchies did appear, they did not spread everywhere immediately, and often provoked significant resistance. Even where societies are ruled by authoritarian structures, resistance is every much a part of the social reality as domination and obedience. Furthermore, the state and authoritarian civilization

---

[16] The victories of the movement and the failure of the IMF and World Bank are argued by David Graeber in "The Shock of Victory," *Rolling Thunder* no. 5, Spring 2008.

are not the last stops on the line. Even though a global revolution has yet to succeed, we have many examples of post-state societies, in which we can make out hints of a stateless future.

Half a century ago, anthropologist Pierre Clastres concluded that the stateless and anti-authoritarian societies he studied in South America were not holdouts from a primordial era, as other Westerners had assumed. He argued that, on the contrary, they were well aware of the possible emergence of the state, and they were organizing themselves to prevent this. It turns out that many of them were in fact post-state societies founded by refugees and rebels who had fled from or overthrown earlier states. Similarly, anarchist Peter Lamborn Wilson hypothesized that anti-authoritarian societies in eastern North America formed in resistance to the hierarchical Hopewell mound-building societies, and recent research seems to be confirming this. What others had interpreted as ahistorical ethnicities were the end results of political movements.

The Cossacks who inhabited the Russian frontiers provide another example of this phenomenon. Their societies were founded by people fleeing serfdom and other inconveniences of government oppression. They learned horsemanship and developed impressive martial skills to survive in the frontier environment and defend themselves against neighboring states. Eventually, they came to be viewed as a distinct ethnicity with a privileged autonomy, and the tsar whom their ancestors renounced sought them out as military allies.

According to Yale political scientist James C. Scott, everything about such societies—from the crops they grow to their kinship systems—can be read as anti-authoritarian social strategies. Scott documents the Hill People of Southeast Asia, an agglomeration of societies existing in rugged terrain where fragile state structures face a severe disadvantage. For hundreds of years, these people have resisted state domination, including frequent wars of conquest or extermination by the Chinese empire and periods of continuous attacks by slavers. Cultural and linguistic diversity is exponentially greater in the hills than in the state-controlled rice paddies of the valleys, where a monoculture holds sway. Hill

People frequently speak multiple languages and belong to multiple ethnicities. Their social organization is suited for quick and easy dispersal and reunification, allowing them to escape assaults and wage guerrilla warfare. Their kinship systems are based on overlapping and redundant relationships that create a strong social network and limit the formalization of power. Their oral cultures are more decentralized and flexible than nearby literate cultures, in which reliance on the written word encourages orthodoxy and gives extra power to those with the resources to keep records.

The Hill People have an interesting relationship with the surrounding states. The people of the valleys view them as "living ancestors," even though they have formed as a response to the valley civilizations. They are post-state, not pre-state, but the ideology of the state refuses to recognize such a category as "post-state" because the state supposes itself to be the pinnacle of progress. Subjects of the valley civilizations frequently "headed for the hills" to live more freely; however the narratives and mythologies of the Chinese, Vietnamese, Burmese, and other authoritarian civilizations in the centuries leading up to World War II seemed to be designed to prevent their members from "going back" to those they perceived as barbarians. According to some scholars, the Great Wall of China was built as much to keep the Chinese in as the barbarians out; yet in the valley civilizations of China and Southeast Asia, myths, language, and rituals that might explain such cultural defections were suspiciously lacking. Culture was used as another Great Wall to hold these fragile civilizations together. No wonder the "barbarians" gave up written language in favor of a more decentralized oral culture: without written records and a specialized class of scribes, history became common property, rather than a tool for indoctrination.

Far from being a necessary social advancement that people readily accept, the state is an imposition that many people try to flee. A proverb from the Burmese encapsulates this: "It is easy for a subject to find a lord, but hard for a lord to find a subject." In Southeast Asia, until recently, the primary goal of warfare was not to capture territory but to capture subjects, as people frequently ran for the hills to create egalitarian societies.[17] It is ironic that so many of us are convinced we have an essential need for the state, when in fact it is the state that needs us.

A broader sense of self

A HUNDRED YEARS AGO, PETER KROPOTKIN, THE RUSSIAN GEOGrapher and anarchist theorist, published his revolutionary book, *Mutual Aid,* which argues that the tendency of people to help one another reciprocally, in a spirit of solidarity, was a greater factor in human evolution than competition. We can see cooperative behaviors similarly playing a role in the survival of many species of mammals, birds, fish, and insects. Still, the belief persists that humans are naturally selfish, competitive, warlike, and male-dominated. This belief is founded upon a misrepresentation of so-called primitive peoples as brutal, and of the state as a necessary, pacifying force. Westerners who see themselves as the pinnacle of human evolution typically view hunter-gatherers and other stateless peoples as relics of the past, even if they are alive in the present. In doing so, they are presuming that history is an inevitable progression from less to more complex, and that Western civilization is more complex than other cultures. If history is organized into the Stone Age, Bronze Age, Iron Age, Industrial Age, Information Age, and so on, someone who does not use metal tools must still be living in the Stone Age, right? But it is eurocentric, to say the least, to assume that a hunter-gatherer who knows the uses of a thousand different plants is less sophisticated than an operator at a nuclear power plant who knows how to push a thousand different buttons but doesn't know where his food comes from.

Capitalism may be capable of feats of production and distribution that have never been possible before, but at the same time this society is tragically unable to keep everyone fed and healthy,

---

17 The paragraphs regarding the Hill People and Southeast Asia are based on James C. Scott, "Civilizations Can't Climb Hills: A Political History of Statelessness in Southeast Asia," lecture at Brown University, Providence, Rhode Island, February 2, 2005.

and has never existed without gross inequalities, oppression, and environmental devastation. One might argue that members of our society are socially stunted, if not outright primitive, when it comes to being able to cooperate and organize ourselves without authoritarian control.

A nuanced view of stateless societies shows them to have their own developed forms of social organization and their own complex histories, both of which contradict Western notions about "natural" human characteristics. The great diversity of human behaviors that are considered normal in different societies calls into question the very idea of human nature.

Our understanding of human nature directly influences what we expect of people. If humans are naturally selfish and competitive, we cannot expect to live in a cooperative society. When we see how differently other cultures have characterized human nature, we can recognize human nature as a cultural value, an idealized and normative mythology that justifies the way a society is organized. Western civilization devotes an immense amount of resources to social control, policing, and cultural production reinforcing capitalist values. The Western idea of human nature functions as a part of this social control, discouraging rebellion against authority. We are taught from childhood that without authority human life would descend into chaos.

This view of human nature was advanced by Hobbes and other European philosophers to explain the origins and purpose of the State; this marked a shift to scientific arguments at a time when divine arguments no longer sufficed. Hobbes and his contemporaries lacked the psychological, historical, archaeological, and ethnographic data that we have today, and their thinking was still heavily influenced by a legacy of Christian teachings. Even now that we have access to an abundance of information contradicting Christian cosmology and statist political science, the popular conception of human nature has not changed dramatically. Why are we still so miseducated? A second question answers the first: who controls education in our society? Nonetheless, anyone who counters the authoritarian dogma faces an uphill battle against the charge of "romanticism."

But if human nature is not fixed, if it can encompass a wide range of possibilities, couldn't we use a romantic dose of imagination in envisioning new possibilities? The acts of rebellion occurring within our society right now, from the Faslane Peace Camp to the Really Really Free Markets, contain the seeds of a peaceful and openhanded society. Popular responses to natural disasters such as Hurricane Katrina in New Orleans show that everyone has the potential to cooperate when the dominant social order is disrupted. These examples point the way to a broader sense of self—an understanding of human beings as creatures capable of a wide range of behaviors.

One might say selfishness is natural, in that people inevitably live according to their own desires and experiences. But egoism need not be competitive or dismissive of others. Our relationships extend far beyond our bodies and our minds—we live in communities, depend on ecosystems for food and water, and need friends, families, and lovers for our emotional health. Without institutionalized competition and exploitation, a person's self-interest overlaps with the interests of her community and her environment. Seeing our relationships with our friends and nature as fundamental parts of ourselves expands our sense of connection with the world and our responsibility for it. It is not in our self-interest to be dominated by authorities, or to dominate others; in developing a broader sense of self, we can structure our lives and communities accordingly.

Recommended Reading:

- Robert K. Dentan, *The Semai: A Nonviolent People of Malaya*. New York: Holt, Rinehart and Winston, 1979.
- Christopher Boehm, "Egalitarian Behavior and Reverse Dominance Hierarchy," *Current Anthropology*, Vol.34, No.3, June 1993.
- Pierre Clastres, *Society Against the State*, (1974), New York: Zone Books, 1987.
- Leslie Feinberg, *Transgender Warriors: Making History*

from Joan of Arc to Dennis Rodman, Boston: Beacon Press, 1997.
- David Graeber, *Fragments of an Anarchist Anthropology*, Chicago: Prickly Paradigm Press, 2004.
- Colin M. Turnbull, *The Forest People,* New York: Simon & Schuster, 1961.
- James C. Scott, *Domination and the Arts of Resistance: Hidden Transcripts*, New Haven: Yale University Press, 1990.
- Bob Black, "The Abolition of Work," 1985. *

2. DECISIONS

ANARCHY IS THE ABSENCE OF RULERS. FREE PEOPLE DO NOT follow orders; they make their own decisions and come to agreements within their communities, and develop shared means for putting these decisions into practice.

How will decisions be made?

THERE SHOULD BE NO DOUBT THAT HUMAN BEINGS CAN MAKE decisions in non-hierarchical, egalitarian ways. The majority of human societies have been stateless, and many stateless societies have not been governed by the dictates of some "Big Man," but by common assemblies using some form of consensus. Numerous consensus-based societies have survived thousands of years, even through European colonialism into the present day, in Africa, Australia, Asia, the Americas, and on the peripheries of Europe.

People from societies in which decision-making power has been monopolized by the state and corporations may initially find it difficult to make decisions in an egalitarian way, but it gets easier with practice. Fortunately, we all have some experience with horizontal decision-making. Most of the decisions we make in daily life, with friends and hopefully with colleagues and family as well, we make on the basis of cooperation rather than authority. Friendship is precious because it is a space in which we interact as equals, where our opinions are valued regardless of our social status. Groups of friends typically use informal consensus to decide how to spend time together, organize activities, assist one another, and respond to challenges in their daily lives. So most of us already understand consensus intuitively; it takes more practice to learn how to come to consensus with people who are significantly different from us, especially in large groups or when it is necessary to coordinate complex activities, but it is possible.

Consensus is not the only empowering way to make decisions. In certain contingencies, groups that are truly voluntary associations can still be empowering for their members when they use majority decision-making. Or one person making her own decisions and acting alone can inspire dozens more people to take similar actions, or to support what she has started, thus avoiding the sometimes stifling weight of meetings. In creative or inspiring circumstances people often succeed in coordinating themselves spontaneously and chaotically, producing unprecedented results. The specific decision-making form is just a tool, and with consensus or individual action as with majority decision-making people can take an active part in using that tool as they see fit.

Korean anarchists won an opportunity to demonstrate people's ability to make their own decisions in 1929. The Korean Anarchist Communist Federation (KACF) was a huge organization at that time, with enough support that it could declare an autonomous zone in the Shinmin province. Shinmin was outside of Korea, in Manchuria, but two million Korean immigrants lived there. Using assemblies and a decentralized federative structure that grew out of the KACF, they created village councils, district councils, and area councils to deal with matters of cooperative agriculture, education, and finance. They also formed an army spearheaded by the anarchist Kim Jwa-Jin, which used guerrilla tactics against Soviet and Japanese forces. KACF sections in China, Korea, and Japan organized international support efforts. Caught between the Stalinists and the Japanese imperial army, the autonomous province was ultimately crushed in 1931. But for two years, large populations had freed themselves from the authority of landlords and governors and reasserted their power to come to collective decisions, to organize their day-to-day life, pursue their dreams, and defend those dreams from invading armies.[18]

One of the most well known anarchist histories is that of the Spanish Civil War. In July 1936, General Franco launched a fascist coup in Spain. From the standpoint of the elite, it was a necessary act; the nation's military officers, landowners, and religious hierarchy were terrified by growing anarchist and socialist movements. The monarchy had already been abolished, but the workers and peasants were not content with representative democracy. The coup did not go smoothly. While in many areas Spain's Republican government rolled over easily and resigned itself to fascism, the anarchist labor union (CNT) and other anarchists working autonomously formed militias, seized arsenals, stormed barracks, and defeated trained troops. Anarchists were especially strong in Catalunya, Aragon, Asturias, and much of Andalucia. Workers also defeated the coup in Madrid and Valencia, where the socialists were strong, and in much of the Basque country. In the anarchist areas, the government effectively ceased to function.

In these stateless areas of the Spanish countryside in 1936, peasants organized themselves according to principles of communism, collectivism, or mutualism according to their preferences and local conditions. They formed thousands of collectives, especially in Aragon, Catalunya, and Valencia. Some abolished all money and private property; some organized quota systems to ensure that everyone's needs were met. The diversity of forms they developed is a testament to the freedom they created themselves. Where once all these villages were mired in the same stifling context of feudalism and developing capitalism, within months of overthrowing government authority and coming together in village assemblies, they gave birth to hundreds of different systems, united by common values like solidarity and self-organization. And they

---

18 Alan MacSimoin, "The Korean Anarchist Movement," a talk in Dublin, September 1991. MacSimoin references Ha Ki-Rak, *A History of the Korean Anarchist Movement*, 1986.

developed these different forms by holding open assemblies and making decisions about their future in common.

The town of Magdalena de Pulpis, for example, abolished money completely. One inhabitant reported, "Everyone works and everyone has the right to what he needs free of charge. He simply goes to the store where provisions and all other necessities are supplied. Everything is distributed free with only a notation of what he took."[19] Recording what everyone took allowed the community to distribute resources equally in times of scarcity, and generally ensured accountability.

Other collectives worked out their own systems of exchange. They issued local money in the form of vouchers, tokens, rationing booklets, certificates, and coupons which carried no interest and were not negotiable outside of the issuing collective. Communities that had suppressed money paid workers in coupons according to the size of the family—a "family wage" based on the needs of the family rather than the productivity of its working members. Abundant local goods like bread, wine, and olive oil were distributed freely, while other items "could be obtained by means of coupons at the communal depot. Surplus goods were exchanged with other anarchist towns and villages."[20] There was much experimentation with new monetary systems. In Aragon, there were hundreds of different kinds of coupon and money systems, so the Aragon Federation of Peasant Collectives unanimously decided to replace local currencies with a standard ration booklet—though each collective retained the power to decide how goods would be distributed and the amount of coupons workers would receive.

All the collectives, once they had taken control of their villages, organized open mass assemblies to discuss problems and plan how to organize themselves. Decisions were made via voting or consensus. Village assemblies generally met between once a week and once a month; foreign observers surveying them remarked that participation was broad and enthusiastic. Many of the collectivized

---

19 Sam Dolgoff, *The Anarchist Collectives*, New York: Free Life Editions, 1974, p. 73.
20 Ditto, p. 73. The statistic on Graus comes from p. 140.

villages joined with other collectives in order to pool resources, aid one another, and arrange trade. The collectives in Aragon donated hundreds of tons of food to the volunteer militias who were holding back the fascists on the front, and also took in large numbers of refugees who had fled the fascists. The town of Graus, for example, with a population of 2,600, took in and supported 224 refugees, only 20 of whom could work.

At assemblies, collectives discussed problems and proposals. Many collectives elected administrative committees, generally consisting of half a dozen people, to manage affairs until the next meeting. The open assemblies:

> allowed the inhabitants to know, to so understand, and to feel so mentally integrated in society, to so participate in the management of public affairs, in the responsibilities, that the recriminations, the tensions which always occur when the power of decision is entrusted to a few individuals… did not happen there. The assemblies were public, the objections, the proposals publicly discussed, everybody being free, as in the syndical assemblies, to participate in the discussions, to criticize, propose, etc. Democracy extended to the whole of social life. In most cases even the individualists [locals who had not joined the collective] could take part in the deliberations. They were given the same hearing as the collectivists.[21]

If not every village inhabitant was a member of the collective, there might be a municipal council in addition to the collective assembly, so that no one would be excluded from decision-making.

In many collectives they agreed that if a member violated a collective rule once, he was reprimanded. If it happened a second time, he was referred to the general assembly. Only the general assembly could expel a member from the collective; delegates and administrators were denied punitive power. The power of the general assembly to respond to transgressions was also used to prevent

---

21 Gaston Leval, *Collectives in the Spanish Revolution*, London: Freedom Press, 1975, pp. 206–207.

people who had been delegated tasks from being irresponsible or authoritarian; delegates or elected administrators who failed to abide by collective decisions or usurped authority were suspended or removed by a general vote. In some villages that were split between anarchists and socialists, the peasants formed two collectives side by side, to allow for different ways of making and enforcing decisions rather than imposing one method on everybody.

Gaston Leval described a general assembly in the village of Tamarite de Litera, in Huesca province, which the non-collective peasants were also allowed to attend. One problem brought up at the meeting was that several peasants who had not joined the collective left their elderly parents in the care of the collective while taking their parents' land to farm as their own. The entire group discussed the matter, and eventually decided to adopt a specific proposal: they would not kick the elderly parents out of the collective, but they wanted to hold those peasants accountable, so they decided that the latter had to take care of their parents or else receive neither solidarity nor land from the collective. In the end, a resolution agreed to by an entire community will carry more legitimacy, and is more likely to be followed, than one handed down by a specialist or a government official.

Important decisions also took place at work in the fields every day:

> The work of the collectives was conducted by teams of workers, headed by a delegate chosen by each team. The land was divided into cultivated zones. Team delegates worked like the others. There were no special privileges. After the day's work, delegates from all the work teams met on the job and made necessary technical arrangements for the next day's work... The assembly made final decisions on all important questions and issued instructions to both the team delegates and the administrative commission."[22]

Many areas also had District Committees that pooled the

---

22 Sam Dolgoff, *The Anarchist Collectives*, New York: Free Life Editions, 1974, p. 113.

resources of all the collectives in a district, basically acting as a clearinghouse to circulate surplus from the collectives that had it to other collectives that needed it. Hundreds of collectives joined federations organized through the CNT or UGT (the socialist labor union). The federations provided economic coordination, pooling resources to allow peasants to build their own fruit and vegetable canneries, gathering information about which items were in abundance and which were in short supply, and organizing uniform exchange systems. This collective form of decision-making proved effective for the approximately seven to eight million peasants involved in this movement. Half the land in anti-fascist Spain—three-quarters of the land in Aragon—was collectivized and self-organized.

In August 1937, just over a year after anarchist and socialist peasants started forming collectives, the Republican government, under control of the Stalinists, had consolidated enough to move against the lawless zones of Aragon. The Karl Marx Brigade, units of the International Brigades, and other units disarmed and dissolved the collectives in Aragon, crushing any resistance and spiriting off numerous anarchists and libertarian socialists to the prisons and torture chambers the Stalinists had set up to use against their revolutionary allies.

Brazil today bears a similarity with Spain in 1936, in that a tiny percentage of the population owns nearly half of all the land while millions of people are without land or sustenance. A major social movement has sprung up in response. The *Movimento dos Trabalhadores Rurais Sem Terra* (MST), or Landless Workers' Movement, is made up of 1.5 million impoverished laborers who occupy unused land to set up farming collectives. Since its founding in 1984, the MST has won land titles for 350,000 families living in 2,000 different settlements. The basic unit of organization consists of a group of families living together in a settlement on occupied land. These groups retain autonomy and self-organize matters of day-to-day living. To participate in regional meetings they appoint two or three representatives, which in principle include a man and a woman though in practice this is not always the case. The MST has a federative structure; there are also State and National Coordinating Bodies. While most of the decision-making takes place at the grassroots level with land occupations, farming, and the establishment of settlements, the MST also organizes at higher levels to coordinate massive protests and highway blockades to pressure the government to give land titles to the settlements. The MST has shown a great deal of innovation and strength, organizing schools and protecting themselves against frequent police repression. They have developed practices of sustainable agriculture, including setting up seed banks for native seeds, and they have invaded and destroyed environmentally harmful eucalyptus forestry plantations and test grounds for genetically modified crops.

Within the logic of democracy, 1.5 million people is considered simply too large a group for everyone to be allowed to participate directly in decision-making; the majority should entrust that power to politicians. But the MST holds an ideal in which all possible decision-making remains on the local level. In practice, however, they often do not meet this ideal. As a massive organization that does not seek to abolish capitalism or overthrow the state but rather to pressure it, the MST has been brought into the game of politics, in which all principles are for sale. Furthermore, a huge portion of their members come from extremely poor and oppressed communities that for generations had been controlled by a combination of religion, patriotism, crime, drug addiction, and patriarchy. These dynamics do not disappear when people enter into the movement, and they cause significant problems within the MST.

Throughout the '80s and the '90s, new MST settlements were created by activists from the organization who would seek landless people in rural areas or especially in the favelas, the urban slums, who wanted to form a group and occupy land. They would go through a base-building period of two months, in which they would hold meetings and debates to try to build a sense of community, affinity, and political common ground. Then they would occupy a piece of unused land owned by a major landlord, choose representatives to federate with the larger organization, and begin farming. Activists working with the MST local would pass through periodically to see if the settlement needed help acquiring tools and materials, resolving internal disputes, or protecting themselves from police, paramilitaries, or major landlords, all of whom frequently conspired to threaten and assassinate MST members.

In part due to the autonomy of each settlement, they have met with a variety of outcomes. Leftists from other countries typically romanticize the MST while the Brazilian capitalist media portray them all as violent thugs who steal land and then sell it. In fact, the capitalist media portrayal is accurate in some cases, though by no means in a majority of cases. It is not unheard of for people in a new settlement to divide up the land and later fight over the allotments. Some might sell their allotment to a local landlord, or open a liquor store on their allotment and fuel alcoholism, or encroach on their neighbor's allotment, and such boundary disputes are sometimes resolved with violence. The majority of settlements divide into completely individualized, separate homesteads rather than working the land collectively or communally. Another common weakness reflects the society from which these landless workers come—many of the settlements are dominated by a Christian, patriotic, and patriarchal culture.

Though its weaknesses need to be addressed, the MST has achieved a long list of victories. The movement has won land and self-sufficiency for a huge number of extremely poor people. Many of the settlements they create enjoy a much higher standard of living than the slums they left behind, and are bound by a sense of solidarity and community. By any measure their accomplishment is a triumph for direct action: by disregarding legality or petitioning the powerful for change, over a million people have won themselves land and control over their lives by going out and doing it themselves. Brazilian society has not collapsed due to this wave of anarchy; on the contrary it has become healthier, although many problems remain, in the society at large and in the settlements. It largely comes down to circumstance whether a particular settlement is empowering and liberated or competitive and oppressive.

According to an MST member who worked for several years in one of the most dangerous regions of Brazil, two months was simply not enough time in most cases to overcome people's anti-social training and create a real sense of community, but it was much better than the prevalent pattern in the subsequent period. As the organization experienced a rush to grow, many activists began slapping together settlements by recruiting groups of strangers, promising them land, and sending them off into the regions with the poorest soil or most violent landlords, often contributing to deforestation in the process. Naturally, this emphasis on quantitative results amplified the worst characteristics of the organization and in many ways weakened it, even as its political power increased.[23]

The context for this watershed in the MST was the election of President Lula of the Workers Party (PT) in 2003. Previously, the MST had been autonomous: they did not cooperate with political parties or allow politicians into the organization, although many organizers used the MST to launch political careers. But with the unprecedented victory of the progressive, socialist Workers Party, the leadership of the MST tried to forbid anyone in the organization from publicly speaking out against the government's new agrarian policy. At the same time, the MST began receiving huge amounts of money from the government. Lula had promised to give land to a certain number of families and the MST leadership rushed to fill this quota and engorge their own organization, abandoning their base and their principles. Many influential MST organizers and leaders, backed by the more radical settlements, criticized this collaboration with the government and pushed for a more anti-authoritarian stance, and in fact by 2005, when the PT's agrarian program proved to be a disappointment, the MST began fiercely challenging the government again.

In the eyes of anti-authoritarians the organization had lost its credibility and proven once again the predictable results of collaboration with the government. But within the movement there are still many causes for inspiration. Many of the settlements continue to demonstrate the ability of people to overcome their capitalist

---

23 The criticisms of the this and the following paragraphs are based on an interview with Marcello, "Criticisms of the MST," February 17, 2009, Barcelona.

and authoritarian socialization, if they take it upon themselves to do so. Perhaps the best example are the Comunas da Terra, a network of settlements that make up a minority within the MST, that farm the land communally, nurture a spirit of solidarity, challenge sexism and capitalist mindsets internally, and create working examples of anarchy. It is notable that the people in the Comunas da Terra enjoy a higher standard of life than those who live in the individualized settlements.

There are contemporary examples of non-hierarchical organizing in North America as well. Throughout the United States today, there exist dozens of anarchist projects that are run on a consensus basis. Consensus decision-making may be used on an ad hoc basis to plan an event or campaign, or more permanently to run an infoshop: an anarchist social center that can serve as a radical bookshop, library, café, meeting space, concert hall, or free store. A typical meeting might begin with volunteers filling the positions of facilitator and note-taker. Many groups also use a "vibes-watcher," someone who volunteers to pay special attention to emotions and interactions within the group, recognizing that the personal is political and that the tradition of suppressing emotions in political spaces derives from the separation of public and private, a separation on which patriarchy and the state are based.

Next, the participants create an agenda in which they list all the topics they want to talk about. For each topic, they start by sharing information. If a decision needs to be made, they talk it over until they find a point where everyone's needs and desires converge. Someone states a proposal that synthesizes everyone's input, and they vote on it: approve, abstain, or block. If one person is opposed, the group looks for another solution. The decisions may not always be everyone's first choice, but everyone must feel comfortable with every decision the group adopts. Throughout this process, the facilitator encourages full participation from everyone and makes sure no one is silenced.

Sometimes, the group is unable to solve a particular problem, but the option of not coming to any decision demonstrates that within consensus, the health of the group is more important than efficiency. Such groups form on the principle of voluntary association—anyone is free to leave if she wishes, in contrast to authoritarian structures that may deny people the right to leave or exempt themselves from an arrangement they do not agree to. According to this principle, it is better to respect the differing views of the members of a group than to enforce a decision that leaves some people excluded or silenced. This might seem impractical to those who have not participated in such a process, but consensus has served many infoshops and similar projects in the US for years. Using consensus, these groups have made the decisions necessary to organize spaces and events, reach out to the surrounding communities, bring in new participants, raise money, and resist attempts by local government and business leaders to shut them down. What's more, it seems like the number of projects using consensus in the US is only growing. Granted, consensus works best for people who know one another and have a common interest in working together, whether they are volunteers who want to run an infoshop, neighbors who want to resist gentrification, or members of an affinity group planning attacks against the system—but it does work.

A common complaint is that consensus meetings take longer, but are they really less efficient? Authoritarian models of decision-making, including majority voting in which the minority is forced to conform to the decision of the majority, hide or externalize their true costs. Communities that use authoritarian means to make their decisions cannot exist without police or some other structure to enforce these decisions. Consensus precludes the need for enforcement and punishment by making sure that everyone is satisfied beforehand. When we take into account all the work hours a community loses maintaining a police force, which is a huge drain on resources, the hours spent in consensus meetings seem like a good usage of time after all.

The rebellion in the southern Mexican state of Oaxaca offers another example of popular decision-making. In 2006, people took over Oaxaca City and much of the state. The population of Oaxaca is over half indigenous, and the struggles there against colonialism and capitalism go back five hundred years. In June 2006, 70,000 striking teachers gathered in Oaxaca de Juarez, the capital, to press their demands for a living wage and better facilities for the students. On June 14, the police attacked the teacher's encampment, but the teachers fought back, forcing the police out of the center of the city, taking over government buildings and evicting politicians, and setting up barricades to keep them out. Oaxaca City was self-organized and autonomous for five months, until federal troops were sent in.

After they forced the police out of the capital city, the striking teachers were joined by students and other workers, and together they formed the Asamblea Popular de los Pueblos de Oaxaca (Popular Assembly of the Peoples of Oaxaca). The APPO became a coordinating body for the social movements of Oaxaca, effectively organizing social life and popular resistance for several months in the vacuum created by the collapse of state control. It brought together delegates from unions, non-governmental organizations, social organizations, and cooperatives across the state, seeking to make decisions in the spirit of indigenous practices of consensus—although most assemblies made decisions with a majority vote. APPO founders rejected electoral politics and called for people throughout the state to organize their own assemblies at every level.[24] Recognizing the role of political parties in co-opting popular movements, the APPO banned them from participating.

According to one activist who helped to found the APPO:

> So the APPO was formed to address the abuses and create an alternative. It was to be a space for discussion, reflection, analysis, and action. We recognized that it shouldn't be just one organization, but rather a blanket coordinating body for many different groups. That is, not one ideology would prevail; we would focus on finding the common ground among diverse social actors. Students, teachers, anarchists, Marxists, churchgoers—everyone was invited.
>
> The APPO was born without a formal structure, but soon developed impressive organizational capacity. Decisions in the APPO are made by consensus within the general assembly, which was privileged as a decision-making body. In

---

24 Wikipedia, "Asamblea Popular de los Pueblos de Oaxaca," [viewed November 6, 2006]

the first few weeks of our existence we created the APPO State Council. The council was originally composed of 260 people—approximately ten representatives from each of Oaxaca's seven regions and representatives from Oaxaca's urban neighborhoods and municipalities.

The Provisional Coordination was created to facilitate the operation of the APPO through different commissions. A variety of commissions were established: judicial, finance, communications, human rights, gender equity, defense of natural resources, and many more. Proposals are generated in smaller assemblies of each sector of the APPO and then brought to the general assembly where they are debated further or ratified.[25]

Time and again, spontaneous popular assemblies such as the one created in Oaxaca have proved capable of making sound decisions and coordinating the activities of an entire population. Naturally, they also attract people who want to take over social movements and people who consider themselves natural leaders. In many revolutions, what begins as a horizontal, libertarian rebellion becomes authoritarian as political parties or self-appointed leaders co-opt and shut down popular decision-making structures. Highly visible participants in popular assemblies can also be pushed towards conservatism by government repression, since they are the most visible targets.

This is one way to interpret dynamics that developed in the APPO after the federal invasion of Oaxaca in late October, 2006. As the repression intensified, some of the more vocal participants in the assembly began calling for moderation, to the dismay of the segments of the movement that were still in the streets. Many APPO members and movement participants complain that the group was taken over by Stalinists and other parasites who use popular movements as tools for their political ambitions. And though the APPO had always taken a stand against political parties, the self-appointed leadership took advantage of the difficult

25 Diana Denham and C.A.S.A. Collective (eds.), *Teaching Rebellion: Stories from the Grassroots Mobilization in Oaxaca*, Oakland: PM Press, 2008, interview with Marcos.

situation to call for participation in the upcoming elections as the only pragmatic course of action.

Many people felt betrayed. Support for collaboration was far from universal within APPO; it was controversial even within the APPO Council, the provisional decision-making group that was emerging as a leadership body. Some people within the APPO created other formations to disseminate anarchist, indigenist, or other anti-authoritarian perspectives, and many just went on with their work and ignored the calls to flock to the voting booths. In the end, the anti-authoritarian ethic that constituted the backbone of the movement and the basis of its formal structures proved stronger. The vast majority of Oaxacans boycotted the elections, and the PRI, the conservative party that already held power, dominated among the few people who came out to cast ballots. The attempt to transform the powerful, liberatory social movements of Oaxaca into a bid for political power was an absolute failure.

A smaller Oaxacan city, Zaachila (pop. 25,000), can provide a closer look at horizontal decision-making. For years, groups had been working together against local forms of exploitation; among other efforts, they had managed to defeat the plan to construct a Coca Cola plant which would have consumed much of the available drinking water. When the rebellion erupted in Oaxaca City, a majority of the residents decided to take action. They convoked Zaachila's first popular assembly with the ringing of the bells, calling everyone together, to share the news of the police attack in Oaxaca City and to decide what to do in their own town. More meetings and actions followed:

> Men, women, children, and city council members joined together to take over the municipal building. A lot of the building was locked and we only used the hallways and the offices that were open. We stayed in the municipal building night and day, taking care of everything. And that's how the neighborhood assemblies were born. We'd say, "It's the neighborhood of La Soledad's turn and tomorrow it's up to San Jacinto." That's how the neighborhood assemblies were first used, and then later they turned into decision-making bodies, which is where we are now.

> The seizing of the municipal building was totally spontaneous. The activists from before played a role and initially directed things, but the popular assembly structure was developed little by little...
>
> Neighborhood assemblies, comprised of a rotating body of five people, were also formed in each section of town and together they would form the permanent popular assembly, the People's Council of Zaachila. The people from neighborhood assemblies may not be activists at all, but little by little, as they follow their obligation to bring information back and forth from the Council, they develop their capacity for leadership. All the agreements made in the Council are studied by these five people and then brought back to the neighborhoods for review. These assemblies are completely open; anyone can attend and have their voice heard. Decisions always go to a general vote, and all the adults present can vote. For example, if some people think a bridge needs to be built, and others think we need to focus on improving electricity, we vote on what the priority should be. The simple majority wins, fifty-percent plus one.[26]

The townsfolk kicked out the mayor while maintaining public services, and also established a community radio station. The city served as a model for dozens of other municipalities throughout the state that soon proclaimed their autonomy.

Years before these events in Zaachila, another group was organizing autonomous villages in the state of Oaxaca. As many as twenty-six rural communities affiliated with the CIPO-RFM (Council of Indigenous Peoples of Oaxaca—Ricardo Flores Magon), an organization that identifies with southern Mexico's tradition of indigenous and anarchist resistance; the name references an indigenous anarchist influential in the Mexican Revolution. Insofar as they can, living under an oppressive regime, the CIPO communities assert their autonomy and help one another to meet their needs, ending private property and working the land communally. Typically, when a village expressed interest in joining the group, someone from the CIPO would come and explain how they

---

26 Ditto, interview with Adán.

worked, and let the villagers decide whether or not they wanted to join. The government frequently denied resources to CIPO villages, hoping to starve them out, but it is no surprise that many people thought they could live more richly as masters of their own lives, even if it meant greater material poverty.

How will decisions be enforced?

THE STATE HAS SO THOROUGHLY OBSCURED THE FACT THAT PEOPLE are capable of implementing their own decisions that those raised in this society are hard-pressed to imagine how this could be done without giving a small minority the authority to coerce people into following orders. On the contrary, the power to enforce decisions should be every bit as universal and decentralized as the power to make those decisions. There have been stateless societies on every continent that used diffuse sanctions rather than specialized enforcers. Only through a long and violent process do states steal this ability from people and monopolize it as their own.

This is how diffuse sanctions work: in an ongoing process, a society decides how it wants to organize and what behaviors it considers unacceptable. This may occur over time or in formal, immediate settings. The participation of everybody in making these decisions is complemented by the participation of everybody in upholding them. If somebody breaks these common standards, everyone is accustomed to reacting. They don't call the police, file a grievance, or wait for someone else to do something; they approach the person they think is in the wrong and tell him, or take another appropriate action.

For example, the people in a neighborhood may decide that each different household will take turns cleaning the street. If one household fails to uphold this decision, everybody else on the block has the ability to ask them to fulfill their responsibility. Depending on how serious the transgression is, other people in the neighborhood might react with criticism, ridicule, or ostracism. If the household has a good excuse for being slack, perhaps someone living there is very sick and the others are busy taking care of her, the neighbors can choose to have sympathy and forgive the lapse. This flexibility and sensitivity are typically lacking in a law-based system. On the other hand, if the negligent household has no excuse, and not only do they never clean the streets, they throw their trash in it, their neighbors might hold a general meeting demanding a change in their behavior, or they might take some action like piling all the trash in front of their door. Meanwhile, in their day-to-day interactions individual neighbors might share their criticisms with members of the offending household, or ridicule them, not invite them to joint activities, or glare at them in the streets. If someone is incorrigibly antisocial, always blocking or contradicting the desires of the rest of the group and refusing to respond to people's concerns, the ultimate response is to kick that person out of the group.

This method is much more flexible, and more liberating, than legalitarian, coercive approaches. Rather than being bound to the blind letter of the law, which cannot take into account specific circumstances or people's needs, and depending on a powerful minority for enforcement, the method of diffuse sanctions allows everyone to weigh for herself how serious the transgression is. It also allows transgressors the opportunity to convince others that their actions were justified, thus providing constant challenges to the dominant morality. By contrast, in a statist system, the authorities don't have to show that something is right or wrong before condemning someone's home or confiscating a drug deemed illegal. All they have to do is cite a statute in a law book that their victims had no hand in writing.

In a horizontal society, people enforce decisions according to how enthusiastic they are about those decisions. If almost everybody strongly supports a decision, it will be upheld vigorously, whereas if a decision leaves most people feeling neutral or unenthusiastic, it will only be partially enforced, leaving open more room for creative transgression and exploring other solutions. On the other hand a lack of enthusiasm in implementing decisions might mean that in practice organization falls on the shoulders of informal powerholders—people who are delegated an unofficial position of leadership by the rest of the group, whether they want it or not. This means that members of horizontal groups, from collective houses to entire societies, must confront the problem of self-discipline. They must hold themselves accountable to the standards they have agreed upon and the criticism of their peers, and risk being unpopular or confronting conflict by criticizing those who do not uphold common standards—calling out the housemate who does not do dishes or the community that does not contribute to road maintenance. It's a difficult process, often lacking in many current anarchist projects, but without it group decision-making is a façade and responsibility is vague and unequally shared. Going through this process, people become more empowered and more connected with those around them.

Groups always contain the possibility for conformity and conflict. Authoritarian groups typically avoid conflict by enforcing greater levels of conformity. Pressures to conform also exist in anarchist groups, but without restrictions on human movement, it is easier for people to leave and join other groups or to act or live on their own. Thus, people can choose the levels of conformity and conflict they want to tolerate, and in the process of finding and leaving groups, people change and challenge social norms.

In the newly created state of Israel, Jews who had participated in socialist movements in Europe took the opportunity to create hundreds of *kibbutzim*, utopian communal farms. In these farms, the members created a strong example of communal living and decision-making. At a typical kibbutz, most decisions were made at a general town meeting, held twice weekly. The frequency and length of meetings stemmed from the fact that so many aspects of social life were open to debate, and the common belief that proper decisions "can only be made after intensive group discussion."[27] There were about a dozen elected positions in the kibbutz, related to managing the commune's financial affairs and coordinating production and trade, but the general policy had to be decided in general meetings. Official positions were limited to terms of a few years, and the members encouraged a culture of "office-hating," a reluctance to take office and a disdain for those who appeared to be power hungry.

---

27 Melford E. Spiro, *Kibbutz: Venture in Utopia*, New York: Schocken Books, 1963, pp. 90–91.

No one in the kibbutz had coercive authority. Neither were there police in the kibbutz, though it was common for everyone to leave their doors unlocked. Public opinion was the most important factor ensuring social cohesion. If there was a problem with a member of the commune, it was discussed at the general meeting, but most of the time even the threat of it being brought up at the general meeting motivated people to work out their differences. In the worst case scenario, if a member refused to accept group decisions, the rest of the collective could vote to kick her out. But this ultimate sanction differs from the coercive tactics used by the state in a key respect: voluntary groups only exist because everyone involved wants to work with everyone else. A person who is excluded is not deprived of the ability to survive or maintain relationships, as there are many other groups she can join. More importantly, she is not forced to abide by collective decisions. In a society based on this principle, people would enjoy a social mobility that is denied to people in statist contexts, in which laws are enforced upon an individual whether she approves of them or not. In any case, expulsion was not common in the kibbutzim, because public opinion and group discussion were sufficient to solve most conflicts.

But the kibbutzim had other problems, which can teach us important lessons about creating collectives. After about a decade, the kibbutzim began to succumb to the pressures of the capitalist world that surrounded them. Although internally the kibbutzim were strikingly communal, they were never properly anti-capitalist; from the beginning, they attempted to exist as competitive producers within a capitalist economy. The need to compete in the economy, and thus to industrialize, encouraged a greater reliance on experts, while influence from the rest of society fostered consumerism.

At the same time, there was a negative reaction to the lack of privacy intentionally structured into the kibbutz—common showers, for example. The purpose of this lack of privacy was to engineer a more communal spirit. But because the designers of the kibbutz did not realize that privacy is as important to people's well-being as social connectedness, kibbutz members began to feel stifled over time, and withdrew from the public life of the kibbutz, including their participation in decision-making.

Another vital lesson of the kibbutzim is that building utopian collectives must involve tireless struggle against contemporary authoritarian structures, or they will become part of those structures. The kibbutzim were founded on land seized by the Israeli state from Palestinians, against whom genocidal policies are still continuing today. The racism of the European founders allowed them to ignore the abuse inflicted on the previous inhabitants of what they saw as a promised land, much the same way religious pilgrims in North America plundered the indigenous to construct their new society. The Israeli state gained incredibly from the fact that nearly all their potential dissidents—including socialists and veterans of armed struggle against Nazism and colonialism—voluntarily sequestered themselves in escapist communes that contributed to the capitalist economy. If these utopians had used the kibbutz as a base to struggle against capitalism and colonialism in solidarity with the Palestinians while constructing the foundations of a communal society, history in the Middle East might have turned out differently.

Who will settle disputes?

ANARCHIST METHODS OF SETTLING DISPUTES OPEN UP A MUCH healthier range of options than are available within a capitalist and statist system. Stateless societies throughout history have come up with numerous methods for settling disputes that seek compromise, allow for reconciliation, and keep power in the hands of the disputants and their community.

The Nubians are a society of sedentary farmers in Egypt. They were traditionally stateless, and even according to recent accounts they consider it highly immoral to bring in the government to solve disputes. In contrast to the individualistic and legalistic ways of viewing disputes in authoritarian societies, the norm in Nubian culture is to consider one person's problem everyone's problem; when there is a dispute, strangers, friends, relatives, or other third parties intercede to help the disputants find a mutually satisfying resolution. According to anthropologist Robert Fernea, Nubian culture regards quarrels between members of a kinship group as dangerous, in that they threaten the supportive social net on which all depend.

This culture of cooperation and mutual responsibility is backed up by economic and social structures as well. Among the Nubians, property such as waterwheels, cattle, and palm trees have traditionally been communally owned, so in the daily work of feeding themselves people are immersed in cooperative social bonds that teach solidarity and the importance of getting along. Additionally, the kinship groups which comprise Nubian society, called "nogs," are interwoven, not atomized like the isolated nuclear families of Western society: "This means that a person's nogs are overlapping and involve diverse, dispersed membership. This feature is very important, for the Nubian community does not easily split into opposing factions."[28] Most disputes are resolved quickly by a third relative. Larger disputes that embroil more people are solved in a family council with all the members of the nog, including women and children. The council is presided over by an elder kinsman, but the goal is to reach consensus and get the disputants to reconcile.

The Hopi of southwestern North America used to be more warlike than in recent times. Factions still exist within Hopi villages, but they overcome conflict through cooperation in rituals, and they use shame and leveling mechanisms with people who are boastful or domineering. When disputes get out of hand, they use ritual clown skits at *kachina* dances to mock the people involved. The Hopi offer an example of a society that gave up feuding and developed rituals to cultivate a more peaceful disposition.[29] The image of clowns and dances being used to solve disputes gives a

28 Robert Fernea, "Putting a Stone in the Middle: the Nubians of Northern Africa," in Graham Kemp and Douglas P. Fry (eds.), *Keeping the Peace: Conflict Resolution and Peaceful Societies around the World*, New York: Routledge, 2004, p. 111.

29 Alice Schlegel, "Contentious But Not Violent: The Hopi of Northern Arizona" in Graham Kemp and Douglas P. Fry (eds.), *Keeping the Peace: Conflict Resolution and Peaceful Societies around the World*, New York: Routledge, 2004.

tantalizing glimpse of humor and art as means for responding to common problems. There is a world of possibilities more interesting than general assemblies or mediation processes! Artistic conflict resolution encourages new ways of looking at problems, and subverts the possibility of permanent mediators or meeting facilitators gaining power by monopolizing the role of arbiter.

Meeting in the streets

POLITICIANS AND TECHNOCRATS ARE CLEARLY NOT CAPABLE OF making responsible decisions for millions of people. They have learned enough from their many past mistakes that governments usually do not collapse under the weight of their own incompetence, but they have hardly created the best of all possible worlds. If they can manage to keep their absurd bureaucracies functioning, it's not a wild jump of logic to think that we could organize our communities at least as well ourselves. The hypothesis of authoritarian society, that a large, diverse population needs specialized institutions to control decision-making, can be disproven many times over. The MST of Brazil shows that in a huge group of people, most decision-making power can reside at the grassroots level, with individual communities that take care of their own needs. The people of Oaxaca showed that an entire modern society can organize itself and coordinate resistance against constant assault by police and paramilitaries, with open assemblies. Anarchist infoshops and Israeli kibbutzim show that groups running complex operations that have to pay rent or meet production schedules while accomplishing social and cultural objectives capitalist enterprises never even attempt, can make decisions in a timely fashion and uphold these decisions without a class of enforcers. The Nuer show that horizontal decision-making can thrive for generations, even after colonization, and that with a shared culture of restorative conflict resolution there is no need for a specialized institution to solve disputes.

For most of human history, our societies have been egalitarian and self-organizing, and we have not lost the capability to make and uphold the decisions that affect our lives, or to imagine new and better forms of organizing. Whenever people overcome alienation and come together with their neighbors, they develop exciting new ways of coordinating and making decisions. Once they liberated themselves from landlords, priests, and mayors, the uneducated and downtrodden peasants of Aragon proved themselves equal to the task of making not just a whole new world, but hundreds of them.

New decision-making methods are usually influenced by pre-existing institutions and cultural values. When people recapture decision-making authority over some aspect of their lives, they should ask themselves what reference points and precedents already exist in their culture, and what ingrained disadvantages they will have to overcome. For example, there might be a tradition of town meetings that can be expanded from symbolic window dressing to real self-organization; on the other hand, people might be starting from a macho culture, in which case they will have to learn how to listen, compromise, and ask questions. Alternately, if a group develops a decision-making method that is totally original and alien to their society, they may face challenges including newcomers and explaining their method to outsiders—this is sometimes a weakness of infoshops in the US, which employ a well thought-out, idealized form of decision-making complex enough to seem foreign even to many participants.

An anti-authoritarian group may use some form of consensus, or of majoritarian voting. Large groups may find voting quicker and more efficient, but it can also silence a minority. Perhaps the most important part of the process is the discussion that happens before the decision; voting does not diminish the importance of methods that allow everyone to communicate and arrive at good compromises. Many autonomous villages in Oaxaca ultimately used voting to make decisions, and they provided an inspiring example of self-organization to radicals who otherwise abhor voting. Though a group's structure doubtlessly influences its culture and outcomes, the formality of voting may be an acceptable expedient if all the discussion that takes place before it is steeped in a spirit of solidarity and cooperation.

In a self-organizing society, not everyone will participate equally in meetings or other formal spaces. A decision-making body can eventually become dominated by certain people, and the assembly itself can become a bureaucratic institution with coercive powers. For this reason, it may be necessary to develop decentralized and overlapping forms of organization and decision-making, and to preserve space for spontaneous organization to occur outside of all pre-existing structures. If there is only one structure in which all decisions are made, an internal culture can develop that is not inclusive to everyone in the society; then experienced insiders can rise to positions of leadership, and human activity external to the structure can be delegitimized. Soon enough, you have a government. The kibbutzim and APPO both evidence the creeping development of bureaucracy and specialization.

But if there are multiple decision-making structures for different spheres of life, and if they can arise or fade out according to need, none of them can monopolize authority. In this regard, power needs to stay in the streets, in the homes, in the hands of the people who exercise it, and in the meeting of people who come together to solve problems.

Recommended Reading:

- Gaston Leval, *Collectives in the Spanish Revolution*, London: Freedom Press, 1975 (translated from the French by Vernon Richards).
- Melford E. Spiro, *Kibbutz: Venture in Utopia*, New York: Schocken Books, 1963.
- Peter Gelderloos, *Consensus: A New Handbook for Grassroots Social, Political, and Environmental Groups*, Tucson: See Sharp Press, 2006.
- Natasha Gordon and Paul Chatterton, *Taking Back Control: A Journey through Argentina's Popular Uprising*, Leeds (UK): University of Leeds, 2004.
- Marianne Maeckelbergh, *The Will of the Many: How the Alterglobalisation Movement is Changing the Face of Democracy*, London: Pluto Press, 2009.

3. ECONOMY

ANARCHISM IS OPPOSED TO CAPITALISM AND TO PRIVATE OWNER-ship of the tools, infrastructure, and resources everyone requires for sustenance. Anarchist economic models range from hunter-gatherer communities and agricultural communes to industrial complexes in which planning is carried out by syndicates and distribution is arranged through quotas or a limited form of currency. All these models are based on the principles of working together to fulfill common needs and rejecting hierarchy of all kinds—including bosses, management, and the division of society into classes such as wealthy and poor or owners and laborers.

Without wages, what is the incentive to work?

SOME WORRY THAT IF WE ABOLISH CAPITALISM AND WAGE-LABOR, no one will work anymore. It is true that work as it exists now for most people would cease to exist; but work that is socially useful offers a number of incentives besides the paycheck. If anything, getting paid to do something makes it less enjoyable. The alienation of labor that is a part of capitalism destroys natural incentives to work such as the pleasure of acting freely and the satisfaction of a job well done. When work puts us in a position of inferiority—to the boss who oversees us and the wealthy people who own our workplace—and we do not have decision-making power in our job but must mindlessly follow orders, it can become excruciatingly odious and mind-numbing. We also lose our natural incentive to work when we are not doing something that is useful for our communities. Of the few workers today who are lucky enough to actually produce something they can see, they are nearly all making something that is profitable to their employers but completely meaningless to them personally. The Fordist or assembly line structuring of labor turns people into machines. Instead of cultivating skills workers can be proud of, it proves more cost-effective to give each person a single repetitive task and put him or her on an assembly line. No wonder so many workers sabotage or steal from their workplaces, or show up with an automatic weapon and "go postal."

The idea that without wages people would stop working is baseless. In the broad timeline of human history, wages are a fairly recent invention yet societies that have existed without currency or wages did not starve to death just because no one paid the workers. With the abolition of wage labor, only the kind of work that no one can justify to himself as useful would disappear; all the time and resources put into making all the useless crap that our society is drowning in would be saved. Think of how much of our resources and labor go into advertising, mass mailings, throwaway packaging, cheap toys, disposable goods—things no one takes pride in making, designed to fall apart in a short time so you have to buy the next version.

Indigenous societies with less division of labor had no problem doing without wages, because the primary economic activities—producing food, housing, clothing, tools—are all easily connected to common needs. In such circumstances, work is a necessary social activity and an apparent obligation from every member of the community who is able. And because it takes place in a flexible, personal setting, work can be adapted to every individual's capabilities, and there is nothing to keep people from transforming work into play. Fixing up your house, hunting, wandering in the woods identifying plants and animals, knitting, cooking a feast—aren't these the things that bored middle-class people do in their leisure hours to forget their loathsome jobs for a moment?

Anti-capitalist societies with greater economic specialization have developed a variety of methods for providing incentives and distributing the products of workers' labor. The aforementioned Israeli kibbutzim offer one example of incentives to work in the absence of wages. One book documenting life and work in a kibbutz identifies four major motivations to work within the cooperative labor teams, which lacked individual competition and profit motive: group productivity affects the whole community's standard of living, so there is group pressure to work hard; members work where they choose, and gain satisfaction from their work; people develop a competitive pride if their branch of work does better than other branches; people gain prestige from work because labor is a cultural value.[30] As described above, the ultimate decline of the kibbutz experiment stemmed largely from the fact that the kibbutzim were socialist enterprises competing within a capitalist economy, and thus subsumed to the logic of competition rather than the logic of mutual aid. A similarly organized commune in a world without capitalism would not face these same problems. In any case, unwillingness to work due to lack of wages was not one of the problems the kibbutzim faced.

Many anarchists suggest that the germs of capitalism are contained in the mentality of production itself. Whether a given type of economy can survive, much less grow, within capitalism is a poor measure of its liberatory potential. But anarchists propose and debate many different forms of economy, some of which can only be practiced to a limited extent because they are wholly illegal within today's world. In the European squatter's movement, some cities have had or continue to have so many squatted social centers and houses that they constitute a shadow society. In Barcelona, for example, as recently as 2008 there were over forty occupied social centers and at least two hundred squatted houses. The collectives of people who inhabit these squats generally use consensus and

---

30 Melford E. Spiro, Kibbutz: *Venture in Utopia*, New York: Schocken Books, 1963, pp. 83–85.

group assemblies, and most are explicitly anarchist or intentionally anti-authoritarian. To a large extent, work and exchange have been abolished from these people's lives, whose networks run into the thousands. Many do not have waged jobs, or they work only seasonally or sporadically, as they do not need to pay rent. For example the author of this book, who has lived within this network for two years, has survived for much of that time on less than one euro a day. Moreover, the great amount of activity they carry out within the autonomous movement is completely unwaged. But they do not need wages: they work for themselves. They occupy abandoned buildings left to rot by speculators, as a protest against gentrification and as anti-capitalist direct action to provide themselves with housing. Teaching themselves the skills they need along the way, they fix up their new houses, cleaning, patching roofs, installing windows, toilets, showers, light, kitchens, and anything else they need. They often pirate electricity, water, and internet, and much of their food comes from dumpster-diving, stealing, and squatted gardens.

In the total absence of wages or managers, they carry on a great deal of work, but at their own pace and logic. The logic is one of mutual aid. Besides fixing up their own houses, they also direct their energies towards working for their neighborhoods and enriching their communities. They provide for many of their collective needs besides housing. Some social centers host bicycle repair workshops, enabling people to repair or build their own bicycles, using old parts. Others offer carpentry workshops, self-defense and yoga workshops, natural healing workshops, libraries, gardens, communal meals, art and theater groups, language classes, alternative media and counterinformation, music shows, movies, computer labs where people can use the internet and learn email security or host their own websites, and solidarity events to deal with the inevitable repression. Nearly all of these services are provided absolutely free. There is no exchange—one group organizes to provide a service to everyone, and the entire social network benefits.

With an astounding amount of initiative in such a passive society, squatters regularly get the idea to organize a communal meal or a bicycle repair shop or a weekly movie showing, they talk with friends and friends of friends until they have enough people and resources to make their idea a reality, and then they spread the word or put up posters and hope as many people as possible will come and partake. To a capitalist mentality, they are avidly inviting people to rob them, but the squatters never stop to question activities that don't put money in their pockets. It is evident that they have created a new form of wealth, and sharing what they make themselves clearly makes them richer.

The surrounding neighborhoods also become richer, as the squatters take the initiative to create projects much quicker than the local government could. In the magazine of a neighborhood association in Barcelona, they praised a local squat for responding to a demand the government had been ignoring for years—building the neighborhood a library. A mainstream news magazine remarked: "the squatters do the work the District forgets about."[31] In that same neighborhood, the squatters proved to be a powerful ally to a rent-paying neighbor who was being pressured out by the landlord. The squatters worked tirelessly with an association of old folks who were facing similar situations of chicanery and illegal eviction by landlords, and they stopped the eviction of their neighbor.

In a trend that seems common to the total abolition of work, the social and the economic blend to become indistinguishable. Labor and services are not valorized or given a dollar value; they are social activities that are carried out individually or collectively as a part of daily life, without any need for accounting or management. The result is that in cities such as Barcelona, people can spend the majority of their time and meet the majority of their needs—from housing to entertainment—within this squatters' social network, without labor and almost without money. Of course not everything can be stolen (not yet), and the squatters are still compelled to sell their labor to pay for things like medical care and court costs. But for many people the exceptional nature

---

31 Gemma Aguilar, "Els okupes fan la feina que oblida el Districte," *Avui*, Saturday 15 December 2007, p. 43.

of those things that cannot be self-produced, scavenged, or stolen, the outrage of having to sell valuable moments of one's life to work for some corporation, can have the effect of increasing the level of conflict with capitalism.

One potential pitfall of any movement powerful enough to create an alternative to capitalism is that its participants can easily become complacent living in their bubble of autonomy and lose the will to fight for the total abolition of capitalism. Squatting itself can easily become a ritual, and in Barcelona the movement as a whole has not applied the same creativity to resistance and attack as it has to many of the practical aspects of fixing up houses and finding subsistence with little or no money. The self-sustaining nature of the network of squatters, the immediate presence of freedom, initiative, pleasure, independence, and community in their lives have by no means destroyed capitalism, but they do reveal it to be a walking corpse, with nothing but the police, in the end, preventing it from becoming extinct and being replaced by far superior forms of living.

Don't people need bosses and experts?

HOW CAN ANARCHISTS ORGANIZE THEMSELVES IN THE WORKPLACE and coordinate production and distribution across an entire economy without bosses and managers? In fact, a great deal of resources are lost through competition and middlemen. Ultimately it is the workers who carry out all the production and distribution, and they know how to coordinate their own work in the absence of bosses.

In and around Turin, Italy, 500,000 workers participated in a factory takeover movement after World War I. Communists, anarchists, and other workers who were pissed off at their exploitation launched wildcat strikes, many of them eventually gaining control of their factories and setting up Factory Councils to coordinate their activities. They were able to run the factories themselves, without bosses. Eventually, the Councils were legalized and legislated out of existence—in part co-opted and absorbed into the labor unions, whose institutional existence was threatened by autonomous workers' power no less than the owners were.

In December 2001, a long-brewing economic crisis in Argentina matured into a run on the banks which precipitated a major popular rebellion. Argentina had been the poster child of neoliberal institutions such as the International Monetary Fund, but the policies that enriched foreign investors and gave middle class Argentinians a First World lifestyle created an acute poverty for much of the country. Anti-capitalist resistance was already widely developed among the unemployed, and after the middle class lost all its savings, millions of people took to the streets, rejecting all the false solutions and excuses offered by politicians, economists, and the media, declaring instead: "Que se vayan todos!" *They all must go!* Dozens were killed by police, but people fought back, shaking off the terror left over from the military dictatorship that ruled Argentina in the '70s and '80s.

Hundreds of factories abandoned by their owners were occupied by workers, who resumed production so they could continue to feed their families. The more radical of these worker-occupied factories equalized wages and shared managerial duties among all workers. They made decisions in open meetings, and some workers taught themselves tasks such as accounting. To ensure that a new managerial class did not arise, some factories rotated managerial tasks, or required that people in managerial roles still work on the factory floor and perform the accounting, marketing, and other tasks after hours. As of this writing, several of these occupied workplaces have been able to expand their workforce and hire additional workers from Argentina's huge unemployed population. In some cases, occupied factories trade needed supplies and products with one another, creating a shadow economy in a spirit of solidarity.

One of the most famous, the Zanon ceramics factory located in southern Argentina, was shut down by the owner in 2001 and occupied by its workers the following January. They began running the factory with an open assembly and commissions made up of workers to manage Sales, Administration, Planning, Security, Hygiene and Sanitation, Purchasing, Production, Diffusion, and Press. Following the occupation, they rehired workers who had been fired before the closing. As of 2004, they numbered 270 workers and produced at

50% of the production rate before the factory was closed. Bringing doctors and psychologists on site, they provided themselves with healthcare. The workers found that they could pay their workforce with just two days of production, so they lowered prices 60% and organized a network of young vendors, many previously unemployed, to market the ceramic tiles throughout the city. In addition to producing tiles, the Zanon factory involves itself with social movements, donating money to hospitals and schools, selling tiles at cost to poor people, hosting films, performances, and art shows, and carrying out solidarity actions with other struggles. They also support the Mapuche struggle for autonomy; and when their clay supplier stopped doing business with them for political reasons, the Mapuche began supplying clay. As of April 2003, the factory had faced four attempted evictions by the police, with the support of the trade unions. All were forcefully resisted by the workers, assisted by neighbors, *piqueteros*, and others.

In July 2001, the workers of the El Tigre supermarket in Rosario, Argentina, occupied their workplace. The owner had shut it down two months earlier and declared bankruptcy, still owing his employees months in wages. After fruitless protesting, the workers opened El Tigre and began running it themselves through an assembly that allowed all workers a part in decision-making. In a spirit of solidarity they lowered prices and began selling fruit and vegetables from a local farmers' cooperative and products made in other occupied factories. They also used part of their space to open a cultural center for the neighborhood, housing political talks, student groups, theater and yoga workshops, puppet shows, a café, and a library. In 2003, El Tigre's cultural center held the national meeting of reclaimed businesses, attended by 1,500 people. Maria, one collective member, said of her experience: "Three years ago, if someone had told me we'd be able to run this place I'd never have believed them… I believed we needed bosses to tell us what to do, now I realize that together we can do it better than them."[32]

---

32 Natasha Gordon and Paul Chatterton, *Taking Back Control: A Journey through Argentina's Popular Uprising*, Leeds (UK): University of Leeds, 2004, p. 45.

In Euskal Herria, the Basque country occupied by the states of Spain and France, a large complex of cooperative, worker-owned businesses has arisen, centered around the small city of Mondragón. Starting with 23 workers in one cooperative in 1956, the Mondragón cooperatives included 19,500 workers in over 100 cooperatives by 1986, surviving despite the heavy recession in Spain at the time and with a survival rate many times better than the average for capitalist firms.

> Mondragón has had a rich experience over many years in manufacturing products as varied as furniture, kitchen equipment, machine tools, and electronic components and in printing, shipbuilding, and metal smelting. Mondragón has created hybrid cooperatives composed of both consumers and workers and of farmers and workers. The complex has developed its own social security cooperative and a cooperative bank that is growing more rapidly than any other bank in the Basque provinces.[33]

The highest authority in the Mondragón cooperatives is the general assembly, with each worker-member getting one vote; the specific management of the cooperative is carried out by an elected governing council, which is advised by a management council and a social council.

There are also many criticisms of the Mondragón complex. To anarchists it comes as no surprise that a democratic structure can house an elite group, and according to Mondragón's critics this is exactly what has happened as the cooperative complex seeks—and achieves—success within a capitalist economy. Although their accomplishment is impressive and gives lie to the assumption that large industries must be organized hierarchically, the compulsion to be profitable and competitive has pushed the cooperatives to manage their own exploitation. For example, after decades of sticking by their egalitarian founding principles regarding pay

---

33 William Foote Whyte and Kathleen King Whyte, *Making Mondragon: The Growth and Dynamics of the Worker Cooperative Complex*, Ithaca, New York: ILR Press, 1988, p. 5.

scales, eventually the Mondragón cooperatives decided to increase the salaries of the managerial and technical experts relative to the manual workers. Their reason was that they had a hard time retaining people who could receive much higher pay for their skills in a corporation. This problem indicates a need to mix manual and intellectual tasks to avoid the professionalization of expertise (i.e. creating expertise as a quality restricted to an elite few); and to build an economy in which people are producing not for profit but for other members of the network, so money loses its importance and people work out of a sense of community and solidarity.

People in today's high-tech societies are trained to believe that examples from the past or from the "under-developed" world have no value for our situation today. Many people who consider themselves educated sociologists and economists dismiss the Mondragón example by classifying Basque culture as exceptional. But there are other examples of the efficacy of egalitarian workplaces, even in the heart of capitalism.

Gore Associates, based in Delaware, is the billion dollar high-tech firm that produces waterproof Gore-Tex fabric, special insulation for computer cables, and parts for the medical, automobile, and semiconductor industries. Salaries are determined collectively, no one has titles, there is no formal management structure, and differentiation between employees is minimized. By all capitalist standards of performance—employee turnover, profitability, product reputation, lists of best companies to work for—Gore is a success.

An important factor in their success is adherence to what some academics call the Rule of 150. Based on the observation that hunter-gatherer groups around the world—as well as successful communities and intentional communes—seem to keep their size between 100 and 150 people, the theory is that the human brain is best equipped to navigate webs of personal relationships of up to 150. Maintaining intimate relationships, remembering names and social status and established codes of conduct and communication—all this takes up mental space; just as other primates tend to live in groups up to a certain size, human beings are probably best suited to keep up with a certain number of companions. All

Gore factories keep their size below 150 employees, so each plant can be entirely self-managing, not just on the factory floor but also including the people responsible for marketing, research, and other tasks.[34]

Skeptics often dismiss the anarchistic example of small-scale "primitive" societies by arguing that it's no longer possible to organize on such a small scale, given the huge population. But there is nothing to stop a large society from organizing itself in many smaller units. Small-scale organization is eminently possible. Even within a high-tech industry, Gore factories can coordinate with one another and with suppliers and consumers while maintaining their small scale organizational structure. Just as each unit is capable of organizing its internal relations, each is capable of organizing its external relations.

Of course, the example of a factory producing successfully within the capitalist system leaves much to be desired. Most anarchists would sooner see all factories burned to the ground than anti-authoritarian forms of organization used to sugarcoat capitalism. But this example should at least demonstrate that even within a large and complex society, self-organization works.

The example of Gore is still problematic because the workers do not own the factory, and also because formal management could be reimposed at any time by the company owners. Anarchists theorize that the problems of capitalism do not exist only in the relationship between workers and owners, but also between workers and managers, and that as long as the manager-worker relationship persists, capitalism can reemerge. This theory is certainly born out by the Mondragón example, where over time managers gained more pay and power and renewed the unequal, profit-focused dynamics typical of capitalism. Taking this into account, several anarchists have designed an outline for a "participatory economy," or parecon, though no one has yet had the opportunity to set up such an economy on any considerable scale. Among other things, parecon emphasizes the importance of empowering all workers by

---

34 Malcolm Gladwell, *The Tipping Point: How Little Things Can Make a Big Difference.* New York: Little, Brown, and Company, 2002, pp. 183–187.

mixing tasks that are creative and rote, mental and manual, thus creating "balanced job complexes" that will prevent the emergence of a managerial class.[35]

During the rebellion in Oaxaca in 2006, people without prior experience organized themselves to run occupied radio and television stations. They were motivated by the social need for free means of communication. The March of Pots and Pans, the legendary women's march on August 1, 2006, culminated with thousands of women spontaneously taking over the state-run television station. Inspired by the sudden sense of power they had won by rebelling against a traditionally patriarchal society, they took over Channel 9, which continuously slandered the social movements while claiming to be the channel of the people. At first, they made the engineers help them run the station, but soon they were learning how to do it themselves. One woman recounted:

> I went daily to the channel to stand guard and help out. The women were organized into different commissions: food, hygiene, production, and security. One thing I liked is that there were no individual leaders. For each task there was a group of several women in charge. We learned everything from the beginning. I remember somebody asking who could use a computer. Then many of the younger girls stepped forward, saying, "me, me, I can!" In Radio Universidad, they announced that we needed people with technical skills, and more people came to help. In the beginning, they were filming headless people, you know. But the experience at Channel 9 showed us that where there's a will, there's a way. Things got done, and they got done well.
>
> In the short time [three weeks] that Channel 9 was running, until Governor Ulises commanded that the antennas be destroyed, we managed to spread a lot of information. Movies and documentaries were shown that you could never have imagined seeing on TV otherwise. About different social movements, about the student massacre in Tlatelolco in Mexico City in 1968, the massacres in Aguas Blancas in Guerrero and Acteal in Chiapas, about

---

35 Michael Albert, *Parecon: Life After Capitalism*, New York: Verso, 2003, pp. 104–105.

> guerrilla movements in Cuba and El Salvador. At this time, Channel 9 wasn't just the women's channel anymore. It was the channel of all the people. The ones participating made their own programs as well. There was a youth program and a program where people from the indigenous communities participated. There was a program of denouncements, where anyone could come and denounce how the government had treated them. A lot of people from the different neighborhoods and communities wanted to participate, there was hardly enough airtime for all of them.[36]

After the occupied television station was taken off the air, the movement responded by occupying all eleven commercial radio stations in Oaxaca. The homogeneity of commercial radio was replaced by myriad voices—a radio station for university students, one for the women's groups, one radio station occupied by the anarchists from a punk squat—and there were more indigenous voices on the radio than ever before. Within a short time, people in the movement decided to return most of the radio stations to their self-styled owners, but kept control of two of them. Their goal was not to suppress the voices that opposed them, as artificial as commercial voices are, but to win themselves the means to communicate. The remaining radio stations operated successfully for months, until government repression shut them down. One university student involved in taking over, running, and defending the radio stations said:

> After the takeover, I read an article that said that the intellectual and material authors of the takeovers of the radios weren't Oaxacan, that they came from somewhere else, and that they received very specialized support. It said that it would have been impossible for anyone without previous training to operate the radios in such a short amount of time, because the equipment is too sophisticated for just anyone to use. They were wrong.[37]

---

36 Diana Denham and C.A.S.A. Collective (eds.), *Teaching Rebellion: Stories from the Grassroots Mobilization in Oaxaca*, Oakland: PM Press, 2008, interview with Tonia.
37 Ditto, interview with Francisco.

Who will take out the trash?

IF EVERYONE IS FREE TO WORK AS THEY CHOOSE, WHO WILL TAKE out the trash or perform other undesirable jobs? Fortunately, in a localized, anti-capitalist economy, we could not *externalize*, or hide, the costs of our lifestyle by paying someone else to clean up after us. We would have to pay for the consequences of all our own actions—rather than paying China to take our toxic waste, for example. If a necessary service like garbage disposal were being neglected, the community would quickly notice and have to decide how to handle the problem. People could agree to reward such work with small perks—nothing that translates into power or authority, but something like getting to be first in line when exotic goods come into town, receiving a massage or a cake or simply the recognition and gratitude for being a stand-up member of the community. Ultimately, in a cooperative society, having a good reputation and being seen by your peers as responsible are more compelling than any material incentives.

Or the community could decide that everyone should involve themselves in these tasks on a rotating basis. An activity like garbage collection does not have to define anyone's "career" in an anti-capitalist economy. Necessary tasks no one wants to perform should be shared by everyone. So instead of a few people having to sort through garbage their entire lives, everyone who was physically able would have to do it for just a couple hours each month.

The Christiania "free state" is a quarter in Copenhagen, Denmark, that has been squatted since 1971. Its 850 inhabitants are autonomous within their 85 acres. They have been taking out their own trash for over thirty years. The fact that they receive about one million visitors a year makes their achievement all the more impressive. The streets, buildings, restaurants, public toilets, and public showers are all reasonably clean—especially for hippies! The body of water that runs through Christiania is not the cleanest, but considering that Christiania is tree-covered and automobile free one suspects most of the pollution comes from the surrounding city that shares the waterway.

Residents have built dozens of the houses now standing in Christiania using innovative eco-designs. They also use:

> solar power, wind power, composting and a whole host of other eco-friendly innovations. A method of filtering sewage through reed beds, which means water coming out of Christiania is as clean as that coming out from the rest of Copenhagen's treatment plants, has helped the commune be shortlisted for a pan-Scandinavian award for ecological living.[38]

Different people interviewed had different conceptions of how Christiania was kept clean, suggesting a sort of dual system. A newcomer said that you cleaned up after yourself, and when you felt like doing some extra picking up, you did. An old-time resident who was more involved in decision-making explained there was a garbage committee, answerable to the "Common Meeting," responsible for the bottom-line of keeping Christiania clean, though clearly voluntary assistance and cleanliness by all the residents was the first line of defense.

Who will take care of the elderly and disabled?

ONLY IN A SOCIETY WITH WHAT IS EUPHEMISTICALLY TERMED A "highly competitive market" are elderly people and disabled people so marginalized. In order to increase profit margins, employers avoid hiring people with disabilities and force older workers into early retirement. When workers are compelled to move frequently in search of jobs, in a culture in which the rite of passage to adulthood is moving into your own house, parents are left alone as they age. Most eventually move into whatever kind of retirement facility they can afford; many die neglected, alone, and indignant, perhaps with bed sores and diapers that have not been changed in two days. In an anarchist, anti-capitalist world, the social fabric would not be so coarse.

---

38 Cahal Milmo, "On the Barricades: Trouble in a Hippie Paradise," *The Independent*, May 31, 2007.

In the plethora of experiments that arose in Argentina in response to the crisis of 2001, the economics of solidarity and care for all members of society flourished. The economic collapse in Argentina did not lead to the dog-eat-dog scenario that capitalists fear. Rather, the result was an explosion of solidarity, and the elderly and disabled have not been left out of this web of mutual aid. In participating in the neighborhood assemblies, elderly and disabled people in Argentina got a chance to secure their own needs and represent themselves in the decisions that would affect their lives. At some assemblies, participants suggested that those who own their own houses withhold their property tax and instead give that money to the local hospital or other care facilities. In parts of Argentina with severe unemployment, movements of unemployed workers have effectively taken over and are building new economies. In General Mosconi, an oil town in the north, unemployment is above 40%, and the area is largely autonomous. The movement has organized over 300 projects to see to people's needs, including those of the elderly and disabled.

Even in the absence of stored wealth or fixed infrastructure, stateless hunter-gatherer societies generally take care of all the members of their community regardless of whether they are economically productive. In fact, grandparents—genetically useless from a Darwinist point of view since they are past the age of reproduction[39]—are a defining characteristic of humankind going back millions of years, and the fossil record from the beginning of our species shows that the elderly were cared for. Modern

---

39 Technically, human elders provide a reproductive function because they store obscure types of information like how to survive natural disasters that only occur once every several generations, and they can also serve to increase social cohesion by increasing the amount of living relations within the community—for example the number of people with the same grandparents is much larger than the number of people with the same parents. However, these survival benefits are not immediately obvious and there is no evidence of any human society making such calculations when deciding whether or not to feed their toothless grannies. In other words, the fact that we avail ourselves of the benefits of the elderly is a reflection of our habitual social generosity.

hunter-gatherers demonstrate not only material care for the elderly, but also something that is invisible in the fossil record: respect. The Mbuti, for example, recognize five age groups—infants, children, youth, adults, and elders—and of these, only the adults carry out significant economic production in the form of gathering and hunting or collecting raw materials like wood; yet social wealth is shared by all regardless of their productivity. It would be unthinkable to let the elderly or disabled starve simply because they do not work. Likewise, the Mbuti include all members of their society in making decisions and participating in political and social life, and the elderly play a special role in conflict resolution and peacemaking.

How will people get healthcare?

CAPITALISTS AND BUREAUCRATS SEE HEALTHCARE AS AN INDUSTRY—a way to extort money from people in need—and also as a way to appease the population and prevent rebellion. It's no surprise that the quality of the healthcare often suffers. In the richest country in the world, millions have no access to healthcare, including this author, and every year hundreds of thousands of people die from preventable or treatable causes.

Since poisonous working and living conditions and lack of healthcare have always been major grievances within capitalism, providing healthcare is generally a chief goal of anti-capitalist revolutionaries. For example, unemployed people and neighborhood assemblies in Argentina commonly set up clinics or take over and fund existing hospitals left defunct by the state.

During the Spanish Civil War, Barcelona's Medical Syndicate, organized largely by anarchists, managed 18 hospitals (6 of which it had created), 17 sanatoria, 22 clinics, 6 psychiatric establishments, 3 nurseries, and one maternity hospital. Outpatient departments were set up in all the principal localities in Catalunya. Upon receiving a request, the Syndicate sent doctors to places in need. The doctor would have to give good reason for refusing the post, "for it was considered that medicine was at the service of the community, and not the other way round."[40] Funds for outpatient clinics came from contributions from local municipalities. The anarchist Health Workers' Union included 8,000 health workers, 1,020 of them doctors, and also 3,206 nurses, 133 dentists, 330 midwives, and 153 herbalists. The Union operated 36 health centers distributed throughout Catalunya to provide healthcare to everyone in the entire region. There was a central syndicate in each of nine zones, and in Barcelona a Control Committee composed of one delegate from each section met once a week to deal with common problems and implement a common plan. Every department was autonomous in its own sphere, but not isolated, as they supported one another. Beyond Catalunya, healthcare was provided for free in agrarian collectives throughout Aragon and the Levant.

Even in the nascent anarchist movement in the US today, anarchists are taking steps to learn about and provide healthcare. In some communities anarchists are learning alternative medicine and providing it for their communities. And at major protests, given the likelihood of police violence, anarchists organize networks of volunteer medics who set up first aid stations and organize roving medics to provide first aid for thousands of demonstrators. These medics, often self-trained, treat injuries from pepper spray, tear gas, clubs, tasers, rubber bullets, police horses, and more, as well as shock and trauma. The Boston Area Liberation Medic Squad (BALM Squad) is an example of a medic group that organizes on a permanent basis. Formed in 2001, they travel to major protests in other cities as well, and hold trainings for emergency first aid. They run a website, share information, and link to other initiatives, such as the Common Ground clinic described below. They are non-hierarchical and use consensus decision-making, as does the Bay Area Radical Health Collective, a similar group on the West Coast.

Between protests, a number of radical feminist groups throughout the US and Canada have formed Women's Health Collectives, to address the needs of women. Some of these collectives teach female anatomy in empowering, positive ways, showing women

---

40 Gaston Leval, *Collectives in the Spanish Revolution*, London: Freedom Press, 1975, p. 270.

how to give themselves gynecological exams, how to experience menstruation comfortably, and how to practice safe methods of birth control. The patriarchal Western medical establishment is generally ignorant of women's health to the point of being degrading and harmful. An anti-establishment, do-it-yourself approach allows marginalized people to subvert a neglectful system by organizing to meet their own needs.

After Hurricane Katrina devastated New Orleans, activist street medics joined a former Black Panther in setting up the Common Ground clinic in one of the neediest neighborhoods. They were soon assisted by hundreds of anarchists and other volunteers from across the country, mostly without experience. Funded by donations and run by volunteers, the Common Ground clinic provided treatment to tens of thousands of people. The failure of the government's "Emergency Management" experts during the crisis is widely recognized. But Common Ground was so well organized it also out-performed the Red Cross, despite the latter having a great deal more experience and resources.[41] In the process, they popularized the concept of mutual aid and made plain the failure of the government. At the time of this writing Common Ground has 40 full-time organizers and is pursuing health in a much broader sense, also making community gardens and fighting for housing rights so that those evicted by the storm will not be prevented from coming home by the gentrification plans of the government. They have helped gut and rebuild many houses in the poorest neighborhoods, which authorities wanted to bulldoze in order to win more living space for rich white people.

What about education?

EDUCATION HAS LONG BEEN A PRIORITY OF ANARCHIST AND OTHER revolutionary movements around the world. But even if people completely neglected the organization of education after the

---

41 Neille Ilel, "A Healthy Dose of Anarchy: After Katrina, nontraditional, decentralized relief steps in where big government and big charity failed," *Reason Magazine*, December 2006.

revolution, that would still be an improvement over the patriotic, degrading, manipulative, and mind-numbing forms of education sponsored by the nation-state. Like everyone else, children are capable of educating themselves, and are motivated to do so in the proper setting. But public schools rarely offer that setting, nor do they educate the students on topics of immediate usefulness, like surviving childhood, expressing emotions healthily, developing their unique creative potentials, taking charge of their own health or caring for sick people, dealing with gender violence, domestic abuse, or alcoholism, standing up to bullies, communicating with parents, exploring their sexuality in a respectful way, finding a job and apartment or making do without money, or other skills young people need to live. In the few classes that teach useful hands-on skills—nearly always electives—students are "tracked." Girls learn how to cook and sew in Home Ec, boys likely to go on to blue collar jobs learn wood-working in Shop. It is safe to say that most boys finish high school ignorant of how to cook or patch up their clothes, and most girls and future white collar workers graduate not knowing how to fix a toilet, mount an electrical installation, repair a bicycle or a car engine, plaster a wall, or work with wood. And in the computer and technology classes, the fact that the students often know more than the teachers is a clear indication that something is wrong with this form of education. Schools do not even teach kids the skills they need for the crappy jobs they will end up working. Most of this, people teach themselves, or learn among friends and peers—that is to say, the school of life is already anarchistic.

The most important lessons consistently taught by schools under the state are to obey arbitrary authority, to accept the imposition of other people's priorities on our lives, and to stop daydreaming. When children start school, they are self-guided, curious about the world they live in, and believe everything is possible. When they finish, they are cynical, self-absorbed, and used to dedicating forty hours of their week to an activity they never chose. They are also likely to be miseducated about a number of things, perhaps unaware that a majority of human societies throughout history have been egalitarian and stateless, that the police have only recently become an important and supposedly necessary institution, that their government has a track record of torture, genocide, and repression, that their lifestyles are destroying the environment, that their food and water are poisoned, or that there is a history of resistance waiting to be uncovered in their very own town.

This systematic miseducation is hardly surprising, given the history of public schools. Though public schools developed gradually from an array of precedents, the regime of Otto von Bismarck is widely credited with first establishing a national public school system. The purpose was to prepare youth for careers in the bureaucracy or military, discipline them, instill them with patriotism, and indoctrinate them in the culture and history of a German nation that had not previously existed. The school system was one of the modernizations that allowed a collection of bickering provinces, some of them practically feudal, to form a state that could threaten the rest of the continent—and large parts of Africa—within a generation.

In response, a number of anarchist theorists set out to design non-hierarchical schools in which teachers would serve as aides helping the students learn and explore their chosen subjects. Some of these anarchist experiments in education in the US were called Modern Schools, on the model of Spanish anarchist Francisco Ferrer's Escuela Moderna. These schools helped educate thousands of students, and played important roles in the anarchist and labor movements. In 1911, shortly after Ferrer's execution in Spain, the first Modern School in the US was founded in New York City by Emma Goldman, Alexander Berkman, Voltairine de Cleyre, and other anarchists. A number of famous artists and writers helped teach there, and pupils included the artist Man Ray. It lasted for several decades, eventually moving out of New York City during a period of intense political repression, and became the center of a rural commune.

More recently, anarchists and other activists in the US have organized "free schools." Some of these are temporary, ad hoc classes, while some are fully organized schools. One, the Albany Free School, has existed for over 32 years in inner-city Albany.

This anti-authoritarian school is committed to social justice as well as education—it offers sliding scale tuition and turns no one away for financial reasons. Most experimental schools are only accessible to the elite, but the student body of the Albany Free School is diverse, including many inner-city kids from poor families. The school has no curriculum or compulsory classes, operating according to the philosophy "'Trust children and they will learn.' Because when you entrust kids with their own so-called "education"—which is not a thing after all, but rather an ever-present action—they will learn continually, each in their own way and rhythm." The Free School teaches children up to 8th grade, and has recently opened a high school, the Harriet Tubman Free School. The school organizes a small organic farm in the city which provides another important learning opportunity for students. Students also work with community service projects such as soup kitchens and daycare centers. Despite financial and other limitations, they have succeeded admirably.

> Our reputation with students that are struggling academically and/or behaviorally, and whose needs the system has failed to meet, is such that an increasing number of kids are coming to us having previously been tagged with labels like ADHD and placed on Ritalin and other biopsychiatric medications. Their parents seek us out because they're concerned about the side effects of the drugs and because they've heard that we work effectively with these children without drugs of any kind. Our active, flexible, individually structured environment renders the drugs entirely unnecessary.[42]

The MST, the Landless Workers' Movement in Brazil, has focused ardently on education in the settlements they have created on occupied land. Between 2002 and 2005, the MST claims to have taught over 50,000 landless workers how to read; 150,000 children are enrolled in 1,200 different schools they have built on

---

42 Albany Free School website (viewed November 24, 2006) http://www.albanyfreeschool.com/overview.shtml

their settlements, and they have also trained over one thousand educators. The MST schools are free from state control, so communities have the power to decide what their children are taught and can develop alternative methods of education as well as curricula free of the racist, patriotic, and capitalist values that are part and parcel of public education. The Brazilian government complains that children in the settlements are taught that genetically modified crops pose a risk to human health and the environment, which suggests that they get a much more relevant and accurate education than their peers in the state run schools. MST schools in the settlements focus on literacy and use the methods of Paulo Freire, who developed the "pedagogy of the oppressed." In São Paulo the MST has built itself an autonomous university which trains farmers nominated by the individual settlements. Rather than teaching, for example, agribusiness, as a capitalist university would, they teach family agriculture with a critique of the exploitative and environmentally destructive techniques prevalent in contemporary agriculture. For other technical courses the MST also helps people get educations in public universities, though they often win the collaboration of leftwing professors to offer more critical lessons of a higher caliber, even enabling them to design their own courses. They emphasize in all these forms of education that it is the responsibility of the students to use what they learn for their community and not for individual profit.

The Movimiento Campesino de Santiago de Estero, MOCASE, is a group of farmers, many of them Quechua, with similarities and connections to the MST. Beginning as a group of farmers fighting for land in the face of expansion by forestry companies from the Global North, they now number 8,000 families in 58 communities active in a broad range of struggles. Working together with the Universidad Transhumante, they set up a Farmers School that helps farmers learn the skills necessary for self-management. The students also learn to teach, so they can help train other farmers. The Universidad Transhumante is interesting in its own right. It is a popular education university, also inspired by Freire, that organized a year-long caravan to 80 cities around Argentina, to present popular education workshops and learn about the problems people face.[43] Outside of the control of the state, education need not be a static, fixed thing. It can be a tool of empowerment, as people are taught how to teach, so they can pass on the lessons they learn rather than being permanently dependent on a class of professional educators. It can be a tool of liberation, as people learn about authority and resistance, and study how to take control over their own lives. It can be a caravan, a circus, as people travel across a country and instead of bringing caged spectacles they bring new ideas and techniques. And it can be a tool for survival, as oppressed peoples learn about their histories and prepare for their futures.

In 1969, Native American activists, organizing under the name "Indians of All Nations," occupied the abandoned Alcatraz island, citing an ignored US law guaranteeing that indigenous people had a right to occupy any land the settler nation abandoned. For six months, the occupation numbered in the hundreds, and though most left because of a government blockade, the occupation ultimately lasted for 19 months, revitalizing indigenous culture and rejecting colonial control. During the early period, the Indian occupiers organized a school that taught indigenous history and culture from their own perspective, without the racist propaganda that filled the textbooks of the government's schools. For the duration of their occupation, they used education as a means of cultural renewal, whereas it had previously been used against them to destroy their identity and conscript the survivors of the genocide into the civilization that had colonized them.

What about technology?

MANY PEOPLE WORRY THAT THE COMPLEXITY OF MODERN DAY TECHnology and the high level integration of infrastructure and production in present day society makes anarchy a dream of the past. In fact, this worry is not at all unfounded. It is not so much the complexity

---

43 Natasha Gordon and Paul Chatterton, *Taking Back Control: A Journey through Argentina's Popular Uprising*, Leeds (UK): University of Leeds, 2004, pp. 43–44.

of the technology, however, that is at odds with the creation of an anarchist society, so much as the fact that technology is not a neutral thing. As Uri Gordon expertly summed it up, the development of technology reflects the interests and needs of ruling members of society, and technology reshapes the physical world in a way that reinforces authority and discourages rebellion.[44] It is no coincidence that the nuclear arms and energy infrastructure creates a need for a centrally organized, high security military organization and disaster management agencies with emergency powers and the ability to suspend constitutional rights; that interstate highways allow the rapid domestic deployment of the military, encourage the transcontinental shipping of goods and private transportation via personal automobiles; that new factories demand unskilled, replaceable laborers who couldn't possibly hold the job until retirement, assuming the boss even wanted to give retirement benefits, because within a few years occupational injuries from repetitive tasks or the unsafe pace of the production line will render them unable to continue.

The subsidies and infrastructure provided by government tend to go towards inventions that increase state power, often to everyone else's misfortune: jet fighters, surveillance systems, pyramid-building. Even the most benevolent forms of government support for invention, such as government subsidies to medical research, at best go to inventing treatments that are patented by corporations with no scruples about letting people die if they cannot afford them—just as they have no scruples over torturing and killing thousands of animals in the testing phase.

The demands of freedom confront us with a much heavier choice than simply changing our decision-making structures. We will have to physically disassemble much of the world we live in and build it anew. Freedom, as well as the ecological balance of the planet and thus our very survival, is incompatible with nuclear energy, reliance on fossil fuels such as oil and coal, and a car culture which estranges public space and fosters a system of exchange where most goods are not produced locally.

---

44 See chapter 5 in Uri Gordon, *Anarchy Alive! Anti-authoritarian Politics from Practice to Theory,* London: Pluto Press, 2008.

This transformation will require a great deal of inventiveness; thus the relevant question becomes, will an anarchist social movement and society be inventive enough to carry out this transformation? I think the answer is yes. After all, the most useful tools in human history were invented before government and capitalism came about.

Capitalism's so-called free market is said to motivate innovation, and market competition does contribute to the proliferation of profitable inventions, which are not necessarily *helpful* inventions. Capitalist competition dictates that every few years all the old gadgets become obsolete as new ones are invented, so people have to throw the old ones away and buy new ones—at great detriment to the environment. Because of this "planned obsolescence," few inventions tend to be well made or fully thought-out in the first place, since they're destined for the trash from the beginning.

The doctrine of intellectual property prevents the spread of useful technologies, allowing them to be controlled or withheld according to what is most profitable. Apologists for capitalism typically argue that intellectual property encourages the development of technology because it gives people the assurance, as incentive, that they can profit from their invention. What kind of cretin would invent something socially useful if he wouldn't get exclusive credit for it and profit from it? But the technological mainstays of our world were developed by groups of people who let their inventions spread freely and didn't take credit for them—everything from the hammer to stringed musical instruments to domesticated grains.

In practice, the capitalist economy itself disproves the assumptions about intellectual property encouraging innovation. Just like any other kind of property, intellectual property usually does not belong to those who produce it: many inventions are made by wage slaves in laboratories who get no credit and no profit because their contracts stipulate that the corporation they work for receives ownership of the patents.

The best people to develop useful innovations are the ones who need them, and they do not need government or capitalism to help them do this. Anarchists themselves have a rich history of inventing solutions to the problems they face. The anarchist bank robbers known as the Bonnot gang invented the getaway car. Makhno, the Ukrainian anarchist, was the first to deploy highly mobile machine guns—he mounted them on tatchankis, the horse-drawn carts used by the peasantry, with devastating effect against superior foes bogged down in traditional tactics. In revolutionary Spain, after they had expropriated the big landlords, collectivized the land, and freed themselves from the need to produce a single export crop, farmers improved the health of the soil and increased their self-sufficiency by intercropping—specifically, growing shade-tolerant crops beneath the orange trees. The Peasant Federation of the Levant, in Spain, set up an agricultural university, and other agricultural collectives founded a center for the study of plant diseases and tree culture.

In the highlands of New Guinea, millions of farmers live with high population densities in steep mountain valleys; their communities are stateless, consensus-based, and, until relatively recently, completely uncontacted by the West. Though they appeared as Stone Age primitives to racist Europeans, they have developed one of the most complex agricultural systems in the world. Their techniques are so precise and numerous that they take years to learn. Self-important Western scientists still do not know the reasons for many of these techniques, which they might dismiss as superstition were they not proven to work. For the past 7,000 years, the highlanders have practiced a dynamic form of sustainable agriculture in response to impacts on their environment that might have caused less innovative societies to collapse. Their methods include complex forms of irrigation, soil retention, intercropping, and more. The highlanders have no chiefs, and make their decisions in long, community discussions. They have developed all their techniques without government or capitalism, via individual and group innovations communicated freely through a large, decentralized society.[45]

---

45 The description of the New Guinea highlanders in Jared Diamond's book (*Collapse: How Societies Choose to Fail or Succeed*, New York, Viking, 2005), particularly the portrayal of their curiosity, wit, and humanity,

Many Westerners might scoff at the thought that people who do not use metal tools could provide a model of technological sophistication. These cynics, however, are simply benighted by Euro/American mythology and superstitions. Technology is not blinking lights and whirring gadgets. Technology is adaptation. By adapting a complex set of techniques that have allowed them to meet all their needs without destroying their environment over 7,000 years, the New Guinea farmers have accomplished something Western civilization has never even approached.

Still, there are plenty of anarchistic examples for the impressed-by-blinking-lights crowd. Consider the recent proliferation of "Open Source" technology. Decentralized networks involving thousands of people working openly, voluntarily, and cooperatively have created some of the better forms of the complicated software on which the Information Age economy depends. The usual approach of major corporations is to keep the source, or code, for their software secret and patented, but Open Source software code is shared, so anyone can review it and improve it. As a result it is often much better, and generally easier to fix. Traditional patented software is more vulnerable to crashing and to viruses, because a smaller pool of brains are able to check for weaknesses, and very few specialists are available to fix problems. Those technical support people you call on the phone when your computer operating system crashes don't get to see the code either, and beyond a little troubleshooting all they can do is direct you to a cumbersome "patch," or advise you to erase your hard drive and reinstall the operating system. Users of Microsoft products, for example, are no doubt familiar with their frequent glitches, and privacy advocates also warn of spyware and the cooperation between technology corporations and the government. Says one anti-authoritarian geek involved in the creation of Open Source software: "The best advertisement for Linux is Microsoft."

Traditionally, much Open Source software has not been especially user-friendly, though generally this has to do with the fact

---

does a great service to dispelling the lingering imagery of so-called primitive peoples as grunting apes or noble savages.

that Open Source resides within, with all due respect, a geek subculture, and its typical users are highly computer literate. However, Open Source and participatory technology are steadily becoming accessible to an extent unprecedented by proprietary software. Wikipedia exemplifies this. Started recently, in 2001, on Open Source Linux software, Wikipedia is already the largest and most accessed encyclopedia in the world, with over 10 million articles in more than 250 languages. Rather than being the exclusive domain of paid experts from a particular academic subculture, Wikipedia is written by everyone. Anyone can author an article or edit an existing article, and by allowing this openness and trust it provides a forum for instantaneous, multiple-peer review. The interests of the broader Wikipedia community of millions provide a self-regulating function, so vandalism—false editing and bogus articles—are quickly cleaned up, and facts lacking citations are challenged. Wikipedia articles avail themselves of a vastly greater body of knowledge than the small and generally elitist circle represented by academia. In a blind, peer-reviewed study it was judged to be as accurate as *Encyclopedia Britannica*.[46]

Wikipedia is "self-organizing" and edited by an open body of peer-elected administrators.[47] There have been a few publicized cases of intentional sabotage, such as when the televised news comedy show *The Colbert Report* rewrote history in one Wikipedia article as a gag for their show; but the prank was quickly fixed, as most false information on the site tends to be. A more lingering problem is posed by corporations who use Wikipedia for public relations purposes, tasking paid personnel to maintain a clean image in the articles about them. However, contradicting interpretations of the facts can be registered in the same article, and Wikipedia contains much more information on corporate misdeeds than any traditional encyclopedia.

---

46 "Wikipedia survives research test," *BBC News* 15 December 2005 news.bbc.co.uk/2/hi/technology/4530930.stm
47 "Editorial administration, oversight and management" Wikipedia, en.wikipedia.org/wiki/Wikipedia:About

How will exchange work?

THERE ARE MANY DIFFERENT WAYS EXCHANGE COULD WORK IN A stateless, anti-capitalist society, depending on the size, complexity, and preferences of the society. Many of these are far more effective than capitalism at ensuring a fair distribution of goods and keeping people from taking more than their fair share. Capitalism has created a greater inequality in access to resources than any other economic system in human history. But the principles of capitalism that economists have indoctrinated the public to accept as laws are not universal.

Many societies have traditionally used gift economies, which can take many different forms. In societies with a modest amount of social stratification, the wealthier families maintain their status by giving gifts, holding lavish feasts, and spreading their wealth; in some cases, they risk the wrath of the others if they are not generous enough. Other gift economies are barely or not at all stratified; the participants simply disown the concept of property and give and take social wealth freely. In his diary, Columbus remarked with amazement that the first indigenous people he encountered in the Caribbean had no sense of property, and gave willingly of all they had; indeed, they came bearing gifts to greet their strange visitors. In such a society, no one could be poor. Now, after hundreds of years of genocide and capitalist development, many parts of the Americas have some of the starkest wealth gaps in the world.

In Argentina, poor people initiated a massive barter network that grew enormously after the economic collapse in 2001 rendered capitalist forms of exchange unworkable. The barter system evolved from simple swap meets into a huge network involving an estimated three million members trading goods and services—everything from homemade crafts, food, and clothing to language lessons. Even doctors, manufacturers, and some railways participated. An estimated ten million people were supported by the barter network at its peak.

The barter club facilitated exchange by developing a credit/currency system. As the network grew, and the capitalist crisis deepened, the network was beset by a number of problems, including people—often from outside the network—stealing or forging the currency. Several years later, after the economy stabilized under President Kirchner, the barter club shrank, but still retained a huge membership considering it was an alternative economy in the country that was once a model for neoliberal capitalism. Rather than giving up, remaining members developed a number of solutions to the problems they had encountered, such as limiting membership to producers so the network is only used by those who contribute to it.

Contemporary anarchists in the US and Europe are experimenting with other forms of distribution that transcend exchange. One popular anarchist project is the "free store" or "give-away shop." Free stores serve as a collection point for donated or scavenged items that people no longer need, including clothes, food, furniture, books, music, even the occasional refrigerator, television, or car. Patrons are free to browse through the store and take whatever they need. Many accustomed to a capitalist economy who come into a free store are perplexed by how it could possibly work. Having been raised with a scarcity mentality, they assume that since people profit by taking stuff and do not profit by donating, a free store would quickly empty out. However this is rarely the case. Countless free stores operate sustainably, and most are overflowing with goods. From Harrisonburg, Virginia, to Barcelona, Catalunya, hundreds of free stores defy capitalist logic on a daily basis. The *Weggeefwinkel*, Giveaway Shop, in Groningen, Netherlands, has operated out of squatted buildings for over three years, opening twice a week to give away free clothes, books, furniture, and other items. Other free stores hold fundraisers if they have to pay rent, which would not be an issue in a completely anarchist society. Free stores are an important resource for impoverished people, who either are denied a job by the whims of the free market or who work a job, or two or three, and still can't afford clothes for their kids.

A more high-tech example of free exchange is the relatively mainstream and wildly successful Freecycle Network. Freecycle is a global network originally formed by an environmental nonprofit group to promote giving away items that might otherwise end up in the trash. As of this writing they have over 4 million members grouped into 4200 local chapters, spread through 50 countries. Using a website to post items wanted or items available to give away, people have circulated prodigious quantities of clothing, furniture, toys, artwork, tools, bicycles, cars, and countless other goods. One of the rules of Freecycle is that everything has to be free, neither bartered nor sold. Freecycle is not a centrally controlled organization; local chapters set themselves up based on the common model, and use the website on which the model is based.

However, as it does come from a liberal nonprofit group without revolutionary aspirations nor any critique of capitalism and the state, we can expect Freecycle to have some problems. In fact, the organization accepts corporate sponsorship from a major recycling company and advertises on its website, and the chairperson has arguably slowed the spread of the Freecycle idea by attacking various member groups or copycat websites with lawsuits, or threats thereof, for trademark infringement; also by collaborating with the notoriously authoritarian Yahoo! Groups to shut down local chapters for not adhering to organizational rules concerning logo and language. Naturally, in an anarchist society there would be no lawsuits for trademark infringement and one chairperson would not be able to tyrannize a network that was maintained by millions of people. In the meantime, Freecycle demonstrates that gift economies can function even within jaded, individualistic Western societies, and can take new forms with the help of the internet.

What about people who don't want to give up a consumerist lifestyle?

Though an anti-capitalist revolution would create new social relationships and values, as well as free people's desires from the control of advertising, some people would probably still want to maintain a consumerist lifestyle—demanding the electronic entertainment, exotic imported foods, and other luxuries that (neo)colonialism currently affords them. By routinizing the act of going to a shop, taking out your wallet, and buying a mahogany dresser or a bar of chocolate, capitalism creates the illusion that human beings naturally possess the ability to procure luxury goods that in actuality are produced by slaves on another continent. It takes a massive infrastructure and multiple institutions of government and colonialism to afford this privilege to a select few. After an anarchist revolution, the slave labor camps that currently produce much of the world's chocolate and tropical hardwoods would no longer exist.

If a person or a group of like-minded people wanted to surround themselves with the consumer goods they still craved, they would be perfectly free to do so; however, without a police force to make others bear the ecological and labor costs of their lifestyle, they would be the ones who would have to procure the resources, produce the goods, and remediate any pollution. Of course, they could make the process more efficient by specializing in one consumer good: for example, a union of chocoholics could produce eco-friendly chocolate—thus not damaging the ecological commons on which the rest of their society depends—and barter off some of that chocolate for, say, video-entertainment equipment produced by a union of TV addicts. Why not? Ultimately, however, all that work and personal responsibility might not mesh with the consumerist mentality; the end result would be a union of producers. When people have to take responsibility for all the costs of their own actions, it removes the pathological insulation from consequences which lies at the root of bourgeois whims. The result is carefully weighed, mature desires.

In anarchist revolutions and stateless, non-capitalist societies throughout history, people used what they could make themselves or trade for from neighboring societies. In the Argentina factory takeovers, various occupied factories began trading their products with one another, allowing the workers access to a variety of manufactured goods. In many of the collectives of the 1936 Spanish revolution, communities decided together how much and what kinds of consumption they could collectively afford, by replacing wages with coupons redeemable for goods at the communal depot. Everyone had a voice in determining how many coupons of various types a person could get, and naturally they were free to trade their coupons with others, so someone who preferred more of one thing, say, cloth, could get more by trading the coupons for something they didn't mind missing, like eggs. Thus there is no imposition of spartan uniformity, as in some communist states; people are free to pursue the lifestyle they want, but only if they can personally bear the costs of it. They are not able to exploit other people, rob their resources, or poison their land to get it.

What about building and organizing large, spread-out infrastructure?

MANY WESTERN HISTORY BOOKS ASSERT THAT CENTRALIZED GOVernment arose out of the need to build and maintain large infrastructure projects, especially irrigation. However, this assertion is based on the assumption that societies need to grow, and that they cannot choose to limit their scale to avoid centralization—an assumption that has been discredited many times over. And while large-scale irrigation projects do require some amount of coordination, centralization is only one form of coordination.

In India and East Africa, local societies built massive irrigation networks that were managed without government or centralization. In the Taita Hills region of what is now Kenya, people created complex irrigation systems that lasted hundreds of years, often until colonial agricultural practices ended them. Households shared day-to-day maintenance, each responsible for the closest section of the irrigation infrastructure, which was common property. Another custom brought people together periodically for major repairs: known as "harambee labor," it was a form of collective, socially motivated work, similar to traditions in many other decentralized societies. The people of the Taita Hills ensured fair use through a number of social arrangements passed on by tradition, which determined how much water each household could take; those who violated these practices faced sanctions from the rest of the community.

When the British colonized the region, they assumed they knew better than the locals and set up a new irrigation system—geared, of course, to cash crop production—based on their engineering expertise and mechanical power. During the drought of the 1960s, the British system failed spectacularly and many locals returned to the indigenous irrigation system to feed themselves. According to one ethnologist, "East African irrigation works seem to have been more extensive and better managed during the precolonial era."[48]

During the Spanish Civil War, workers in occupied factories coordinated an entire wartime economy. Anarchist organizations that had been instrumental in bringing about the revolution, namely the CNT labor union, often provided the foundations for the new society. Especially in the industrial city of Barcelona, the CNT lent the structure for running a worker-controlled economy—a task for which it had been preparing years in advance. Each factory organized itself with its own chosen technical and administrative workers; factories in the same industry in every locality organized into the Local Federation of their particular industry; all the Local Federations of a locality organized themselves into a Local Economic Council "in which all the centers of production and services were represented"; and the local Federations and Councils organized into parallel National Federations of Industry and National Economic Federations.[49]

The Barcelona congress of all Catalan collectives, on August 28, 1937, provides an example of their coordinating activities and decisions. The collectivized shoe factories needed 2 million pesetas credit. Because of a shortage of leather, they had to cut down on hours, though they still paid all their workers full time salaries. The Economic Council studied the situation, and reported that there was no surplus of shoes. The congress agreed to grant credit to purchase leather and to modernize the factories in order to lower the prices of the shoes. Later, the Economic Council outlined plans to build an aluminum factory, which was necessary for the war effort. They had located available materials, secured the cooperation of chemists, engineers, and technicians, and decided

---

48 Patrick Fleuret, "The Social Organization of Water Control in the Taita Hills, Kenya," *American Ethnologist*, Vol. 12, 1985.
49 Sam Dolgoff, *The Anarchist Collectives*, New York: Free Life Editions, 1974, p. 66.

to raise the money through the collectives. The congress also decided to mitigate urban unemployment by working out a plan with agricultural workers to bring new areas into cultivation with the help of unemployed workers from the cities.

In Valencia, the CNT organized the orange industry, with 270 committees in different towns and villages for growing, purchasing, packing, and exporting; in the process, they got rid of several thousand middlemen. In Laredo, the fishing industry was collectivized—workers expropriated the ships, cut out the middlemen who took all the profit, and used those profits to improve the ships and other equipment or to pay themselves. Catalunya's textile industry employed 250,000 workers in scores of factories. During collectivization, they got rid of high-paid directors, increased their wages by 15%, reduced their hours from 60 to 40 hours per week, bought new machinery, and elected management committees.

In Catalunya, libertarian workers showed impressive results in maintaining the complex infrastructure of the industrial society they had taken over. The workers who had always been responsible for these jobs proved themselves capable of carrying on and even improving their work in the absence of bosses. "Without waiting for orders from anyone, the workers restored normal telephone service within three days [after heavy street fighting ended]... Once this crucial emergency work was finished a general membership meeting of telephone workers decided to collectivize the telephone system."[50] The workers voted to raise the salaries of the lowest paid members. The gas, water, and electricity services were also collectivized. The collective managing water lowered rates by 50% and was still able to contribute large amounts of money to the anti-fascist militia committee. The railway workers collectivized the railroads, and where technicians in the railroads had fled, experienced workers were chosen as replacements. The replacements proved adequate despite their lack of formal schooling, because they had learned through the experience of working together with the technicians to maintain the lines.

50 Ditto, p. 88.

Municipal transportation workers in Barcelona—6,500 out of 7,000 of whom were members of the CNT—saved considerable money by kicking out the overpaid directors and other unnecessary managers. They then reduced their hours to 40 per week, raised their wages between 60% (for the lowest income bracket) and 10% (for the highest income bracket), and helped out the entire population by lowering fares and giving free rides to schoolchildren and wounded militia members. They repaired damaged equipment and streets, cleared barricades, got the transportation system running again just five days after fighting ceased in Barcelona, and deployed a fleet of 700 trolleys—up from the 600 on the streets before the revolution—repainted red and black. As for their organization:

> the various trades coordinated and organized their work into one industrial union of all the transport workers. Each section was administered by an engineer designated by the union and a worker delegated by the general membership. The delegations of the various sections coordinated operations in a given area. While the sections met separately to conduct their own specific operations, decisions affecting the workers in general were made at general membership meetings.

The engineers and technicians, rather than comprising an elite group, were integrated with the manual workers. "The engineer, for example, could not undertake an important project without consulting the other workers, not only because responsibilities were to be shared but also because in practical problems the manual workers acquired practical experience which technicians often lacked." Public transportation in Barcelona achieved greater self-sufficiency too: before the revolution, 2% of maintenance supplies were made by the private company, and the rest had to be purchased or imported. Within a year after socialization, 98% of repair supplies were made in socialized shops. "The union also provided free medical services, including clinics and home nursing care, for the workers and their families."[51]

---

51 All the quotes and statistics in the paragraph come from Sam Dolgoff,

For better or worse, the Spanish revolutionaries also experimented with Peasant Banks, Labor Banks, and Councils of Credit and Exchange. The Levant Federation of Peasant Collectives started a bank organized by the Bank Workers Union to help farmers draw from a broad pool of social resources needed for certain infrastructure- or resource-intensive types of farming. The Central Labor Bank of Barcelona moved credit from more prosperous collectives to socially useful collectives in need. Cash transactions were kept to a minimum, and credit was transferred as credit. The Labor Bank also arranged foreign exchange, and importation and purchase of raw materials. Where possible, payment was made in commodities, not in cash. The bank was not a for-profit enterprise; it charged only 1% interest to defray expenses. Diego Abad de Santillan, the anarchist economist, said in 1936: "Credit will be a social function and not a private speculation or usury... Credit will be based on the economic possibilities of society and not on interests or profit... The Council of Credit and Exchange will be like a thermometer of the products and needs of the country."[52] In this experiment, money functioned as a symbol of social support and not as a symbol of ownership—it signified resources being transferred between unions of producers rather than investments by speculators. Within a complex industrial economy such banks make exchange and production more efficient, though they also present the risk of centralization or the reemergence of capital as a social force. Furthermore, *efficient production and exchange* as a value should be viewed with suspicion, at the least, by people interested in liberation.

There are a number of methods that could prevent institutions such as labor banks from facilitating the return of capitalism, though unfortunately the onslaught of totalitarianism from both the fascists and Communists deprived Spanish anarchists of the chance to develop them. These might include rotating and mixing tasks to prevent the emergence of a new managing class, developing fragmented structures that cannot be controlled at a central

The Anarchist Collectives, New York: Free Life Editions, 1974, pp. 88–92.
52 Ditto, pp. 75–76

or national level, promoting as much decentralization and simplicity as possible, and maintaining a firm tradition that common resources and instruments of social wealth are never for sale.

But as long as money is a central fact of human existence, myriad human activities are reduced to quantitative values and value can be massed as power, and thus alienated from the activity that created it: in other words, it can become capital. Naturally anarchists do not agree on how to strike a balance between practicality and perfection, or how deep to cut in order to root out capitalism, but studying all the possibilities, including those that might be doomed to failure or worse, can only help.

How will cities work?

MANY PEOPLE BELIEVE THAT AN ANARCHIST SOCIETY MIGHT WORK in theory, but the modern world contains too many obstacles that prevent such a total liberation. Large cities are chief among these putative stumbling blocks. Industrial capitalist cities are a tangled mess of bureaucracies supposedly only kept running by the authorities. But the maintenance of a large city is not as mystifying as we are led to believe. Some of the biggest cities in the world are largely composed of self-organizing slums stretching for miles. Their quality of life leaves much to be desired, but they do show that cities do not simply collapse in the absence of experts.

Anarchists have some experience maintaining large cities; the solution seems to lie in maintenance workers taking over the organization of the infrastructure for which they are responsible, and neighborhoods forming assemblies so that nearly all other decisions can be made at a local level, where everyone can participate. It is probable that an anarchist revolution will be accompanied by a process of deurbanization as cities shrink to more manageable sizes. Many people will probably return to the land as industrial agriculture decreases or ceases, to be replaced by sustainable agriculture—or "permaculture"—which can support a higher population density in rural areas.

In such a period, it might be necessary to make new social arrangements in a hurry, but it won't be the first time anarchists have made a town or city from scratch. In May 2003, as envoys of the eight leading world governments prepared for the "G8" summit in Evian, France, the anti-capitalist movement set up a series of connected villages to serve as a foundation for protest and an example of collective, anti-capitalist living; these took the name VAAAG (Village Alternatif, Anticapitalist et AntiGuerres). For the duration of the mobilization, thousands of people lived in these villages, organizing food, housing, childcare, debate forums, media, and legal services, and making decisions communally. The project was widely regarded as a success. The VAAAG also exhibited the dual form of organization suggested above. Specific "neighborhoods," each with fewer than 200 people, organized around a community kitchen, while village-wide services—"inter-neighborhood collective spaces" such as the legal and medical space—were organized by those involved in providing those services. This experience was replicated during the 2005 mobilizations against the G8 in Scotland, and the 2007 mobilizations in northern Germany, when nearly six thousand people lived together in Camp Reddelich.

These protest villages had precedents in the German anti-nuclear movement of the previous generation. When the state wanted to build a massive nuclear waste storage complex at Gorleben in 1977, local farmers began to protest. In May 1980, five thousand people set up an encampment on the site, building a small city from trees cut for construction and naming their new home The Free Republic of Wendland. They issued their own passports, set up illegal radio shows and printed newspapers, and held common debates to decide how to run the camp and respond to police aggression. People shared food and did away with money in their daily lives. One month later, eight thousand police assaulted the protestors, who had decided to resist nonviolently. They were brutally beaten and cleared out. Subsequent manifestations of the antinuclear movement were less inclined to pacifism.[53]

---

53 George Katsiaficas, *The Subversion of Politics: European Autonomous Social Movements and the Decolonization of Everyday Life*. Oakland: AK Press, 2006, pp. 84–85

In England, a yearly festival of travellers and hippies that converged at Stonehenge to mark the summer solstice became a major counter-cultural autonomous zone and an experiment in "collective anarchy." Beginning in 1972, the Stonehenge Free Festival was a gathering that lasted for the month of June until the solstice. More than a music festival, it was a non-hierarchical space for the creation of music, art, and new relationships, as well as spiritual and psychedelic exploration. It became an essential ritual and social event in England's growing traveller culture. By 1984, it drew 30,000 participants who created a self-organized village for the month. In the words of one participant, it was "Anarchy. And it worked."[54] The Thatcher regime saw it as a threat; in 1985 they banned the 14th annual Stonehenge Free Festival, brutally attacking the several hundred people who came to set it up in an assault known as the Battle of the Beanfield.

These examples of impromptu camps are not as marginal as they might seem at first. Hundreds of millions of people throughout the world live in informally organized cities, sometimes called shantytowns or favelas, which are self-organizing, self-created, and self-sustaining. The social issues posed by these shantytowns are very complex. Millions of farmers are forced off their land yearly and have to move to the cities, where the peripheral shantytowns are the only place they can afford to settle; but a great many people also move to the city voluntarily to escape the more culturally rigid rural areas and build a new life. Many shantytowns are plagued by health problems caused by poor access to clean water, healthcare, and nutrition. However, many of these problems are peculiar to capitalism rather than the structure of the shantytowns, as the inhabitants are often ingenious in providing for themselves in spite of artificially limited resources.

Privatized electricity and water are generally too expensive, and even where these utilities are public the authorities often refuse to provide access to informal settlements. Shanty dwellers get around this problem by constructing their own wells and pirating

---

54 The Stonehenge Free Festivals, 1972–1985. http://www.ukrockfestivals.com/henge-menu.html Viewed 8 May 2008.

electricity. Medical care is highly professionalized in capitalist societies and distributed in exchange for money rather than on the basis of need; consequently, there are rarely fully trained doctors in the shantytowns. But the folk medicine and healers that are present are often available on a basis of mutual aid. Access to food is also artificially limited, because small-scale horticulture for local consumption has been replaced by large-scale production of cash crops, depriving people throughout the Global South of diverse and affordable sources of local food. This problem is exacerbated in famine areas, because food aid from the US, in line with military and economic strategies, consists of imports rather than subsidies for local production. But within the settlements, available food is frequently shared rather than traded. An anthropologist estimated that in one informal settlement in Ghana people gave away almost one third of all their resources. This makes perfect sense. Police rarely have control of shantytowns, and some armed force is required to uphold an unequal distribution of resources. In other words, those who hoard resources are likely to be robbed. With few resources, little security, and no guarantees of property rights, people can live better by giving away a large portion of whatever resources they come across. Gift-giving increases their social wealth: friendships and other relationships that create a safety network which cannot be stolen.

In addition to mutual aid, the anarchist objectives of decentralization, voluntary association, hands-on production rather than professionalization of skills and services, and direct democracy are guiding principles in many shantytowns. It is also important to note that, in an era of growing environmental devastation, shantytown dwellers subside on just a fraction of a percent of the resources consumed by suburbanites and formal city dwellers. Some may even have a negative ecological footprint, in that they recycle more waste than they generate.[55] In a world without capitalism, informal settlements would have the potential to be much healthier places. Even today, they disprove the capitalist myths

---

55 The Curious George Brigade, *Anarchy In the Age of Dinosaurs*, CrimethInc. 2003, pp. 106–120. The statistic from Ghana appears on page 115.

that cities can only be held together by experts and central organization, and that people can only live at today's population levels by continuing to surrender our lives to the control of authorities.

One inspiring example of an informal city is El Alto, Bolivia. El Alto sits on the Altiplano, the plateau overlooking La Paz, the capital. A few decades ago El Alto was just a small town, but as global economic changes caused the shutting down of mines and small farms, huge numbers of people came here. Unable to reside in La Paz, they built settlements up on the plateau, changing the town into a major urban area with 850,000 residents. Seventy percent of the people who have jobs here make their living through family businesses in an informal economy. Land use is unregulated, and the state provides little or no infrastructure: most neighborhoods do not have paved roads, garbage removal services, or indoor plumbing, 75% of the population lacks basic health care, and 40% are illiterate.[56] Faced with this situation, the residents of the informal city took their self-organization to the next step, by creating neighborhood councils, or juntas. The first juntas in El Alto go back to the '50s. In 1979 these juntas started to coordinate through a new organization, the Federation of Neighborhood Councils, FEJUVE. Now there are nearly 600 juntas in El Alto. The juntas allow neighbors to pool resources to create and maintain necessary infrastructure, like schools, parks, and basic utilities. They also mediate disputes and levy sanctions in cases of conflict and social harm. The federation, FEJUVE, pools the resources of the juntas to coordinate protests and blockades and constitute the slum dwellers as a social force. In just the first five years of the new millennium, FEJUVE took a lead role in establishing a public university in El Alto, blocking new municipal taxes, and deprivatizing the water services. FEJUVE also was instrumental in the popular movement that forced the government to nationalize the natural gas resources.

Each junta typically contains at least 200 people and meets

---

[56] Emily Achtenberg, "Community Organizing and Rebellion: Neighborhood Councils in El Alto, Bolivia," *Progressive Planning*, No.172, Summer 2007.

every month, making general decisions through public discussion and consensus. They also elect a committee which meets more frequently and has an administrative role. Political party leaders, merchants, real estate speculators, and those who collaborated with the dictatorship are not allowed to be committee delegates. More men than women sit on these committees; however a greater percentage of women take on leadership roles in FEJUVE than in other Bolivian popular organizations.

Parallel to the organization in neighborhood councils is the organization of infrastructure and economic activity in unions or syndicates. The street vendors and transportation workers, for example, self-organize in their own base unions.

> Both the neighborhood councils and their counterparts in the informal economy are patterned after the traditional communitarian organization of rural indigenous communities (ayllu) in terms of territoriality, structure and organizational principles. They also reflect the traditions of radical miners' unions, which for decades led Bolivia's militant labor movement. Fusing these experiences, El Alto's migrants have reproduced, transplanted and adapted their communities of origin to facilitate survival in a hostile urban environment. [...] Through the neighborhood juntas, El Alto has developed as a self-constructed city run by a network of micro-governments[57] independent of the state. In Raúl Zibechi's view, the autonomous organization of labor in the informal sector, based on productivity and family ties instead of the hierarchical boss-worker relationship, reinforces this sense of empowerment: Citizens can self-manage and control their own environment[58]

Horizontal networks "without traditional leadership" also play a

---

57 Although the author of this piece chooses the term government, the underlying concept should not be given parity with what in Western society is considered to be government. In the ayllu tradition, leadership is not a privileged social position or a position of command, but a form of "community service."

58 Emily Achtenberg, "Community Organizing and Rebellion: Neighborhood Councils in El Alto, Bolivia," *Progressive Planning*,

major role complementary to these formal structures in both the organization of daily life and the coordination of protest, blockades, and struggle against the state.

Now that Bolivia has an indigenous president and progressive government led by MAS, the Movement Towards Socialism, FEJUVE faces the danger of incorporation and recuperation that typically neutralizes horizontal movements without explicitly anti-state goals and means. However, while supporting Evo Morales' reversals of neoliberal policy, as of this writing FEJUVE remains critical of MAS and the government, and it remains to be seen to what extent they will be recuperated.

In South Africa, there are many other examples of informal urban settlements that organize themselves to create a better life and struggle against capitalism. Specific movements of shack dwellers in South Africa are often born out of moments of violent resistance that take on an extended life as people who met in the streets to stop an eviction or a water shut-off continue to meet in order to create structures for home care for the sick, fire watch, security patrols, burial services, education, gardens, sewing collectives, and food distribution. This was the case with the movement Abahlali base Mjondolo, which arose in 2005 out of a road blockade to stop the eviction of the settlement to make way for development in preparation for the 2010 World Cup.

The Symphony Way settlement of Capetown is a squatted community of 127 families who had been forcibly evicted from their previous home by the government, which is trying to meet its 2020 target under the Millennium Development Goals to eradicate all slums. The government relocated some of the evictees in a tent camp surrounded by armed guards and razor wire, and the rest in the Transit Relocation Areas, described by one resident as "a lost place in hell" with high crime and frequent rape of children.[59]

No.172, Summer 2007.

59 All the quotes on Symphony Way come from Daria Zelenova, "Anti-Eviction Struggle of the Squatters Communities in Contemporary South Africa," paper presented at the conference "Hierarchy and Power in the History of Civilizations," at the Russian Academy of Sciences, Moscow, June 2009.

Refusing to negotiate with the highly distrusted political parties or to live in either of the officially provided hell holes, the Symphony Way families decided to illegally occupy an area along a road to set up their community. They organize their community with mass assemblies in which everyone participates, as well as a high degree of individual initiative. For example, Raise, a nurse who lives in Symphony Way, volunteers as a teacher within the community center, helps organize a girl's netball team, a boy's soccer team, a drum band, a children's daycamp during holidays, and assists in childbirth. Children are very important within the settlement, and they have their own committee to discuss the problems they are confronted with. "In the committee we solve our everyday problems, when children fight or something. We come together and talk. There are children from other settlements, not only from this road," explains one member of the committee. The community is multiracial and multireligious, including Rastafarians, Muslims, and Christians, who work together to foster a culture of respect among the different groups. The settlement has a nightwatch to discourage antisocial crime and put out unattended fires. The residents told a visiting Russian anarchist that they felt much safer in their community than they would in one of the camps offered by the government, where crime is rampant, because at Symphony Way the community worked together to protect itself. "When someone is in trouble everyone is here," explained Raise. The sense of community is one reason why the squatters do not want to move to a government camp, despite the threat of police violence, and even though in the tent camp the government provides food and water for free. "The community is strong and we made it strong, living and working together, but we didn't know each other when we first came here. This year and a half made us all a big family."

There are thousands of examples of people creating cities, living with a high population density, and meeting their basic needs with scant resources, with mutual aid and direct action. But what about the bigger picture? How would densely populated cities feed themselves without subjugating or exploiting the surrounding countryside? It may be that the subjugation of rural areas by cities played a role in the emergence of the state thousands of years ago. But cities do not have to be as unsustainable as they are now. The 19th century anarchist Peter Kropotkin wrote about a phenomenon that suggested interesting possibilities for anarchist cities. Urban gardeners in and immediately around Paris supplied most of the city's vegetables via intensive agriculture supported by plentiful manure from the city, as well as industrial products, such as glass for greenhouses, that was too costly for farmers in rural areas. These suburban gardeners lived close enough to the city that they could come in every week to sell their produce at market. The spontaneous development of this system of gardening was one of Kropotkin's inspirations in writing about anarchist cities.

In Cuba, centralized industrial agriculture collapsed after the fall of the Soviet Bloc, which had been Cuba's main supplier of petroleum and machinery. The subsequent tightening of the US embargo only exacerbated the situation. The average Cuban lost 20 pounds. Quickly, much of the country shifted to small-scale intensive urban agriculture. As of 2005, half of the fresh produce consumed by the 2 million residents of Havana was produced by about 22,000 urban gardeners within the city itself.[60] The Parisian example chronicled by Kropotkin shows that such shifts can also occur without state guidance.

What about drought, famine, or other catastrophes?

GOVERNMENTS ASSERT ADDITIONAL CONTROL THROUGH "EMERgency powers," on the premise that greater centralization is necessary in emergencies. On the contrary, centralized structures are less agile in responding to chaotic situations. Studies show that after natural disasters most rescues are carried out by common people, not government experts or professional aid workers. More humanitarian aid is offered by people than by governments. Government aid often facilitates political agendas such as supporting political

---

60 Oxfam America, "Havana's Green Revelation," http://www.oxfamamerica.org/whatwedo/where_we_work/camexca/news_publications/art6080.html [viewed December 5, 2005]

allies against their opponents, spreading genetically modified foods, and undermining local agriculture with huge shipments of free food that are quickly replaced by commercial imports monopolizing the upset market. For that matter, a significant portion of the international arms trade is disguised in government aid shipments.

It is possible that people would be better off in catastrophes without governments. We can also develop effective alternatives to government assistance based on the principle of solidarity. If one anarchist community is struck by a catastrophe, it can count on help from others. Whereas in a capitalist context catastrophe is an occasion for politically motivated forms of aid, if not outright opportunism, anarchists give assistance freely with the assurance that it will be reciprocated when the time comes.

Spain in 1936 again provides a good example. In Mas de las Matas, as in other parts, the Cantonal (district) Committee kept track of shortages and surpluses and made arrangements for even distribution. Part of its work was to make sure all collectives were taken care of in the event of natural disasters.

> For example: this year the principal crops of Mas de las Matas, Seno, and La Ginebrosa were destroyed by hailstorms. In a capitalist regime, such natural disasters would have meant endless privations, heavy debts, foreclosures, and even emigration of some workers for several years. But in the regime of libertarian solidarity, these difficulties were overcome by the efforts of the whole district. Provisions, seeds, [...] everything needed to repair the damage, were furnished in the spirit of brotherhood and solidarity—without conditions, without contracting debts. The Revolution has created a new civilization![61]

Anarchism is one of the few revolutionary ideas that does not require modernization; anarchist societies are free to organize themselves at any sustainable level of technology. This means that

---

61 Sam Dolgoff, *The Anarchist Collectives*, New York: Free Life Editions, 1974, pp. 163–164.

societies currently existing as hunter-gatherers, or groups of people who choose to adopt such a lifestyle, can practice this most efficient and ecological form of subsistence, the most conducive to a resilient ecosystem that is less vulnerable to natural disasters.

Meeting our needs without keeping count

CAPITALISM HAS PRODUCED SOME AMAZING GADGETS, BUT THE military and the police are almost always the first to use new technologies, and often the wealthiest people are the only ones who benefit from them. Capitalism has produced undreamed of wealth, but it is hoarded by parasites who did not produce it and who lord over the slaves and wage laborers who created it. Currently, the 85 richest people in the world have as much wealth as the poorest 3.5 billion combined.

Competition may seem to be a useful principle for encouraging efficiency—but efficiency for what purpose? Beneath the mythology it has created, capitalism is not actually a competitive system. Workers are divided and played against each other, while the elite cooperate to maintain their subjection. The wealthy may compete for bigger slices of the pie, but they regularly take up arms together to ensure that every day the pie is baked and brought to their table. When capitalism was still a new phenomenon, one could describe it more honestly, without being confused by decades of propaganda about its supposed virtues: Abraham Lincoln, hardly an anarchist, could see clearly enough that "capitalists generally act harmoniously and in concert to fleece the people."

Capitalism has failed horribly at meeting people's needs and arranging a fair distribution of goods. Throughout the world, millions die from treatable diseases because they cannot afford the medicine that would save them, and people starve to death while their countries export cash crops. Under capitalism, everything is for sale—culture is a commodity that can be manipulated to sell lingerie or skin cream, nature is a resource to be sucked dry and destroyed for profit. People must sell their time and energy to the owning class in order to buy back a fraction of what they produce. This is a deeply rooted system that shapes our values and relationships and defies most attempts to abolish it. The socialist revolutions in the USSR and China did not go deep enough: as they never fully abolished capitalism, it reemerged, stronger than before. Many anarchist attempts have not gone deep enough either; capitalism may well have resurfaced in these experiments if hostile governments had not crushed them first.

Power and alienation must be pursued to their roots. It is not enough for the workers to own their factories collectively if they are controlled by managers and the work still reduces them to machines. Alienation is not simply the absence of legal ownership of the means and fruits of production—it is the lack of control over one's relationship with the world. Worker ownership of a factory is meaningless if it is still administered by others on their behalf. The workers must organize themselves and control the factory directly. And even if they control the factory directly, alienation persists where the broader economic relationships, the factory itself, dictates the form their labor takes. Can a person truly be free working on an assembly line, denied creativity and treated as a machine? The form of work itself must change, so that people can pursue the skills and activities that give them joy.

The separation of work from other human activities is one of the roots of alienation. Production itself becomes a sort of obsession that justifies exploiting people or destroying the environment for the sake of efficiency. If we view happiness as a human need no less than food and clothing, then the division between productive and nonproductive activity, between work and play, melts away. The squatting movement in Barcelona and the gift economies of many indigenous societies provide examples of the blurring of work and play.

In a free society, exchange is simply a symbolic assurance that everyone is contributing to the common resources—people don't hoard resources or take advantage of others, because they have to give in order to receive. But exchange can present problems by attaching a quantitative value to every object and experience, thus stripping them of their subjective value.

Where once an ice cream cone was worth a delicious ten minutes of finger licking goodness in the sun, and a book was worth several afternoons of enjoyment and reflection and possibly even life-changing insight, after these goods are assessed according to the regime of exchange, an ice cream cone is worth a fourth of a book. Further into this process, to make the exchanges more efficient, while consequently fixing the quantitative value as inherent rather than comparative, an ice cream cone is worth one unit of currency and a book four units of currency. The monetary value replaces the subjective value of the object—the pleasure people find in it. On one hand, people and their desires are taken out of the equation, while on the other hand all values—pleasure, usefulness, inspiration—are absorbed into a quantitative value, and money itself becomes a symbol for all these other values.

In effect, possessing money comes to symbolize having access to enjoyment or the fulfillment of a desire; but money, by affixing a quantitative value, robs objects of the sense of fulfillment they might bring, because humans cannot experience quantitative, abstract value. In eating an ice cream cone, the pleasure is in the act—but in buying a commodity, the pleasure is in the purchase, in the magical moment that an abstract value is transformed into a tangible possession. Money exerts such a powerful influence on notions of value that consumption itself is always anticlimactic: once the commodity is purchased, it loses its value, especially as people come to prioritize abstract value over subjective value. Furthermore, having purchased it, you lose money, and your total holdings of symbolic value decrease—hence the nagging feeling of guilt that accompanies spending money.

In addition to alienation, exchange creates power-over: if one person accumulates more quantitative value, they have accrued the right to a greater portion of the community's resources. Systems of exchange and currency, like the barter network in Argentina or the coupon system for purchasing goods in parts of anarchist Spain, rely on customs and social arrangements to prevent the reemergence of capitalism. For example, a gift economy could function at a local level, with exchange used only for regional trade. People could deliberately set up work environments that encourage personal development, creativity, fun, and self-organization, while decentralized federations of such workplaces could award one another with coupons for the goods they produce so each person has access to the wealth created by all.

But it is a worthwhile challenge to do away with exchange and currency altogether. Within free stores or Freecycle, the symbolic assurance provided by exchange or barter is unnecessary. The assurance that everyone will contribute to the common wealth springs from the culture of the spaces themselves. As a participant, you express the desire to give and to receive, and your inclusion in the social space increases as you carry out both of these activities. In such contexts, giving pleases a person just as much as receiving.

The world is bountiful enough to provide for everyone's needs. Scarcity is a dangerous illusion that functions as a self-fulfilling prophecy. Once people stop giving and begin hoarding, collective wealth declines. If we overcome the fear of scarcity, scarcity itself disappears. Common resources will be bountiful if everyone shares and contributes, or even if most people do. People like to be active, to create and improve things. If people are ensured access to common resources and spared the poverty of wage slavery, they will create plenty of the things they need and that give them pleasure, as well as the infrastructure required to make and distribute these things.

Recommended Reading:

- Sam Dolgoff, *The Anarchist Collectives*, New York: Free Life Editions, 1974.
- Natasha Gordon and Paul Chatterton, *Taking Back Control: A Journey Through Argentina's Popular Uprising*. Leeds, UK: University of Leeds, 2004.
- Michael Albert, *Parecon: Life After Capitalism,* New York: Verso, 2003.
- Peter Kropotkin, *Fields, Factories and Workshops Tomorrow*. London: Freedom Press, 1974.
- Jac Smit, Annu Ratta and Joe Nasr, *Urban Agriculture: Food, Jobs and Sustainable Cities,* UNDP, Habitat II Series, 1996.

- The Curious George Brigade, *Liberate, Not Exterminate*, New York: CrimethInc., 2005.
- Gonzalo Casanova, *Armarse Sobre Las Ruinas: Historia del movimiento autónomo en Madrid (1985–1999)*. Madrid: Potencial Hardcore, 2002.
- VV.AA *Colectividades y Ocupación Rural*, Madrid: Traficantes de Sueños, 1999.
- Marcel Mauss, *The Gift: forms and functions of exchange in archaic societies*. 1924 (English version London: Routledge Press, 1990).
- p.m., *Bolo'Bolo*. Zurich: Paranoia City Verlag, 1983.

4. ENVIRONMENT

NO PHILOSOPHY OR MOVEMENT FOR LIBERATION CAN IGNORE the connection between human exploitation of the environment and our exploitation of one another, nor can it ignore the suicidal ramifications of industrial society. A free society must forge a respectful and sustainable relationship with its bioregion, on the understanding that humans depend on the health of the entire planet.

What's to stop someone from destroying the environment?

SOME PEOPLE OPPOSE CAPITALISM ON ENVIRONMENTAL GROUNDS, but think some sort of state is necessary to prevent ecocide. But the state is itself a tool for the exploitation of nature. Socialist states such as the Soviet Union and People's Republic of China have been among the most ecocidal regimes imaginable. That these two societies never escaped the dynamics of capitalism is itself a feature of the state structure—it necessitates hierarchical, exploitative economic relationships of control and command, and once you start playing that game nothing beats capitalism. However the state does present the possibility of forcibly changing people's behavior on a massive scale, and this power is attractive to some environmentalists. There have been a few states in world history that enforced protective measures domestically, when saving the environment coincided with their strategic interests. One of the foremost is Japan, which halted and reversed deforestation in the archipelago around the Meiji period. But in this case and other cases, domestic environmental protections enforced by the state were coupled with greater exploitation abroad. Japanese society consumed increasing amounts of imported wood, fueling deforestation in other countries and providing an incentive for the development of an imperial military to secure these vital resources. This led not only to environmental devastation but also to warfare and genocide. Similarly in Western Europe, statist environmental protections came at the expense of colonial exploitation, which also resulted in genocide.

In smaller-scale societies, the existence of an elite tends to fuel environmental exploitation. The renowned social collapse on Easter Island was caused in large part by the elite, who compelled the society to build statues in their honor. This statue-building complex deforested the island, as large numbers of logs were needed for scaffolding and transportation of the statues, and farmland to feed the laborers came at the expense of more forests. Without forests, soil fertility plummeted, and without food the human population plunged as well. But they didn't just starve or decrease their birth rate—the clan elites warred with one another, knocking down rival statues and carrying out raids that culminated in cannibalism, until nearly the entire society died off.[62]

A decentralized, communal society with a commonly held ecological ethos is the best equipped to prevent environmental destruction. In economies that value local self-sufficiency over trade and production, communities have to deal with the environmental consequences of their own economic behaviors. They cannot pay others to take their garbage or starve so they can have an abundance.

---

62 This theory for the fate of Easter Island is convincingly argued in Jared Diamond, *Collapse: How Societies Choose to Fail or Succeed*, New York, Viking, 2005.

Local control of resources also discourages overpopulation. Studies have shown that when the members of a society can directly see how having too many children will diminish the resources available for everyone, they keep their families within a sustainable limit. But when these localized societies are incorporated into a globalized economy in which most resources and wastes are imported and exported, and scarcity results from seemingly arbitrary price fluctuations rather than the depletion of local resources, populations climb unsustainably, even if more effective forms of contraception are also available.[63] In *Seeing Like a State*, James Scott explains how governments enforce "legibility"—a uniformity that enables comprehension from above, in order to control and track subjects. As a result, such societies lose the local knowledge necessary to understand problems and situations.

Capitalism, Christianity, and Western science all share a certain mythology regarding nature, which encourages exploitation and contempt, and views the natural world as dead, mechanical, and existing to satisfy human consumption. This megalomania masquerading as Reason or Divine Truth has revealed itself beyond all doubt to be suicidal. What is needed instead is a culture that respects the natural world as a living, interconnected thing, and understands our place within it. Bruce Stewart, a Maori writer and activist, told an interviewer, pointing to a flowering vine he had planted by his house,

---

63 Eric Alden Smith, Mark Wishnie, "Conservation and Subsistence in Small-Scale Societies," *Annual Review of Anthropology*, Vol. 29, 2000, pp. 493–524. "As population density and political centralization increases, communities may exceed the size and homogeneity needed for endogenous systems of communal management" (p. 505). The authors also pointed out that colonial and postcolonial interference ended many systems of communal resource management. Bonnie Anna Nardi, "Modes of Explanation in Anthropological Population Theory: Biological Determinism vs. Self-Regulation in Studies of Population Growth in Third World Countries," *American Anthropologist*, vol. 83, 1981. Nardi points out that as decision-making, society, and identity go from small-scale to a national scale, fertility control loses its effectiveness (p. 40).

> This vine no longer has a name. Our Maori name has been lost, so we'll have to find another. Only one of this plant remained in the world, living on a goat-infested island. The plant could go any day. So I got a seed and planted it here. The vine has grown, and although it normally takes twenty years to bloom, this one is blooming after seven.
>
> ...If we are to survive, each of us must become *kaitiaki*, which to me is the most important concept in my own Maori culture. We must become caretakers, guardians, trustees, nurturers. In the old days each *whanau*, or family, used to look after a specific piece of terrain. One family might look after a river from a certain rock down to the next bend. And they were the kaitiaki of the birds and fish and plants. They knew when it was time to take them to eat, and when it was not. When the birds needed to be protected, the people put a *rahui* on them, which means the birds were temporarily sacred. And some birds were permanently *tapu*, which means they were full-time protected. This protection was so strong that people would die if they broke it. It's that simple. It needed no policing. In their eagerness to unsavage my ancestors Christian missionaries killed the concept of tapu along with many others.[64]

Tikopia, a Pacific island settled by Polynesian people, provides a good example of a decentralized, anarchic society that has successfully dealt with life-and-death environmental problems. The island is only 1.8 square miles in area and supports 1,200 inhabitants—that is, 800 people per square mile of farmland. The community has existed sustainably for 3,000 years. Tikopia is covered in multi-storied orchard-gardens that mimic the natural rainforests. At first sight, most of the island appears to be covered in forest, though true rainforests only remain on a few steep parts of the island. Tikopia is small enough that all its inhabitants can become familiar with their entire ecosystem. It is also isolated, so for a long time they could not import resources or export the consequences of their lifestyle. Each of the four clans have chiefs,

---

64 Bruce Stewart, quoted in Derrick Jensen, *A Language Older Than Words*, White River Junction, Vermont: Chelsea Green Publishing Company, 2000, p.162.

though these have no coercive powers and play a ceremonial role as the custodians of tradition. Tikopia is among the least socially stratified of the Polynesian islands; for example, the chiefs still have to work and produce their own food. Population control is a common value, and parents feel it is immoral to have more than a certain number of children. In one striking example of the power of these collectively held and reinforced values, around the year 1600 the islanders reached a collective decision to end pig-breeding. They slaughtered all the pigs on the island, even though pig meat was a highly valued food source, because keeping pigs was a major strain on the environment.[65] In a more stratified, hierarchical society, this might have been impossible, because the elite would typically force poorer people to suffer the consequences of their lifestyles rather than give up an esteemed luxury product.[66]

Before colonization and the disastrous arrival of missionaries, population control methods on Tikopia included natural contraception, abortion, and abstinence for younger people—though this was a compassionate celibacy that amounted to a prohibition on reproduction rather than on sex. Tikopians also used other forms of population control, such as infanticide, that many people in other societies would find impermissible, but Tikopia can still provide us with a perfectly valid example because with the effectiveness of modern contraception and abortion techniques, no other methods are necessary for a decentralized approach to population control. The most important feature of the Tikopian example is their ethos: their recognition that they lived on an island and resources were limited, so that increasing their population was tantamount to suicide. Other Polynesian island societies ignored that fact and subsequently died off. The planet Earth, in this sense, is also an island; accordingly, we need to develop both global consciousness and localized economies, so we can avoid exceeding the

---

[65] Jared Diamond, *Collapse: how societies choose to fail or succeed*, New York: Viking, 2005, pp. 292–293

[66] For example, the United States and Western Europe, responsible for most of the world's greenhouse gases, are currently forcing hundreds of millions of people to die every year rather than curtailing their car cultures and reducing their emissions.

capacity of the land and stay aware of the other living things with whom we share this island.

Today most of the world is not organized into communities that are structured to be sensitive to the limits of the local environment, but it is possible to recreate such communities. There is a growing movement of ecologically sustainable communities, or "ecovillages," organized on horizontal, non-hierarchical lines, in which groups of people ranging from a dozen to several hundred come together to create anarchic societies with organic, sustainable designs. The construction of these villages maximizes resource efficiency and ecological sustainability, and also cultivates sensitivity to the local environment on a cultural and spiritual level. These ecovillages are at the forefront of developing sustainable technologies. Any alternative community can degenerate into yuppie escapism, and ecovillages are vulnerable to this, but a leading part of the ecovillage movement seeks to develop and spread innovations that are relevant to the world at large rather than to close itself off from the world. To help proliferate ecovillages and adapt them to all regions of the globe, and to facilitate coordination between existing ecovillages, 400 delegates from 40 countries met in Findhorn, Scotland, in 1995 and established the Global Ecovillage Network.

Each ecovillage is a little different, but a few examples can provide an idea of their diversity. The Farm, in rural Tennessee, has 350 residents. Established in 1971, it contains mulch gardens, solar-heated showers, a sustainable shiitake mushroom business, straw bale houses, and a center for training people from around the world to build their own ecovillages. Old Bassaisa, in Egypt, contains a few hundred residents and has existed for thousands of years. The residents have perfected an ecological and sustainable village design from traditional methods. Old Bassaisa now contains a Future Studies center, and they are developing new sustainable technologies like a methane gas producing unit that extracts gases from cow manure to save themselves from having to use scarce firewood. They use the leftover slurry as fertilizer for their fields. Ecotop, near Dusseldorf in Germany, is an entire suburb with hundreds of residents living in several four-story apartment buildings and a few detached homes. The architecture fosters a sense of community and freedom, with a number of communal and private spaces. Between the buildings, in a sort of village center, is a multi-use courtyard/playground/pedestrian zone, as well as community gardens and an abundance of plants and trees. The buildings, which have a completely modern, urban aesthetic, were constructed with natural materials and designed with passive heating and cooling and biological on-site wastewater treatment.

Earthhaven, with about sixty residents, was founded in 1995 in North Carolina by permaculture designers. It is composed of several neighborhood clusters set in the steep Appalachian hills. Most of the land is covered in forest, but the residents recently made the difficult decision to clear some of the forest for gardens so they could come closer to food self-sufficiency rather than exporting the costs of their lifestyle by purchasing food from elsewhere. They talked about it a long time, prepared themselves spiritually, and attempted to clear the land in a respectful way. This sort of attitude, which capitalist ideology would dismiss as sentimental and inefficient, is exactly what could prevent destruction of the environment in an anarchist society.

Also necessary are fierceness and the willingness to take direct action to defend the environment. On the isthmus of Tehuantepec, in Oaxaca, Mexico, anarchist and anti-authoritarian indigenous people have shown exactly these qualities in protecting the land against a series of threats. Organizations such as the Union of Indigenous Communities of the Northern Zone of the Isthmus, UCIZONI, which includes one hundred communities in Oaxaca and Veracruz, and later the anarchist/Magonista group CIPO-RFM, have fought against the environmentally devastating construction of wind farms, shrimp farms, eucalyptus plantations, and the expropriation of land by the lumber industry. They have also reduced economic pressures to exploit the environment by setting up corn and coffee cooperatives and building schools and clinics. Meanwhile, they have created a network of autonomous community radio stations to educate people about dangers to the environment and inform the surrounding communities about new industrial projects that would destroy more land. In 2001, the indigenous communities defeated the construction of a highway that was part of Plan Puebla Panama, a neoliberal megaproject intended to connect North and South America with transportation infrastructure designed to increase the flow of commodities. During the Zapatista rebellion of 1994, they shut down transportation lines to slow down the movement of troops, and they also blocked highways and shut down government offices to support the 2006 rebellion throughout Oaxaca.

In 1998, the Minnesota Department of Transportation wanted to reroute a highway through a park in Minneapolis along the confluence of the Minnesota and Mississippi rivers. The proposed reroute would destroy an area that contained old trees, a precious oak savanna ecosystem, an ancient freshwater spring, and sites sacred to Native Americans—a vital wild space in the middle of the city that also served as a refuge for many neighbors. Indigenous activists with the American Indian Movement and the Mendota Mdewakanton Dakota Community came together to work in coalition with white residents, environmentalists from Earth First!, and anarchists from all over the country to help stop the construction. The result was the Minnehaha Free State, an autonomous zone that became the first and longest-lasting urban anti-road occupation in US history. For a year and a half, hundreds of people occupied the land to prevent the Department of Transportation from cutting down the trees and building the highway, and thousands more supported and visited the Free State. The occupation empowered countless participants, reconnected many Dakota people with their heritage, won the support of many neighbors, created a yearlong autonomous zone and self-organizing community, and significantly delayed the destruction of the area—buying time during which many people were able to discover and enjoy the space in an intimate and spiritual way.

To crush the occupation, the state was forced to resort to a variety of repressive tactics. The people at the encampment were subjected to harassment, surveillance, and infiltration. An army of police officers raided and destroyed the camps repeatedly; tortured, hospitalized, and almost killed people; and carried out over a hundred arrests. In the end, the state cut down the trees and built the highway, but the protestors did manage to save Coldwater Spring, which is a sacred site to the area's indigenous peoples and an important part of the local watershed. The Native participants declared an important spiritual victory.

People throughout Minneapolis who had initially supported the destructive project because of its supposed benefits to the transportation system were won over by the resistance to save the park, and came to oppose the highway. If the decision had been up to them, the highway would not have been built. The Free State created and nurtured coalitions and community bonds that last to this day, shaping new generations of radical community and inspiring similar efforts around the world.

Outside Edinburgh, Scotland, eco-anarchists have had even more success saving a forest. The Bilston Glen anti-roads camp has existed for over seven years as of this writing, drawing the participation of hundreds of people and stopping the construction of a bypass desired by large biotech facilities in the area. To allow people to live there permanently with a lower impact on the forest, and to make it harder for police to evict them, the activists have built houses up in the trees which people occupy year round. The village is certainly low technology, but it is also low impact, and some of the houses are clearly works of love, comfortable enough to be considered permanent homes. The dozen or so inhabitants have also been tending the forest, removing invasive species and encouraging the growth of native species. The Bilston Glen tree village is just one in a long line of anti-road occupations and ecological direct actions in the UK that create a collective force that makes the state think twice about building new roads or evicting protestors. The village also crosses the line between simply opposing government policy and creating new social relations with the environment: in the course of defending it, dozens of people have made the forest their home, and hundreds more people have personally seen the importance of relating with nature in a respectful way and defending it from Western civilization.

What about global environmental problems, like climate change?

ANARCHISTS DO NOT YET HAVE EXPERIENCE DEALING WITH GLOBAL problems because our successes so far have only been local and temporary. Stateless, anarchic societies once covered the world, but this was long before the existence of global environmental problems like those created by capitalism. Today, members of many of these indigenous societies are at the forefront of global resistance to the ecological destruction caused by governments and corporations.

Anarchists also coordinate resistance globally. They organize international protests against major polluters and their state backers, such as the mobilizations during the G8 summits that have convened hundreds of thousands of people from dozens of countries to demonstrate against the states most responsible for global warming and other problems. In response to the global activity of transnational corporations, ecologically-minded anarchists share information globally. In this manner, activists around the world can coordinate simultaneous actions against corporations, targeting a polluting factory or mine on one continent, retail stores on another continent, and an international headquarters or shareholders' meeting on another continent.

For example, major protests, boycotts, and acts of sabotage against Shell Oil were coordinated among people in Nigeria, Europe, and the North America throughout the 1980s and '90s. In 1986, autonomists in Denmark carried out multiple simultaneous fire bombings of Shell stations across the country during a worldwide boycott to punish Shell for supporting the government responsible for apartheid in South Africa. In the Netherlands, the clandestine anti-authoritarian group RARA (Revolutionary Anti-Racist Action) carried out a campaign of nonlethal bombings against Shell Oil, playing a crucial role in forcing Shell to pull out of South Africa. In 1995, when Shell wanted to dump an old oil rig in the North Sea, it was forced to abandon its plans by protests in Denmark and the UK, an occupation of the oil rig by Greenpeace activists, and a fire bombing and a shooting attack against Shell stations in two different cities in Germany as well as a boycott that lowered sales by ten percent in that country.⁶⁷ Efforts such as these prefigure the decentralized global networks that could protect the environment in an anarchist future. If we succeed in abolishing capitalism and the state, we will have removed the greatest systemic ravagers of the environment as well as the structural barriers that currently impede popular action in defense of nature.

There are historical examples of stateless societies responding to large scale, collective environmental problems through decentralized networks. Though the problems were not global, the relative distances they faced—with information traveling at a pedestrian's pace—were perhaps greater than the distances that mark today's world, in which people can communicate instantaneously even if they live on opposite sides of the planet.

Tonga is a Pacific archipelago settled by Polynesian peoples. Before colonization, it had a centralized political system with a hereditary leader, but the system was far less centralized than a state, and the leader's coercive powers were limited. For 3,200 years, the people of Tonga were able to maintain sustainable practices over an archipelago of 288 square miles with tens of thousands of inhabitants.⁶⁸ There was no communications technology, so information travelled slowly. Tonga is too large for a single farmer to have knowledge of all the islands or even all of any of its large islands. The leader was traditionally able to guide and ensure sustainable practices not through recourse to force, but because he had access to information from the entire territory, just as a federation or general assembly would if the islanders organized themselves in that way. It was up to the individuals who made up the society to implement particular practices and support the idea of sustainability.

The fact that a large population can protect the environment in a diffuse or decentralized manner, without leadership, is amply

---

67 The ten percent figure and mention of the two attacks in Germany come from Nathaniel C. Nash, "Oil Companies Face Boycott Over Sinking of Rig," *The New York Times*, June 17, 1995.
68 Jared Diamond, *Collapse: How Societies Choose to Fail or Succeed*, New York: Viking, 2005, p. 277.

demonstrated by the aforementioned New Guinea highlanders. Agriculture usually leads to deforestation as land is cleared for fields, and deforestation can kill the soil. Many societies respond by clearing more land to compensate for lower soil productivity, thus aggravating the problem. Numerous civilizations have collapsed because they destroyed their soil through deforestation. The danger of soil erosion is accentuated in mountainous terrain, such as the New Guinea highlands, where heavy rains can wash away denuded soil en masse. A more intelligent practice, which the farmers in New Guinea perfected, is silvaculture: integrating trees with the other crops, combining orchard, field, and forest to protect the soil and create symbiotic chemical cycles between the various cultivated plants.

The people of the highlands developed special anti-erosion techniques to keep from losing the soil of their steep mountain valleys. Any particular farmer might have gained a quick advantage by taking shortcuts that would eventually cause erosion and rob future generations of healthy soil, yet sustainable techniques were used universally at the time of colonization. Anti-erosion techniques were spread and reinforced using exclusively collective and decentralized means. The highlanders did not need experts to come up with these environmental and gardening technologies and they did not need bureaucrats to ensure that everyone was using them. Instead, they relied on a culture that valued experimentation, individual freedom, social responsibility, collective stewardship of the land, and free communication. Effective innovations developed in one area spread quickly and freely from valley to valley. Lacking telephones, radio, or internet, and separated by steep mountains, each valley community was like a country unto itself. Hundreds of languages are spoken within the New Guinea highlands, changing from one community to the next. Within this miniature world, no one community could make sure that other communities were not destroying their environment—yet their decentralized approach to protecting the environment worked. Over thousands of years, they protected their soil and supported a population of millions of people living at such a high population density that the first Europeans to fly overhead saw a country they likened to the Netherlands.

Water management in that lowland northern country in the 12th and 13th centuries provides another example of bottom-up solutions to environmental problems. Since much of the Netherlands is below sea level and nearly all of it is in danger of flooding, farmers had to work constantly to maintain and improve the water management system. The protections against flooding were a common infrastructure that benefited everybody, yet they also required everyone to invest in the good of the collective to maintain them: an individual farmer stood to gain by shirking water management duties, but the entire society would lose if there were a flood. This example is especially significant because Dutch society lacked the anarchistic values common in indigenous societies. The area had long been converted to Christianity and indoctrinated in its ecocidal, hierarchical values; for hundreds of years it had been under the control of a state, though the empire had fallen apart and in the 12th and 13th centuries the Netherlands were effectively stateless. Central authority in the form of church officials, feudal lords, and guilds remained strong in Holland and Zeeland, where capitalism would eventually originate, but in northern regions such as Friesland society was largely decentralized and horizontal.

At that time, contact between towns dozens of miles apart—several days' travel—could be more challenging than global communication in the present day. Despite this difficulty, farming communities, towns, and villages managed to build and maintain extensive infrastructure to reclaim land from the sea and protect against flooding amid fluctuating sea levels. Neighborhood councils, by organizing cooperative work bands or dividing duties between communities, built and maintained the dykes, canals, sluices, and drainage systems necessary to protect the entire society; it was "a joint approach from the bottom-up, from the local communities, that found their protection through organizing themselves in such a way."[69] Spontaneous horizontal organizing

---

69 H. Van Der Linden, "Een Nieuwe Overheidsinstelling: Het Waterschap circa 1100–1400" in D.P. Blok, *Algemene Geschiednis der Nederlanden*, deel III. Haarlem: Fibula van Dishoeck, 1982, p. 64. Author's translation.

even played a major role in the feudal areas such as Holland and Zeeland, and it is doubtful that the weak authorities who did exist in those parts could have managed the necessary water works by themselves, given their limited power. Though the authorities always take credit for the creativity of the masses, spontaneous self-organization persists even in the shadow of the state.

The only way to save the planet

WHEN IT COMES TO PROTECTING THE ENVIRONMENT, NEARLY ANY social system would be better than the one we have now. Capitalism is the first social arrangement in human history to endanger the survival of our species and life on earth in general. Capitalism provides incentives to exploit and destroy nature, and creates an atomized society that is incapable of protecting the environment. Under capitalism, ecocide is literally a right. Environmental protections are "trade barriers"; preventing a corporation from clear-cutting land it has purchased is a violation of private property and free enterprise. Companies are allowed to make millions of tons of plastic, most of it for throwaway packaging, despite the fact that they have no plan for disposing of it and not even any idea what will happen with it all; plastic does not decompose, so plastic trash is filling up the ocean and appearing in the bodies of marine creatures, and it may last millions of years. To save endangered rhinoceros from poachers, game wardens have started sawing off their valuable horns; but the poachers are killing them anyway because once they are extinct, the value of the few remaining bits of rhinoceros ivory will go through the roof.

And despite all this, universities have the audacity to indoctrinate students to believe that a communal society would be incapable of protecting the environment because of the so-called tragedy of the commons. This myth is often explained thus: imagine a society of sheepherders owns the grazing land in common. They benefit collectively if each grazes a smaller number of sheep, because the pasture stays fertile, but any one of them benefits individually if he overgrazes, because he will receive a greater share of the product—thus collective ownership supposedly leads to depletion of resources. The historical examples intended to corroborate this theory are generally drawn from colonial and postcolonial situations in which oppressed people, whose traditional forms of organization and stewardship have been undermined, are crowded onto marginal land, with predictable results. The sheepherding scenario assumes a situation that is extremely rare in human history: a collective comprised of atomized, competitive individuals who value personal wealth over social bonds and ecological health, and lack social arrangements or traditions that can guarantee sustainable, shared use.

Capitalism has already caused the biggest wave of extinctions to hit the planet since an asteroid collision killed off the dinosaurs. To prevent global climate change from bringing about total ecological collapse, and stop pollution and overpopulation from killing off most of the planet's mammals, birds, amphibians, and marine life, we have to abolish capitalism, hopefully within the next few decades. Human-caused extinctions have been apparent for at least a hundred years now. The greenhouse effect has been widely acknowledged for nearly two decades. The best that the reputed ingenuity of free enterprise has come up with is carbon trading, a ridiculous farce. Likewise, we cannot trust some world government to save the planet. A government's first concern is always its own power, and it builds the base of this power upon economic relationships. The governing elite must maintain a privileged position, and that privilege depends on the exploitation of other people and of the environment.

Localized, egalitarian societies linked by global communication and awareness are the best chance for saving the environment. Self-sufficient, self-contained economies leave almost no carbon footprint. They don't need petroleum to ship goods in and waste out, or huge amounts of electricity to power industrial complexes to produce goods for export. They must produce most of their energy themselves via solar, wind, biofuel, and similar technologies, and rely more on what can be done manually than on electrical appliances. Such societies pollute less because they have fewer incentives to mass production and lack the means to dump their byproducts on others' land. In place of busy airports, traffic-clogged highways, and long commutes to work, we can imagine bicycles, buses, interregional trains, and sailboats. Likewise, populations will not spiral out of control, because women will be empowered to manage their fertility and the localized economy will make apparent the limited availability of resources.

An ecologically sustainable world would have to be anti-authoritarian, so no society could encroach on its neighbors to expand its resource base; and cooperative, so societies could band together in self-defense against a group developing imperialist tendencies. Most importantly, it would demand a common ecological ethos, so people would respect the environment rather than regarding it simply as raw material to exploit. We can begin building such a world now, by learning from ecologically sustainable indigenous societies, sabotaging and shaming polluters, spreading a love for nature and an awareness of our bioregions, and establishing projects that allow us to meet our needs for food, water, and energy locally.

Recommended Reading:

- Nirmal Sengupta, *Managing Common Property: Irrigation in India and The Philippines*, New Delhi: Sage, 1991.
- Winona LaDuke, *Recovering the Sacred: The Power of Naming and Claiming*, Cambridge: South End Press, 2005.
- Jan Martin Bang, *Ecovillages: A Practical Guide to Sustainable Communities*. Edinburgh: Floris Books, 2005.
- Heather C. Flores, *Food Not Lawns: How To Turn Your Yard Into A Garden And Your Neighborhood Into A Community*. White River Jct., Vermont: Chelsea Green, 2006.
- Jared Diamond, *Collapse: How Societies Choose to Fail or Succeed*, New York, Viking, 2005.
- Murray Bookchin, *The Ecology of Freedom: the Emergence and Dissolution of Hierarchy*, Palo Alto, CA: Cheshire Books, 1982.

- Elli King, ed., *Listen: The Story of the People at Taku Wakan Tipi and the Reroute of Highway 55, or, The Minnehaha Free State*, Tucson, AZ: Feral Press, 2006.
- Bill Holmgren and David Mollison, *Permaculture One: a Perennial Agriculture for Human Settlements*. Sydney: Corgi books, 1978.

5. CRIME

PRISON IS THE INSTITUTION THAT MOST CONCRETELY SYMBOLizes domination. Anarchists wish to create a society that can protect itself and resolve internal problems without police, judges, or prisons; a society that does not view its problems in terms of good and evil, permitted and prohibited, law-abiders and criminals.

Who will protect us without police?

IN OUR SOCIETY, POLICE BENEFIT FROM A TREMENDOUS AMOUNT of hype, whether it's biased and fear-mongering media coverage of crime or the flood of movies and television shows featuring cops as heroes and protectors. Yet many people's experiences with police contrast starkly with this heavy-handed propaganda.

In a hierarchical society, whom do police protect? Who has more to fear from crime, and who has more to fear from police? In some communities, the police are like an occupying force; police and crime form the interlocking jaws of a trap that prevents people from escaping oppressive situations or rescuing their communities from violence, poverty, and fragmentation.

Historically, police did not develop out of a social necessity to protect people from rising crime. In the United States, modern police forces arose at a time when crime was already diminishing. Rather, the institution of police emerged as a means to give the ruling class greater control over the population and expand the state's monopoly on the resolution of social conflict. This was not a response to crime or an attempt to solve it; on the contrary, it coincided with the creation of new forms of crime. At the same time police forces were being expanded and modernized, the ruling class began to criminalize predominantly lower class behaviors that had previously been acceptable such as vagrancy, gambling, and public drunkenness.[70] Those in authority define "criminal activity" according to their own needs, then present their definitions as neutral and timeless. For example, many more people may be killed by pollution and work-related accidents than by drugs, but drug dealers are branded a threat to society, not factory owners. And even when factory owners break the law in a way that kills people, they are not sent to prison.[71]

Today, over two-thirds of prisoners in the US are locked up for nonviolent offenses. It is no surprise that the majority of prisoners are poor people and people of color, given the criminalization of drugs and immigration, the disproportionately harsh penalties for the drugs typically used by poor people, and the greater chance people of color have of being convicted or sentenced more harshly for the same crimes.[72] Likewise, the intense presence of militarized

---

70 This analysis is well documented by Kristian Williams in *Our Enemies in Blue*. Brooklyn: Soft Skull Press, 2004.

71 In 2005, 5,734 workers were killed by traumatic injury on the job, and an estimated 50,000 to 60,000 died from occupational diseases, according to the AFL-CIO "Facts About Worker Safety and Health 2007." http://www.aflcio.org/issues/safety/memorial/upload/wmd_safetyfacts.pdf

Of all the killings of workers by employer negligence between 1982 and 2002, fewer than 2000 were investigated by the government, and of these only 81 resulted in convictions and only 16 resulted in jailtime, though the maximum allowed sentence was six months, according to David Barstow, "U.S. Rarely Seeks Charges for Deaths in Workplace," New York Times, December 22, 2003.

72 These are widely available statistics from US Census bureau, Justice Department, independent researchers, Human Rights Watch, and

police in ghettos and poor neighborhoods is connected to the fact that crime stays high in those neighborhoods while rates of incarceration increase. The police and prisons are systems of control that preserve social inequalities, spread fear and resentment, exclude and alienate whole communities, and exercise extreme violence against the most oppressed sectors of society.

Those who can organize their own lives within their communities are better equipped to protect themselves. Some societies and communities that have won autonomy from the state organize volunteer patrols to help people in need and discourage aggressions. Unlike the police, these groups generally do not have coercive authority or a closed, bureaucratic structure, and are more likely to be made up of volunteers from within the neighborhood. They focus on protecting people rather than property or privilege, and in the absence of a legal code they respond to people's needs rather than inflexible protocol. Other societies organize against social harm without setting up specific institutions. Instead they utilize diffuse sanctions—responses and attitudes spread throughout the society and propagated in the culture—to promote a safe environment.

Anarchists take an entirely different view of the problems that authoritarian societies place within the framework of crime and punishment. A crime is the violation of a written law, and laws are imposed by elite bodies. In the final instance, the question is not whether someone is hurting others but whether she is disobeying the orders of the elite. As a response to crime, punishment creates hierarchies of morality and power between the criminal and the dispensers of justice. It denies the criminal the resources he may need to reintegrate into the community and to stop hurting others.

In an empowered society, people do not need written laws; they have the power to determine whether someone is preventing them from fulfilling their needs, and can call on their peers for help resolving conflicts. In this view, the problem is not crime,

other organizations. They can be found, for example, on drugwarfacts.org [viewed 30 December, 2009].

but social harm—actions such as assault and drunk driving that actually hurt other people. This paradigm does away with the category of victimless crime, and reveals the absurdity of protecting the property rights of privileged people over the survival needs of others. The outrages typical of capitalist justice, such as arresting the hungry for stealing from the wealthy, would not be possible in a needs-based paradigm.

During the February 1919 general strike in Seattle, workers took over the city. Commercially, Seattle was shut down, but the workers did not allow it to fall into disarray. On the contrary, they kept all vital services running, but organized by the workers without the management of the bosses. The workers were the ones running the city every other day of the year, anyway, and during the strike they proved that they knew how to conduct their work without managerial interference. They coordinated citywide organization through the General Strike Committee, made up of rank and file workers from every local union; the structure was similar to, and perhaps inspired by, the Paris Commune. Union locals and specific groups of workers retained autonomy over their jobs without management or interference from the Committee or any other body. Workers were free to take initiative at the local level. Milk wagon drivers, for example, set up a neighborhood milk distribution system the bosses, restricted by profit motives, would never have allowed.

The striking workers collected the garbage, set up public cafeterias, distributed free food, and maintained fire department services. They also provided protection against anti-social behavior—robberies, assaults, murders, rapes: the crime wave authoritarians always forecast. A city guard comprised of unarmed military veterans walked the streets to keep watch and respond to calls for help, though they were authorized to use warnings and persuasion only. Aided by the feelings of solidarity that created a stronger social fabric during the strike, the volunteer guard were able to maintain a peaceful environment, accomplishing what the state itself could not.

This context of solidarity, free food, and empowerment of the common person played a role in drying up crime at its source. Marginalized people gained opportunities for community involvement, decision-making, and social inclusion that were denied to them by the capitalist regime. The absence of the police, whose presence emphasizes class tensions and creates a hostile environment, may have actually decreased lower-class crime. Even the authorities remarked on how organized the city was: Major General John F. Morrison, stationed in Seattle, claimed that he had never seen "a city so quiet and so orderly." The strike was ultimately shut down by the invasion of thousands of troops and police deputies, coupled with pressure from the union leadership.[73]

In Oaxaca City in 2006, during the five months of autonomy at the height of the revolt, the APPO, the popular assembly organized by the striking teachers and other activists to coordinate their resistance and organize life in Oaxaca City, established a volunteer watch that helped keep things peaceful in especially violent and divisive circumstances. For their part, the police and paramilitaries killed over ten people—this was the only bloodbath in the absence of state power.

The popular movement in Oaxaca was able to maintain relative peace despite all the violence imposed by the state. They accomplished this by modifying an indigenous custom for the new situation: they used *topiles,* rotating watches that maintain security in indigenous communities. The teacher's union already used *topiles* as security volunteers during the encampment, before the APPO was formed, and the APPO quickly extended the practice as part of a security commission to protect the city against police and paramilitaries. A large part of the *topiles'* duty included occupying government buildings and defending barricades and occupations. This meant they often had to fight armed police and paramilitaries with nothing but rocks and firecrackers.

---

73 Wikipedia "Seattle General Strike of 1919," http://en.wikipedia.org/wiki/Seattle_general_strike_of_1919 [viewed 21 June 2007]. Print sources cited in this article include Jeremy Brecher, *Strike!* Revised Edition. South End Press, 1997; and Howard Zinn, *A People's History of the United States,* Perrenial Classics Edition, 1999.

> Some of the worst attacks happened in front of the occupied buildings. We were guarding the Secretary of the Economy building, when we realized that somewhere inside the building there was a group of people preparing to attack us. We knocked on the door and no one responded. Five minutes later, an armed group drove out from behind the building and started shooting at us. We tried to find cover, but we knew if we backed away, all the people at the barricade in front of the building—there must have been around forty people—would be in serious danger. So we decided to hold our position, and defended ourselves with rocks. They kept firing at us until their bullets ran out and drove away, because they saw that we weren't going anywhere. Several of us were wounded. One guy took a bullet in his leg and the other got shot in the back. Later, some reinforcements arrived, but the hit men had already retreated.
>
> We didn't have any guns. At the Office of the Economy, we defended ourselves with stones. As time went on and we found ourselves under attack by gunfire more and more frequently, so we started making things to defend ourselves with: firecrackers, homemade bottle-rocket launchers, molotov cocktails; all of us had something. And if we didn't have any of those things, we defended people with our bodies or bare hands.[74]

After such attacks, the *topiles* would help take the wounded to first aid centers.

The security volunteers also responded to common crime. If someone was being robbed or assaulted, the neighbors would raise the alarm and the neighborhood *topiles* would come; if the assailant was on drugs he would be tied up in the central plaza for the night, and the next day made to pick up garbage or perform another type of community service. Different people had different ideas on what long-term solutions to institute, and as the rebellion in Oaxaca was politically very diverse, not all these ideas were

---

74 Diana Denham and C.A.S.A. Collective (eds.), *Teaching Rebellion: Stories from the Grassroots Mobilization in Oaxaca*, Oakland: PM Press, 2008, interview with Cuatli.

revolutionary; some people wanted to hand robbers or assaulters over to the courts, though it was widely believed that the government released all law-breakers and encouraged them to go back and commit more anti-social crimes.

The history of Exarchia, a neighborhood in central Athens, shows throughout the years that the police do not protect us, they endanger us. For years, Exarchia has been the stronghold of the anarchist movement and the counterculture. The neighborhood has protected itself from gentrification and policing through a variety of means. Luxury cars are regularly burned if they are parked there overnight. After being targeted with property destruction and social pressure, shop and restaurant owners no longer try to remove political posters from their walls, kick out vagrants, or otherwise create a commercial atmosphere in the streets; they have conceded that the streets belong to the people. Undercover cops who enter Exarchia have been brutally beaten on a number of occasions. During the run-up to the Olympics the city tried to renovate Exarchia Square to turn it into a tourist spot rather than a local hangout. The new plan, for example, included a large fountain and no benches. Neighbors began meeting, came up with their own renovation plan, and informed the construction company that they would use the local plan rather than the city government's plan. Repeated destruction of the construction equipment finally convinced the company who was boss. The renovated park today has more green space, no touristy fountain, and nice, new benches.

Attacks against police in Exarchia are frequent, and armed riot police are always stationed nearby. Over the past years, police have gone back and forth between trying to occupy Exarchia by force, or maintaining a guard around the borders of the neighborhood with armed groups of riot cops constantly ready for an attack. At no point have the police been able to carry out normal policing activities. Police do not patrol the neighborhood on foot, and rarely drive through. When they enter, they come prepared to fight and defend themselves. People spray graffiti and put up posters in broad daylight. It is to a large extent a lawless zone, and people commit crimes with an astonishing frequency and openness.

However, it is not a dangerous neighborhood. The crimes of choice are political or at least victimless, like smoking weed. It is safe to walk there alone at night, unless you are a cop, people in the streets are relaxed and friendly, and personal property faces no great threat, with the exception of luxury cars and the like. The police are not welcome here, and they are not needed here.

And it is exactly in this situation that they demonstrate their true character. They are not an institution that responds to crime or social need, they are an institution that asserts social control. In past years, police tried to flood the area, and the anarchist movement in particular, with addictive drugs like heroin, and they have directly encouraged junkies to hang out in Exarchia Square. It was up to anarchists and other neighbors to defend themselves from these forms of police violence and stop the spread of addictive drugs. Unable to break the rebellious spirit of the neighborhood, police have resorted to more aggressive tactics, taking on the characteristics of a military occupation. On December 6, 2008, this approach produced its inevitable conclusion when two cops shot 15-year-old anarchist Alexis Grigoropoulos to death in the middle of Exarchia. Within a few hours, the counterattacks began, and for days the police throughout Greece were pummeled with clubs, rocks, molotov cocktails, and in a couple of incidents, gunfire. The liberated zones of Athens and other Greek cities are expanding, and the police are afraid to evict these new occupations because the people have proven themselves to be stronger. Currently, the media is waging a campaign of fear, increasing coverage of antisocial crime and trying to conflate these crimes with the presence of autonomous areas. Crime is a tool of the state, used to scare people, isolate people, and make government seem necessary. But government is nothing but a protection racket. The state is a mafia that has won control over society, and the law is the codification of everything they have stolen from us.

The Rotuman are a traditionally stateless people who live on the island of Rotuma in the South Pacific, north of Fiji. According to anthropologist Alan Howard, members of this sedentary society are socialized not to be violent. Cultural norms promote respectful and gentle behavior towards children. Physical punishment is extremely rare, and almost never intended to actually hurt the misbehaving child. Instead, Rotuman adults use shame instead of punishment, a strategy that raises children with a high degree of social sensitivity. Adults will especially shame children who act like bullies, and in their own conflicts adults try very hard not to make others angry. From Howard's perspective as an outsider from the more authoritarian West, children are given "an astonishing degree of autonomy" and the principle of personal autonomy extends throughout the society: "Not only do individuals exercise autonomy within their households and communities, but villages are also autonomous in relation to one another, and districts are essentially autonomous political units."75 The Rotuman themselves probably describe their situation with different words, though we could find no insider accounts. Perhaps they might emphasize the horizontal relationships that connect households and villages, but to observers raised in a Euro/American culture and trained in the belief that a society is only held together by authority, what stands out most is the autonomy of the different households and villages.

Though the Rotuman currently exist under an imposed government, they avoid contact with it and dependence on it. It is probably no coincidence that the Rotuman murder rate stands at the low level of 2.02 per 100,000 people per year, three times lower than in the US. Howard describe the Rotuman view of crime as being similar to that of many other stateless peoples: not as the violation of a code or statute, but as something causing harm or hurting social bonds. Accordingly, mediation is important to solving disputes peacefully. Chiefs and sub-chiefs act as mediators, though distinguished elders may intervene in that role as well. Chiefs are not judges, and if they do not appear impartial they will lose their followers, as households are free to switch between groups. The most important conflict resolution mechanism is the

---

75 Alan Howard, "Restraint and Ritual Apology: the Rotumans of the South Pacific," in Graham Kemp and Douglas P. Fry (eds.), *Keeping the Peace: Conflict Resolution and Peaceful Societies around the World*, New York: Routledge, 2004, p. 42.

public apology. The public apology has great weight attached to it; depending on the seriousness of the offense, it may be accompanied by ritual peace offerings as well. Apologizing properly is honorable, while denying an apology is dishonorable. Members maintain their standing and status in the group by being accountable, being sensitive to group opinion, and resolving conflicts. If some people acted in a way that we might expect in a society based on police and punishment, they would isolate themselves and thus limit their harmful influence.

For two months in 1973, maximum-security prisoners in Massachusetts showed that supposed criminals may be less responsible for the violence in our society than their guards. After the prison massacre at Attica in 1971 focused national attention on the dramatic failure of the prison system to correct or rehabilitate people convicted of crimes, the governor of Massachusetts appointed a reformist commissioner to the Department of Corrections. Meanwhile, the inmates of Walpole state prison had formed a prisoners' union. Their goals included protecting themselves from the guards, blocking the attempts of prison administrators to institute behavioral modification programs, and organizing prisoners' programs for education, empowerment, and healing. They sought more visitation rights, work or volunteer assignments outside the prison, and the ability to earn money to send to their families. Ultimately, they hoped to end recidivism—ex-prisoners getting convicted again and returning to prison—and to abolish the prison system itself.

Black prisoners had formed a Black Power education and cultural group to create unity and counter the racism of the white majority, and this proved instrumental in the formation of the union in the face of repression from guards. First of all, they had to end the race war between the prisoners, a war that was encouraged by the guards. Leaders from all groups of prisoners brokered a general truce which they guaranteed with the promise to kill any inmate who broke it. The prison union was supported by an outside group of media-savvy civil rights and religious activists, though communication between the two groups was sometimes hampered by the latter's service-provider mentality and orthodox commitment to nonviolence. It helped that the Corrections commissioner supported the idea of a prisoners' union, rather than opposing it outright as most prison administrators would have.

Early on in the life of the Walpole prisoners' union, the prison superintendent attempted to divide the prisoners by putting the prison under an arbitrary lockdown just as the black prisoners were preparing their Kwanzaa celebration. The white prisoners had already had their Christmas celebrations undisturbed, and the black prisoners had spent all day cooking, eagerly anticipating family visits. In an amazing display of solidarity, all the prisoners went on strike, refusing to work or leave their cells. For three months, they suffered beatings, solitary confinement, starvation, denial of medical care, addiction to tranquilizers handed out by the guards, and disgusting conditions as excrement and refuse piled up in and around their cells. But the prisoners refused to be broken or divided. Eventually the state had to negotiate; they were running out of the license plates Walpole prisoners normally produced and they were getting bad press over the crisis.

The prisoners won their first demand: the prison superintendent was forced to resign. Quickly they won additional demands for expanded visiting rights, furlough, self-organized programs, review and release of those in segregation, and civilian observers inside the prison. In exchange, they cleaned up the prison, and brought what the guards never had: peace.

In protest of their loss of control, the guards walked off the job. They thought this act would prove how necessary they were, but embarrassingly for them, it had the exact opposite effect. For two months, the prisoners ran the prison themselves. For much of that time, the guards were not present within the cell blocks, though state police controlled the prison perimeter to prevent escapes. Civilian observers were inside the prison twenty-four hours a day, but they were trained not to intervene; their role was to document the situation, talk with prisoners, and prevent violence from guards who sometimes entered the prison. One observer recounted:

> The atmosphere was so relaxed—not at all what I expected. I find that my own thinking has been so conditioned by

society and the media. These men are not animals, they are not dangerous maniacs. I found my own fears were really groundless.

Another observer insisted "It is imperative that none of the personnel formerly in Block 9 [a segregation block] ever return. It's worth paying them to retire. The guards are the security problem."[76]

Walpole had been one of the most violent prisons in the country, but while the prisoners were in control, recidivism dropped dramatically and murders and rapes fell to zero. The prisoners had disproved two fundamental myths of the criminal justice system: that people who commit crimes should be isolated, and that they should be recipients of enforced rehabilitation rather than the ones who control their own healing.

The guards were eager to end this embarrassing experiment in prison abolition. The guards' union was powerful enough to provoke a political crisis, and the Corrections commissioner could not fire any of them, even those who engaged in torture or made racist statements to the press. To keep his job, the commissioner had to bring the guards back into the prison, and he eventually sold out the prisoners. Major elements of the power structure including the police, guards, prosecutors, politicians, and media opposed the prison reforms and made them impossible to achieve within democratic channels. The civilian observers unanimously agreed that the guards brought chaos and violence back to the prison, and that they intentionally disrupted the peaceful results of prisoner self-organization. In the end, to crush the prisoners' union, the guards staged a riot and the state police were called in, shooting several prisoners and torturing key organizers. The most recognizable leader of the black prisoners only saved his life through armed self-defense.

Many of the civilian observers and the Corrections commissioner, who was soon forced out of his job, ultimately came to

---

76 Both observer quotes from Jamie Bissonette, *When the Prisoners Ran Walpole: a true story in the movement for prison abolition*, Cambridge: South End Press, 2008, p. 160.

favor prison abolition. The prisoners who took over Walpole continued to fight for their freedom and dignity, but the guards' union ended up with greater power than before, the media ceased talking about prison reform, and as of this writing Walpole prison, now MCI Cedar Junction, still warehouses, tortures, and kills people who deserve to be in their communities, working towards a safer society.

What about gangs and bullies?

SOME FEAR THAT IN A SOCIETY WITHOUT AUTHORITIES, THE STRONGEST people would run amok, taking and doing whatever they wanted. Never mind that this describes what generally goes on in societies with government! This fear derives from the statist myth that we are all isolated. The government would very much like you to believe that without its protection you are vulnerable to the whims of anyone stronger than you. However, no bully is stronger than an entire community. A person who shatters the social peace, disrespects another person's needs, and acts in an authoritarian, bullying way can be defeated or kicked out by neighbors working together to restore the peace.

In Christiania, the anti-authoritarian, autonomous quarter in Denmark's capital, they have been dealing with their own problems, and the problems associated with all the visitors they receive and the resulting high social mobility. Many people come as tourists, and many more come to buy hash—there are no laws in Christiania and soft drugs are easy to come by, though hard drugs have been successfully banned. Within Christiania there are numerous workshops that produce a variety of goods, most famously their high-quality bicycles; there are also restaurants, cafés, a kindergarten, a clinic, a health food shop, a book shop, an anarchist space, and a concert venue. Christiania has never been successfully dominated by gangs or resident bullies. In 1984 a motorcycle gang moved in, hoping to exploit the lawlessness of the autonomous zone and monopolize the hash trade. After several conflicts, the residents of Christiania succeeded in kicking out the bikers, using mostly peaceful tactics.

The worst bullying has come from the police, who recently resumed entering Christiania to arrest people for marijuana and hash, generally as a pretext to escalate tensions. Local real estate developers would love to see the free state destroyed because it sits on land that has become very valuable. Decades ago, the residents of Christiania had a heated debate about how to deal with the problem of hard drugs coming in from outside. Over much opposition, they decided to ask the police for help, only to find that the police concentrated on locking people up for soft drugs and protected the spread of hard drugs like heroin, presumably in the hope that an addiction epidemic would destroy the autonomous social experiment.[77] It is by no means the first time police or other agents of the state have spread addictive drugs while suppressing soft or hallucinogenic drugs; in fact this seems universally to be a part of police strategies for repression. In the end, the residents of Christiania kicked out the police and dealt with the hard drug problem themselves, by keeping out dealers and using social pressure to discourage hard drug use.

In Christiania as elsewhere, the state presents the greatest danger to the community. Unlike the individual bullies one imagines terrorizing a lawless society, the state cannot be easily defeated. Typically, the state seeks a monopoly on force on the pretext of protecting citizens from other bullies; this is the justification for prohibiting anyone outside the state apparatus from using force, especially in self-defense against the government. In return for relinquishing this power, citizens are directed to the court system as a means of defending their interests; but of course, the court system is part of the state, and protects its interests above all others. When the government comes to seize your land to build a shopping mall, for example, you can take the matter to court or even bring it before the city council, but you might find yourself talking to someone who stands to profit from the shopping mall. The bully's courts will not be fair to the bully's victims, and they

---

[77] One can't help but compare this to the British spreading opium in China or the US government spreading whiskey among indigenous people and, later, heroin in ghettos.

will not sympathize with you if you defend yourself against the eviction. Instead, they will lock you up.

In this context, those who want resolution often have to seek it outside the courts. A military dictatorship seized power in Argentina in 1976 and waged a "Dirty War" against leftists, torturing and killing 30,000 people; the officers responsible for the torture and executions were pardoned by the democratic government that succeeded the dictatorship. The Mothers of the Plaza de Mayo, who began gathering to demand an end to the disappearances and to know what happened to their children, were an important social force in ending the reign of terror. As the government has never taken serious steps to hold the murderers and torturers accountable, people have elaborated a popular justice that builds on and goes beyond the protests and memorials organized by the Mothers.

When a participant in the Dirty War is located, activists put up posters throughout the neighborhood informing everyone of his presence; they may ask local shops to refuse the person entry, and follow and harass him. In a tactic known as "escrache," hundreds or even thousands of participants will march to the house of a Dirty War participant with signs, banners, puppets, and drums. They sing, chant, and make music for hours, shaming the torturer and letting everyone know what he has done; the crowd may attack his house with paint bombs.[78] Despite a justice system that protects the powerful, the social movements in Argentina have organized collectively to shame and isolate the very worst bullies.

What's to stop someone from killing people?

MUCH VIOLENT CRIME CAN BE TRACED BACK TO CULTURAL FACTORS. Violent crime, such as murder, would probably decrease dramatically in an anarchist society because most of its causes—poverty, televised glorification of violence, prisons and police,

---

78 Natasha Gordon and Paul Chatterton, Taking Back Control: A Journey through Argentina's Popular Uprising, Leeds (UK): University of Leeds, 2004, pp. 66–68.

warfare, sexism, and the normalization of individualistic and anti-social behaviors—would disappear or decrease.

The differences between two Zapotec communities illustrates that peace is a choice. The Zapotec are a sedentary agrarian indigenous nation living on land that is now claimed by the state of Mexico. One Zapotec community, La Paz, has a yearly homicide rate of 3.4/100,000. A neighboring Zapotec community has the much higher homicide rate of 18.1/100,000. What social attributes go along with the more peaceful way of life? Unlike their more violent neighbors, the La Paz Zapotec do not beat children; accordingly, children see less violence and use less violence in their play. Similarly, wife-beating is rare and not considered acceptable; women are considered equal to men, and enjoy an autonomous economic activity that is important to the life of the community so they are not dependent on men. Regarding child-rearing, the implications of this particular comparison are corroborated by at least one cross-cultural study on socialization, which found that warm, affectionate socialization techniques correlate with low levels of conflict in society.[79]

The Semai and the Norwegians were both previously mentioned as societies with low homicide rates. Until colonialism the Semai were stateless, whereas Norway is ruled by a government. Socialization is relatively peaceful among the Semai and the Norwegians alike. The Semai use a gift economy so wealth is evenly distributed, while Norway has one of the lowest wealth gaps of any capitalist country on account of its socialist domestic policies. A further similarity is a reliance on mediation rather than punishment, police, or prisons to solve disputes. Norway does have police and a prison system, but compared with most states there is a high reliance on conflict mediation mechanisms not unlike those that flourish in peaceful, stateless societies. Most civil disputes in Norway must be brought before mediators before they can be taken to court, and thousands of criminal cases are taken

---

79 Graham Kemp and Douglas P. Fry (eds.), Keeping the Peace: Conflict Resolution and Peaceful Societies around the World, New York: Routledge, 2004, pp. 73–79. The cross-cultural study is M.H. Ross, The Culture of Conflict, New Haven: Yale University Press, 1993.

to mediators as well. In 2001, agreement was reached in 89% of the mediations.[80]

Therefore in an anarchist society, violent crime would be less common. But when it did occur, would society be more vulnerable? After all, one might argue, even when violence is no longer a rational social response, psychopathic killers might still occasionally appear. Let it suffice to say that any society capable of overthrowing a government would hardly be at the mercy of lone psychopathic killers. And societies that do not come about from a revolution but enjoy a strong sense of community and solidarity are capable of protecting themselves as well. The Inuit, hunter-gatherers indigenous to the arctic regions of North America, provide an example of what a stateless society can do in the worst-case scenario. According to their traditions, if a person committed a murder, the community would forgive him and make him reconcile with the family of the victim. If that person commits another murder, he would be killed—usually by members of his own family group, so there would be no bad blood or cause for feud.

The state's punitive methods for dealing with crime make things worse, not better. The restorative methods for responding to social harm that are used in many stateless societies open new possibilities for escaping the cycles of abuse, punishment, and harm that are all too familiar to many of us.

What about rape, domestic violence, and other forms of harm?

MANY ACTIONS THAT ARE CONSIDERED CRIMES BY OUR GOVERNment are completely harmless; some crimes, such as stealing from the wealthy or sabotaging instruments of warfare, can actually decrease harm. Still, a number of transgressions that are now considered crimes do constitute real social harm. Of these, murder is highly sensationalized but rare compared to other more common problems.

---

80 Graham Kemp and Douglas P. Fry (eds.), Keeping the Peace: Conflict Resolution and Peaceful Societies around the World, New York: Routledge, 2004, p. 163.

Sexual and domestic violence are rampant in our society, and even in the absence of government and capitalism these forms of violence will continue unless they are specifically addressed. Currently, many forms of sexual and domestic violence are commonly tolerated; some are even subtly encouraged by Hollywood, relgions, and other mainstream institutions. Hollywood often sexualizes rape and, along with other corporate media and most major religions, glorifies female passivity and servility. In the discourse these institutions influence, the severe problem of spousal rape is ignored, and as a result many people even believe that a husband cannot rape a wife because they are joined in a contractual sexual union. News media and Hollywood movies regularly portray rape as an act committed by a stranger—especially a poor, non-white stranger. In this version, a woman's only hope is to be protected by the police or a boyfriend. But in fact, the vast majority of rapes are committed by boyfriends, friends, and family members, in situations that fall in the gray area between the mainstream definitions of consent and force. More frequently, Hollywood ignores the problems of rape, abuse, and domestic violence altogether, while perpetuating the myth of love at first sight. In this myth, the man wins over the woman and the two fulfill all of each other's emotional and sexual needs, making a perfect match without having to talk about consent, work on communication, or navigate emotional and sexual boundaries.

Police and other institutions purporting to protect women from rape counsel women not to resist for fear of aggravating their attacker, when all evidence and common sense suggest that resistance is often one's best chance. The state rarely offers self-defense classes to women, while frequently prosecuting women who kill or injure attackers in self-defense. People who go to the state to report sexual or physical assault face added humiliations. Courts question the honesty and moral integrity of women who bravely go public after being sexually assaulted; judges award custody of children to abusive fathers; police ignore domestic violence calls, even standing by as husbands beat wives. Some local regulations require the police to arrest someone, or even both involved parties, in a domestic violence call; often a woman who calls for help is herself sent to jail. Transgender people are betrayed even more regularly by the legal system, which refuses to respect their identities and often forces them into prison cells with people of different genders. Working class and homeless transgender people are systematically raped by agents of the legal system.

A great deal of abuse not directly caused by the authorities is a result of people taking out their anger on those below them in the social hierarchy. Children, who tend to be at the bottom of the pyramid, ultimately receive a great deal of this abuse. The authorities who are supposed to keep them safe—parents, relatives, priests, teachers—are the most likely to abuse them. Seeking help may only make things worse, because at no point does the legal system allow them to regain control over their lives, even though it is this control that survivors of abuse most need. Instead, each case is decided by social workers and judges with little knowledge of the situation and hundreds of other cases to arbitrate.

The current paradigm of punishing offenders and ignoring the needs of victims has proven a total failure, and increased enforcement of laws would not change this. People who abuse were often abused themselves; sending them to prison does not make them any less likely to act abusively. People who survive abuse may benefit from having a safe space, but sending their abusers to prison removes the chance of reconciliation, and if they depend economically on their abusers, as is often the case, they may choose not to report the crime for fear of ending up homeless, poor, or in foster care.

Under the state, we address sexual and domestic violence as crimes—violations of the victims' state-mandated rights, unacceptable because they defy the commandments of the state. In contrast, many stateless societies have used a needs-based paradigm. This paradigm frames these forms of violence as social harm, thus focusing on the needs of the survivor to heal and the need of the offender to become a healthy person who can relate with the broader community. Because these acts of social harm do not happen in isolation, this paradigm draws in the entire community and seeks to restore a broad social peace, while respecting the autonomy and self-defined needs of each individual.

The Navajo method of "peacemaking" has survived for centuries, despite the violence of colonialism. They are currently reviving this method to deal with social harm and decrease their dependence on the US government; and people studying restorative justice are looking to the Navajo example for guidance. In the Navajo practice of restorative justice, a person respected by all parties as fair and impartial acts as a peacemaker. A person might seek out a peacemaker if she is seeking help with a problem on her own volition, if her community or family is concerned about her behavior, if she has hurt someone or been hurt by someone, or if she is in a dispute with another person that the two need help solving. Contrast this with the statist system of punitive justice, in which people only receive attention—and always negative attention—when they commit a statutory offense. The harm itself and the reasons they are causing it are irrelevant to the judicial process.

The purpose of the Navajo process is to meet the needs of those who come to the peacemaker and to find the root of the problem. "When members of the Navajo community try to explain why people do harm to themselves or others, they say that those responsible for a harm behave that way because they have become disconnected from the world around them, from the people they live and work with. They say that that person 'acts as if he has no relatives.'" The peacemakers solve this by "talking things out" and helping the person who harmed to reconnect with his community and regain the support and groundedness he needs to act in a healthy way. Additionally they provide support for the person who was harmed, looking for ways to help that person feel safe and whole again.

To this end, the peacemaking process involves the family and friends of those involved. People present their stories, their perspectives on the problem, and their feelings. The ultimate goal is to find a practical solution that restores people's relationships. To aid this, the peacemaker delivers a homily that often draws on Navajo creation stories to show how traditional figures have dealt with the same problems in the past. In cases where there is clearly someone who acted wrongly and harmed another person, at the end of the process the offender often pays an agreed amount of restitution, or *nalyeeh*. However, *nalyeeh* is not a form of punishment in the spirit of "an eye for an eye," but rather a way to "make things right for the person who has suffered a loss." 104 of the 110 chapters, or semi-autonomous communities, of the Navajo Nation currently have designated peacemakers, and in many instances in the past respected family members have been called on to settle disputes in an unofficial capacity.[81]

Critical Resistance is an anti-authoritarian organization in the US formed by ex-prisoners and family members of prisoners with the purpose of abolishing the prison system and its causes. As of this writing, the group is working on setting up "harm free zones." The purpose of a harm free zone is to provide "tools and trainings to local communities to strengthen and develop their ability to resolve conflicts without the need for the police, court system, or prison industry. The harm free zone practices an abolitionist approach to developing communities, which means building models today that can represent how we want to live now and in the future."[82] By building stronger relationships among neighbors and intentionally creating common resources, people in a neighborhood can keep out drug dealers, provide support for those suffering from addiction, intervene in abusive family situations, set up childcare and alternatives to joining gangs, and increase face to face communication.

Other anti-authoritarian groups, some inspired by this model, have begun the hard work of setting up harm free zones in their own cities. Of course, even if there were no violent crime at all, a racist, capitalist government would still find excuses to lock people up: creating internal enemies and punishing rebels have always been functions of the government, and nowadays so many private companies are invested in the prison system that it has become a growth-based industry. But when people are no longer dependent

---

81 All quotes and statistics on the Navajo come from Dennis Sullivan and Larry Tifft, *Restorative Justice: Healing the Foundations of Our Everyday Lives*, Monsey, NY: Willow Tree Press, 2001, pp. 53–59.
82 http://www.harmfreezone.org/wiki/index.php/HarmFreeZone:About (viewed November 24, 2006)

on police and prisons, when communities are no longer crippled by self-inflicted social harm, it is much easier to organize resistance.

Throughout the United States and other countries, feminists have organized an event called "Take Back the Night" to address violence against women. Once a year, a large group of women and their supporters march through their neighborhood or campus at night—a time many women associate with increased risk of sexual assault—to reclaim their environment and make the issue visible. These events usually include education about the prevalence and causes of violence against women. Some Take Back the Night groups also address our society's rampant violence against transgender people. The first Take Back the Night march took place in Belgium in 1976, organized by women attending the International Tribunal on Crimes against Women. The event takes much from the tradition of Walpurgisnacht protests in Germany. Known as Witches' Night, April 30, the night before May Day, is a traditional night for pranks, rioting, and pagan and feminist resistance. In 1977, German feminists involved with the autonomous movement marched on Walpurgisnacht under the banner "Women take back the night!" The first Take Back the Night in the US occurred November 4, 1977, in San Francisco's red light district.

Such an action is an important first step to creating a collective force capable of changing society. Under patriarchy, every family is isolated, and though many people suffer the same problems, they do so alone. Gathering together to talk about a problem that has been unspeakable, to reclaim a public space that has been denied to you—the nighttime streets—is a living metaphor for the anarchist society, in which people come together to overcome any authority figure, any oppressor.

Sexual violence affects everyone in a patriarchal society. It occurs in radical communities that are opposed to sexism and sexual violence. Unless they sincerely focus on unlearning patriarchal conditioning, self-professed radicals often respond to rape, harassment, and other forms of abuse and sexual violence with the same behavior that is all too common in the rest of society: ignoring them, justifying them, refusing to take a stand, not believing or even blaming the survivor. In order to combat this, feminists and anarchists in Philadelphia formed two groups. The first, Philly's Pissed, works to support survivors of sexual violence:

> All of Philly's Pissed's work is done confidentially unless the survivor requests otherwise. We are not certified "experts," but a group of people whose lives have been repeatedly affected by sexual assault and are doing our best to make a safer world. We respect our own and others' knowledge to figure out what feels safest for each person. Philly's Pissed supports survivors of sexual assault by meeting their immediate needs as well as helping them to articulate and facilitate what they need to make them feel safe and in control of their lives again.[83]

If a survivor has demands to make of his or her assaulter—e.g., that he or she receive counseling, publicly apologize, or never come near the survivor again—the support group delivers them. If the survivor wishes, the group may publicize the identity of the assaulter to warn other people or prevent that person from hiding his actions.

The second group, Philly Stands Up, works with people who have committed sexual assault to support them through the process of taking responsibility for their actions, learning from them and changing their behaviors, and restoring healthy relationships with their community. The two groups also hold workshops in other cities to share their experiences responding to sexual assault.

Beyond individual justice

THE NOTION OF JUSTICE IS PERHAPS THE MOST DANGEROUS PRODUCT of authoritarian psychology. The state's worst abuses occur in its prisons, its inquisitions, its forced corrections and rehabilitations. Police, judges, and prison guards are key agents of coercion and violence. In the name of justice, uniformed thugs terrorize entire communities while dissidents petition the very government

---

83 Philly's Pissed, http://www.phillyspissed.net/ [Viewed May 20, 2008]

that represses them. Many people have internalized the rationalizations of state justice to such an extent that they are terrified of losing the protection and arbitration states supposedly provide.

When justice becomes the private sphere of specialists, oppression is not far behind. In stateless societies on the cusp of developing the coercive hierarchies that lead to government, the common feature seems to be a group of respected male elders permanently entrusted with the role of resolving conflicts and meting out justice. In such a context privilege can become entrenched, as those who enjoy it may shape the social norms that preserve and amplify their privilege. Without that power, individual wealth and power rest on a weak foundation that everyone can challenge.

State justice begins with a refusal to engage with human needs. Human needs are dynamic and can only be fully understood by those who experience them. State justice, by contrast, is the execution of universal prescriptions codified into law. The specialists who interpret the laws are supposed to focus on the original intention of the lawmakers rather than the situation at hand. If you need bread and stealing is a crime, you will be punished for taking it, even if you take it from someone who doesn't need it. But if your society focuses on people's needs and desires rather than on the enforcement of static laws, you have the opportunity to convince your community that you needed bread more than the person you took it from. In this way the actor and those affected remain at the center of the process, always empowered to explain themselves and to challenge the community's norms.

Justice, in contrast, hinges on judgment, privileging a powerful decision-maker over the accusers and defendants who powerlessly await the outcome. Justice is the enforcement of morality—which, in its origins, is justified as divinely ordained. When societies shift away from religious rationales, morality becomes universal, or natural, or scientific—spheres ever further removed from the influence of the general public—until it is shaped and packaged almost exclusively by the media and government.

The notion of justice and the social relations it implies are inherently authoritarian. In practice, justice systems always give unfair advantages to the powerful and inflict terrible wrongs on the powerless. At the same time, they corrupt us ethically and cause our powers of initiative and sense of responsibility to atrophy. Like a drug, they make us dependent while mimicking the fulfillment of a natural human need, in this case the need to resolve conflicts. Thus, people beg to the justice system for reforms, no matter how unrealistic their expectations are, rather than taking matters into their own hands. To heal from abuse, the injured person needs to regain control over her life, the abuser needs to restore healthy relations with his peers, and the community needs to examine its norms and power dynamics. The justice system prevents all this. It hoards control, alienates entire communities, and obstructs examination of the roots of problems, preserving the status quo above all.

Police and judges may provide a limited degree of protection, especially for people privileged by racism, sexism, or capitalism; but the greatest danger facing most human beings is the system itself. For example, thousands of workers are killed every year by employer negligence and unsafe working conditions, but employers are never punished as murderers and virtually never even charged as criminals. The most workers' families might hope for is a monetary settlement from a civil court. Who decides that a boss who profits from the deaths of workers should face no worse than a lawsuit, while a wife who shoots her abusive husband goes to prison and a black teenager who kills a police officer in self-defense gets the death penalty? It certainly isn't workers, women, or people of color.

For every human need, a totalitarian system must provide it, subdue it, or substitute a surrogate. In the above example, the justice system frames the killing of workers as a problem to be addressed with regulations and bureaucracies. The media assist by focusing grossly disproportionate coverage on serial killers and "cold-blooded murderers," almost always poor and usually not white, thus changing people's perceptions of the risks they face. Consequently many people fear other poor people more than their own bosses, and are willing to support the police and courts in targeting them.

To be sure, in some cases the police and courts respond when workers or women are killed—though this is often to offset popular outrage and discourage people from seeking their own solutions. Even in these cases, the responses are often half-hearted or counterproductive.

Meanwhile, the justice system serves quite effectively as a tool for reshaping society and controlling lower class populations. Consider the "War on Drugs" waged from the 1980s up to the present day. Compared with work and rape, most illegal drugs are relatively harmless; in the case of those that can be harmful, medical attention has been thoroughly demonstrated to be a more effective response than prison time. But the justice system has declared this war to shift public priorities: it justifies the police occupation of poor neighborhoods, the mass imprisonment and enslavement of millions of poor people and people of color, and the expansion of the powers of police and judges.

What do the police do with this power? They arrest and intimidate the most powerless elements of society. Poor people and people of color are overwhelmingly the victims of arrests and convictions, not to mention daily harassment and even murder at the hands of police. Attempts to reform the police rarely do more than feed their budgets and streamline their methods for imprisoning people. And what happens to the millions of people in prison? They are isolated, killed slowly by poor diets and miserable conditions or swiftly by guards who are almost never convicted. Prison guards encourage gangs and racial violence to help them maintain control, and often smuggle in and sell addictive drugs to fill their wallets and sedate the population. Tens of thousands of prisoners are locked up in solitary confinement, some for decades.

Countless studies have found that treating drug addiction and other psychological problems as criminal matters is ineffective and inhumane; mistreating prisoners and depriving them of human contact and educational opportunities has been proven to increase recidivism.[84] But for every study that showed how to end crime

---

84 George R. Edison, MD, "The Drug Laws: Are They Effective and Safe?" *The Journal of the American Medial Association*. Vol. 239 No. 24, June 16, 1978. A.W. MacLeod, *Recidivism: a Deficiency Disease*, Philadelphia:

and reduce prison populations, the government has gone and done the exact opposite: they cut educational programs, increased the use of solitary confinement, lengthened sentences, and curtailed visiting rights. Why? Because in addition to a control mechanism, prison is an industry. It funnels billions of dollars of public money to institutions that strengthen state control, such as the police, the courts, surveillance and private security companies, and it provides a slave labor force that produces goods for the government and private corporations. Forced labor is still legal in the prison system, and most prisons contain factories where prisoners have to work for a few cents an hour. Prisons also have the modern equivalent of the company store, where prisoners have to spend all the money they make and the money their families send them, buying clothing, food, or phone calls, all at inflated prices.

The prison system is beyond hope of reform. Reformist prison bureaucrats have given up or else come to support prison abolition. One high ranking bureaucrat who directed juvenile corrections departments in Massachusetts and Illinois concluded that:

> Prisons are violent, outmoded bureaucracies that don't protect public safety. There's no way to rehabilitate anyone in them. The facility produces violence that calls for more of the facility. It's a self-fulfilling prophecy. Prisons offer themselves as a solution to the very problems they've created. Institutions are set up to make people fail. That's their latent purpose.[85]

These are not problems to be solved with reforms or changes of law. The justice system has set its priorities and arranged its laws with the specific purpose of controlling and abusing us. The problem is law itself.

University of Pennsylvania Press, 1965.

85 Jamie Bissonette, *When the Prisoners Ran Walpole: A True Story in the Movement for Prison Abolition*, Cambridge: South End Press, 2008, p. 201. Also consider the stories of John Boone and other bureaucrats presented in this story.

Often, people who live in a statist society assume that without a centralized justice system following clear laws, it would be impossible to resolve conflicts. Without a common set of laws, everyone would fight for her own interests, resulting in perpetual feuding. If methods of dealing with social harm are decentralized and voluntary, what's to keep people from "taking justice into their own hands?"

An important leveling mechanism in stateless societies is that people sometimes *do* take justice into their own hands, especially in dealing with those in leadership positions who are acting authoritarian. Anyone can abide by her conscience and take action against a person she perceives to be harming the community. At best, this can push others to acknowledge and confront a problem they had tried to ignore. At worst, it can divide the community between those who think such action was justified and those who think it was harmful. Even this, though, is better than institutionalizing imbalances of power; in a community in which everyone has the power to take things into their own hands, in which everyone is equal, people will find it is much easier to talk things out and try to change the opinions of their peers than to do whatever they want or cause conflicts by acting as a vigilante. The reason this method is not used in democratic, capitalist societies is not because it does not work, but because there are certain opinions that must not be changed, certain contradictions that must not be addressed, and certain privileges that can never be challenged.

In many stateless societies, bad behavior is not dealt with by specialized defenders of justice, but by everyone, through what anthropologists call diffuse sanctions—sanctions or negative reactions that are diffused throughout society. Everyone is accustomed to responding to injustice and harmful behavior, and thus everyone is more empowered and more involved. When there is no state to monopolize the day-to-day maintenance of society, people learn how to do this for themselves, and teach one another.

We do not need to define abuse as a crime to know that it hurts us. Laws are unnecessary in empowered societies; there are other models for responding to social harm. We can identify the problem as an infringement on others' needs rather than a violation of written code. We can encourage broad social involvement in the resolution of the problem. We can help those who have been hurt to express their needs and we can follow their lead. We can hold people accountable when they hurt others, while supporting them and giving them opportunities to learn and reestablish respectful relationships with the community. We can see problems as the responsibility of the entire community rather than the fault of one person. We can reclaim the power to heal society, and break through the isolation imposed on us.

Recommended Reading:

- Kristian Williams, *Our Enemies in Blue.* Brooklyn: Soft Skull Press, 2004.
- Jamie Bissonette, *When the Prisoners Ran Walpole: A True Story in the Movement for Prison Abolition,* Cambridge: South End Press, 2008.
- Dennis Sullivan and Larry Tifft, *Restorative Justice: Healing the Foundations of Our Everyday Lives*, Monsey, NY: Willow Tree Press, 2001.
- Graham Kemp and Douglas P. Fry (eds.), *Keeping the Peace: Conflict Resolution and Peaceful Societies around the World,* New York: Routledge, 2004.
- Michel Foucault, *Discipline and Punish: the Birth of the Prison,* New York: Pantheon Books, 1977.
- Ammon Hennacy, *The Book of Ammon.* Salt Lake City: Catholic Worker Books, 1970.
- Fred Woodworth, *The Match!* an anarchist periodical published in Tucson.

6. REVOLUTION

To put an end to all coercive hierarchies and open space for organizing a horizontal, liberated society, people must overcome the repressive powers of the state, abolish all institutions of capitalism, patriarchy, and white supremacy, and create communities that organize themselves without new authorities.

How could people organized horizontally possibly overcome the state?

IF ANARCHISTS BELIEVE IN VOLUNTARY ACTION AND DECENTRALized organization, how could they ever be strong enough to topple a government with a professional army? In fact, strong anarchist and anti-authoritarian movements have defeated armies and governments in a number of revolutions. Often this occurs in periods of economic crisis, when the state lacks vital resources, or political crisis, when the state has lost the illusion of legitimacy.

The Soviet revolution of 1917 did not begin as the authoritarian terror it became after Lenin and Trotsky hijacked it. It was a multiform rebellion against the Tsar and against capitalism. It included such diverse actors as Socialist Revolutionaries, republicans, syndicalists, anarchists, and Bolsheviks. The soviets themselves were spontaneous non-party worker councils that organized along anti-authoritarian lines. The Bolsheviks gained control and ultimately suppressed the revolution by playing an effective political game that included co-opting or sabotaging the soviets, taking over the military, manipulating and betraying allies, and negotiating with imperialist powers. The Bolsheviks adeptly established themselves as the new government, and their allies made the mistake of believing their revolutionary rhetoric.

One of the first actions of the Bolshevik government was to sign a backstabbing peace treaty with the German and Austrian Empires. To pull out of World War I and free up the army for domestic action, the Leninists ceded the imperialists a treasure trove of money and strategic resources, and bequeathed them the country of Ukraine—without consulting the Ukrainians. Peasants in southern Ukraine rose up in revolt, and it was there that anarchism was strongest during the Soviet revolution. The rebels called themselves the Revolutionary Insurgent Army. They were commonly described as Makhnovists, after Nestor Makhno, their most influential military strategist and a skilled anarchist organizer. Makhno had been released from prison after the revolution in February 1917, and he returned to his hometown to organize an anarchist militia to fight the occupying German and Austrian forces.

As the insurrectionary anarchist army grew, it developed a more formal structure to allow for strategic coordination along several fronts, but it remained a volunteer militia, based on peasant support. Guiding questions of policy and strategy were decided in general meetings of peasants and workers. Aided rather than hindered by their flexible, participatory structure and strong support from the peasants, they liberated an area roughly 300 by 500 miles across, containing 7 million inhabitants, centered around the town of Gulyai-Polye. At times, the cities surrounding this anarchist zone—Alexandrovsk and Ekaterinoslav (now named Zaporizhye and Dnipropetrovsk, respectively) as well as Melitopol, Mariupol and Berdyansk, were freed from the control of the state, though they changed hands several times throughout the war. Self-organization along anarchist lines was deployed more consistently in the rural areas in these tumultuous years. In Gulyai-Polye, the anarchists set up three secondary schools and gave money expropriated from banks to orphanages. Throughout the area, literacy increased among the peasants.

In addition to taking on the Germans and Austrians, the anarchists also fought off the forces of nationalists who tried to subjugate the newly independent country under a homegrown Ukrainian government. They went on to hold the southern front against the armies of the White Russians—the aristocratic, pro-capitalist army funded and armed largely by the French and Americans—while their supposed allies, the Bolsheviks, withheld guns and ammunition and began purging anarchists to stop the spread of anarchism emanating from the Makhnovist territory. The White Russians eventually broke through the starved southern front, and reconquered Gulyai-Polye. Makhno retreated to the West, drawing off a large portion of the White armies, the remainder of which beat back the Red Army and advanced steadily towards Moscow. At the battle of Peregenovka, in western Ukraine, the anarchists obliterated the White army pursuing them. Although they were outnumbered and outgunned, they carried the day by effectively executing a series of brilliant maneuvers developed by Makhno, who had no military education or expertise. The volunteer anarchist army raced back to Gulyai-Polye, liberating the countryside and several major cities from the Whites. This sudden reversal cut off the supply lines of the armies that had almost reached Moscow, forcing them to retreat and saving the Russian Revolution.

For another year, an anarchist society again flourished in and around Gulyai-Polye, despite the efforts of Lenin and Trotsky to repress the anarchists there the way they had repressed them throughout Russia and the rest of Ukraine. When another White incursion under General Wrangel threatened the revolution, the Makhnovists again agreed to join the Communists against the imperialists, despite the earlier betrayal. The anarchist contingent accepted a suicide mission to take out enemy gun positions on the Perekop isthmus of Crimea; they succeeded in this and went on to capture the strategic city of Simferopol, again playing a crucial role in defeating the Whites. After the victory, the Bolsheviks surrounded and massacred most of the anarchist contingent, and occupied Gulyai-Polye and executed many influential anarchist organizers and fighters. Makhno and a few others escaped and confounded the massive Red Army with an effective campaign of guerrilla warfare for many months, even causing several major defections; in the end, however, the survivors decided to escape to the West. Some peasants in Ukraine retained their anarchist values, and raised the anarchist banner as part of the partisan resistance against Nazis and Stalinists during the Second World War. Even today, the red and black flag is a symbol of Ukrainian independence, though few people know its origins.

The Makhnovists of southern Ukraine maintained their anarchist character under extremely difficult conditions: constant warfare, betrayal and repression by supposed allies, lethal pressures that required them to defend themselves with organized violence. In these circumstances they continued to fight for liberty, even when it was not in their military interests. They repeatedly interceded to prevent pogroms against Jewish communities while the Ukrainian nationalists and Bolsheviks fanned the flames of anti-Semitism to provide a scapegoat for the problems they themselves were exacerbating. Makhno personally killed a neighboring warlord and potential ally upon learning he had ordered pogroms, even at a time when he desperately needed allies.[86]

> During October and November [1919], Makhno occupied Ekaterinoslav and Aleksandrovsk for several weeks, and thus obtained his first chance to apply the concepts of anarchism to city life. Makhno's first act on entering a large town (after throwing open the prisons) was to dispel

[86] Some mainstream sources still contest that the Makhnovists were behind anti-Semitic pogroms in Ukraine. In *Nestor Makhno, Anarchy's Cossack*, Alexandre Skirda traces this claim to its roots in anti-Makhno propaganda, while citing unfriendly contemporary sources who acknowledged that the Makhnovists were the only military units not carrying out pogroms. He also references propaganda put out by the Makhnovists attacking anti-Semitism as a tool of the aristocracy, Jewish militias that fought among the Makhnovists, and actions against pogromists personally carried out by Makhno.

any impression that he had come to introduce a new form of political rule. Announcements were posted informing the townspeople that henceforth they were free to organize their lives as they saw fit, that the Insurgent Army would not "dictate to them or order them to do anything." Free speech, press, and assembly were proclaimed, and in Ekaterinoslav half a dozen newspapers, representing a wide range of political opinion, sprang up overnight. While encouraging freedom of expression, however, Makhno would not countenance any political organization which sought to impose their authority on the people. He therefore dissolved the Bolshevik "revolutionary committees" (*revkomy*) in Ekaterinoslav and Aleksandrovsk, instructing their members to "take up some honest trade."[87]

The Makhnovists stuck to defending the region, leaving socio-economic organization to the individual towns and cities; this hands-off approach to others was matched by an internal emphasis on direct democracy. Officers were elected from within every subgroup of fighters, and they could be recalled by that same group; they were not saluted, they did not receive material privileges, and they could not lead from behind to avoid the risks of combat.

In contrast, officers in the Red Army were appointed from above and received privileges and higher pay on the scale of the Tsarist Army. In fact the Bolsheviks had essentially taken over the structure and personnel of the Tsarist Army after the October Revolution. They retained most of the officers but reformed it into a "people's army" by adding political officers responsible for identifying "counter-revolutionaries" to be purged. They also adopted the imperialist practice of stationing soldiers far across the continent from their homes, in areas where they did not speak the language, so they would be more likely to obey orders to repress locals and less likely to desert.

To be sure, the Revolutionary Insurgent Army enforced a strict discipline, shooting suspected spies and those who abused the peasants for personal gain such as embezzlers and rapists. The insurgents must have held many of the same powers over the

---

87 Paul Avrich, *The Russian Anarchists*, Oakland: AK Press, 2005, p. 218.

civilian population as does any army. Among their many opportunities to abuse that power, some of them probably did. However, their relationship with the peasants was unique among the military powers. The Makhnovists could not survive without popular support, and during their lengthy guerrilla war against the Red Army many peasants provided them with horses, food, lodging, medical help, and intelligence gathering. In fact the peasants themselves provided the majority of the anarchist fighters.

It is also debated how democratic the Makhnovist organizations were. Some historians say Makhno exerted substantial control over the "free soviets"—the non-party assemblies where workers and peasants made decisions and organized their affairs. Even sympathetic historians relate anecdotes of Makhno bullying delegates he saw as counter-revolutionary in meetings. But one must weigh these against the many occasions Makhno refused positions of power, or the fact that he left the Military Revolutionary Soviet, the assembly that decided military policy for the peasant militias, in an attempt to save the movement from the Bolshevik repression.[88]

One criticism the Bolsheviks had of the Makhnovists was that their Military Revolutionary Soviet, the closest thing they could have had to a dictatorial organization, wielded no real power—it was really just an advisory group—while individual workers' groups and peasant communities retained their autonomy. More charitable is the description by Soviet historian Kubanin: "the supreme body of the insurgent army was its Military Revolutionary Soviet, elected at a general assembly of all insurgents. Neither the overall command of the army nor Makhno himself truly ran the movement; they merely reflected the aspirations of the mass, acting as its ideological and technical agents." Another Soviet historian, Yefimov, says "No decision was ever taken by just one individual. All military matters were debated in common."[89]

---

88 Makhno hoped that Lenin and Trotsky were motivated by a personal vendetta against him rather than an absolute desire to crush the free soviets, and would call off the repression if he left.
89 Alexandre Skirda, *Nestor Makhno, Anarchy's Cossack: The Struggle for Free*

Grossly outnumbered and outgunned volunteer anarchist militias successfully defeated the armies of the Germans, the Austrians, the Ukrainian nationalists, and the White Russians. It took a professional army supplied by the world's greatest industrial powers and simultaneous betrayal by their allies to stop them. If they had known then what we know now—that authoritarian revolutionaries can be as tyrannical as capitalist governments—and Russian anarchists in Moscow and St. Petersburg had succeeded in preventing the Bolsheviks from hijacking the Russian Revolution, things might have turned out differently.

Even more impressive than the example provided by the Makhnovists is the victory won by several indigenous nations in 1868. In a two year war, thousands of warriors from the Lakota and Cheyenne nations defeated the US military and destroyed several army forts during what became known as Red Cloud's War. In 1866, the Lakota met with the US government at Fort Laramie because the latter wanted permission to build a military trail through the Powder River country to facilitate the influx of white settlers who were seeking gold. The US military had already defeated the Arapaho in its attempt to open the area for white settlers, but they had been unable to defeat the Lakota. During the negotiations it became apparent that the US government had already started the process of building military forts along this trail, without even having secured permission for the trail itself. The Oglala Lakota war chief Red Cloud promised to resist any white attempts to occupy the area. Nonetheless in the summer of 1866 the US military began sending more troops to the region and constructing new forts. Lakota, Cheyenne, and Arapaho warriors following the direction of Red Cloud began a campaign of guerrilla resistance, effectively closing down the Bozeman trail and harassing the troops stationed in the forts. The military sent down the order for an aggressive winter campaign, and on December 21, when their wood train was attacked yet again, an army of about one hundred US soldiers decided to pursue. They met a decoy party including the Oglala warrior Crazy Horse and took the bait.

Soviets in the Ukraine 1917–1921, London: AK Press, 2005, p. 314.

The entire force was defeated and killed by a force of 1,000–3,000 warriors that waited in ambush. The commanding officer of the white soldiers was knifed to death in hand to hand combat. The Lakota covered the body of a young bugle boy who fought with just his bugle in a buffalo robe as a sign of honor—with such acts the indigenous warriors demonstrated the possibility of a much more respectful form of warfare, in contrast with the white soldiers and settlers who often cut out fetuses from pregnant women and used the amputated genitals of unarmed victims as tobacco pouches.

In the summer of 1867 US troops with new repeating rifles fought the Lakota to a standstill in two battles, but they failed to carry out any successful offensives. In the end, they asked for peace talks, which Red Cloud said he would only grant if the new military forts were abandoned. The US government agreed, and in the peace talks they recognized the rights of the Lakota to the Black Hills and Powder River country, a huge area currently occupied by the states of North Dakota, South Dakota, and Montana.

During the war, the Lakota and Cheyenne organized without coercion or military discipline. But contrary to the typical dichotomies, their relative lack of hierarchy did not hamper their ability for organization. On the contrary, they held together during a brutal war on the basis of a collective, self-motivated discipline and varying forms of organization. In a Western army, the most important unit is the military police or the officer who walks behind the troops, pistol loaded and ready to shoot anyone who turns and runs. The Lakota and Cheyenne had no need for discipline imposed from above. They were fighting to defend their land and way of life, in groups bound by kinship and affinity.

Some fighting groups were structured with a chain of command, while others operated in a more collective fashion, but all of them voluntarily rallied around individuals with the best organizational abilities, spiritual power, and combat experience. These war chiefs did not control those who followed them so much as inspire them. When morale was low or a fight looked hopeless, groups of warriors often went home, and they were always free to do so. If a chief declared war, he had to go, but no one else did, so a leader who could not convince anyone to follow him to war was engaging in an embarrassing and even suicidal venture. In contrast, politicians and generals in Western society frequently start unpopular wars, and they are never the ones to suffer the consequences.

The warrior societies played an important role in the indigenous organization of warfare, but women's societies were vital as well. They played a role similar to that of the Quartermaster in Western armies, provisioning food and materials, except that where the Quartermaster is a simple cog obeying orders, the Lakota and Cheyenne women would refuse to cooperate if they disagreed with the reasons for a war. Considering that one of Napoleon's most important contributions to European warfare was the insight that "an army marches on its stomach," it becomes apparent that Lakota and Cheyenne women exercised more power in the affairs of their nations than the histories written by men and white people would lead us to believe. Additionally, women who chose to could fight alongside the men.

Despite being impossibly outnumbered by the US military and white settler paramilitaries, the Native Americans won. After Red Cloud's War, the Lakota and Cheyenne enjoyed nearly a decade of autonomy and peace. Contrary to pacifist allegations about militant resistance, the victors did not begin oppressing one another or creating uncontrollable cycles of violence just because they had violently fought off the white invaders. They won themselves several years of freedom and peace.

In 1876, the US military again invaded the Lakota territory to attempt to force them to live on the reservations, which were being transformed into concentration camps as part of the campaign of genocide against the indigenous populations. Several thousand troops were involved, and they met with several early defeats, the most notable of which was the Battle of Greasy Grass Creek, also known as the Battle of the Little Bighorn. Around 1,000 Lakota and Cheyenne warriors, defending themselves from an attack, decimated the cavalry unit commanded by George A. Custer and killed several hundred soldiers. Custer himself had previously invaded Lakota lands to spread reports of gold and provoke another wave of white settlers, who were a major driving force for the genocide. The settlers, aside from being an armed paramilitary force responsible for a large share of the encroachments and murders, provided a sufficient pretext for bringing in the military. The logic was that those poor humble homesteaders, in the act of invading another country, had to be defended from "marauding Indians." The US government ultimately won the war against the Lakota, by attacking their villages, invading their hunting grounds, and instituting strong repression against the people living on the reservations. One of the last to surrender was the Oglala warrior Crazy Horse, who had been one of the most effective leaders in the fight against the US military. After his group agreed to come into the reservation, Crazy Horse was arrested and assassinated.

Their ultimate defeat does not indicate a weakness in the horizontal organization of the Lakota and Cheyenne so much as the fact that the white American population trying to exterminate them outnumbered these indigenous groups by a thousand to one, and had the ability to spread disease and drug addiction on their home turf while destroying their food source.

Lakota resistance never ended, and they may win their war in the end. In December 2007, a group of Lakota again asserted their independence, informing the US State Department that they were withdrawing from all treaties, which had already been broken by the settler government, and seceding, as a necessary measure in the face of "colonial apartheid conditions."[90]

Some of the most uncompromising struggles against the state are indigenist. Current indigenist struggles have created some of the only zones in North America that enjoy physical and cultural autonomy and have successfully defended themselves in periodic confrontations with the state. These struggles typically do not identify themselves as anarchist, and perhaps for this reason anarchists have even more to learn from them. But if learning is not to be another commodity relation, an act of acquisition, it must

---

90 Amy Goodman, "Lakota Indians Declare Sovereignty from US Government," *Democracy Now!*, December 26, 2007.

be accompanied by horizontal relationships of reciprocity, which is to say, solidarity.

The Mohawk nation have long fought against colonization and in 1990 they won a major victory against the forces of the settler state. In Kanehsatake territory, near Montreal, white people in the town of Oka wanted to expand a golf course at the expense of a forested area in which a Mohawk graveyard was located, sparking native protests. In the spring of 1990, Mohawks set up a camp there and blocked the road. On July 11, 1990, Quebec police attacked the encampment with tear gas and automatic weapons, but the Mohawk defenders were armed and dug in. One cop was shot and killed and the rest ran away. The police cars, which they had left behind in panic, were used to build new barricades. Meanwhile, Mohawk warriors at Kahnawake blocked Mercier Bridge, halting commuter traffic to Montreal. Police began a seige of the Mohawk communities, but more warriors came, smuggling in supplies. The resisters organized food, medical care, and communications services, and the blockades persisted. White mobs formed in neighborhing towns and rioted, demanding police violence to open the bridge and restore traffic. Later in August, these mobs attacked a group of Mohawks while police stood by.

On August 20, the blockades were still going strong, and the Canadian military took over the siege from the police. In total 4,500 troops were deployed, backed by tanks, armored personnel carriers, helicopters, fighter jets, artillery, and naval ships. On September 18, Canadian soldiers raided Tekakwitha Island, shooting tear gas and bullets. The Mohawks fought back and the soldiers had to be evacuated by helicopter. Across Canada, native people protested in solidarity with the Mohawk, occupying buildings, blocking railroads and highways, and carrying out acts of sabotage. Unknown people burned down railway bridges in British Colombia and Alberta, and cut down five hydro-electric towers in Ontario. On September 26, the remaining besieged Mohawk declared victory and walked out, having burned their weapons. The golf course was never expanded, and most of those arrested were acquitted of weapons and riot charges. "Oka served to revitalize the warrior spirit of indigenous peoples and our will to resist."[91]

At the end of the '90s, the World Bank threatened not to renew a major loan on which the Bolivian government depended if they did not agree to privatize all water services in the city of Cochabamba. The government conceded and signed a contract with a consortium headed up by corporations from England, Italy, Spain, the US, and Bolivia. The water consortium, lacking knowledge of local conditions, immediately raised the rates, to the point where many families had to pay a fifth of their monthly earnings just for water. On top of this they enforced a policy of shutting off the water of any household that did not pay. In January 2000, major protests erupted against the water privatization. Primarily indigenous peasants converged on the city, joined by retired workers, sweatshop employees, street vendors, homeless youth, students, and anarchists. Protestors seized the central plaza and barricaded major roads. They organized a general strike which paralyzed the city for four days. On February 4 a major protest march was attacked by police and soldiers. Two hundred demonstrators were arrested, while seventy people and fifty-one cops were injured.

In April people again seized the central plaza of Cochabamba, and when the government began arresting organizers, protests spread to the cities of La Paz, Oruro, and Potosí, as well as many rural villages. Most major highways throughout the country were blockaded. On April 8, the Bolivian president declared a 90 day state of siege, banning meetings of more than 4 people, restricting political activity, allowing arbitrary arrests, establishing curfews, and putting the radio stations under military control. Police occasionally joined the demonstrators to demand higher pay, even participating in some riots. Once the government raised their salaries, they returned to work and continued beating and arresting their erstwhile comrades. Across the country people fought against the police and military with stones and molotov cocktails, suffering many injuries and multiple deaths. On April 9, soldiers trying to

---

91 From an anonymous illustrated pamphlet, "The 'Oka Crisis' "

remove a roadblock encountered resistance and shot two protestors to death, injuring several others. Neighbors attacked the soldiers, seized their weapons, and opened fire. Later they stormed a hospital and seized an army captain they had wounded, and lynched him.

As violent protests only showed signs of growing despite, and often because of, repeated killings and violent repression by the police and military, the state cancelled its contract with the water consortium and on April 11 annulled the law that had authorized the privatization of water in Cochabamba. Management of the water infrastructure was turned over to a community coordinating group that had arisen from the protest movement. Some participants in the struggle subsequently travelled to Washington, D.C. to join antiglobalization protestors in the demonstration intended to shut down the annual World Bank meeting.[92]

The complaints of the protestors moved far beyond water privatization in one city. The resistance had generalized to a social rebellion that included socialist rejections of neoliberalism, anarchist rejections of capitalism, farmers' rejections of their debts, poor people's demands for lower fuel prices and the end of multinational ownership of Bolivia's gas, and indigenous demands for sovereignty. Similarly fierce resistance in subsequent years defeated Bolivia's political elite on a number of occasions. Farmers and anarchists armed with dynamite took over banks to win the forgiveness of their debts. Under intense popular pressure, the government nationalized the extraction of gas, and a powerful union of indigenous farmers defeated the US-backed program of coca eradication. The coca farmers even got their leader, Evo Morales, elected president, giving Bolivia its first indigenous head of state. Because of this, Bolivia is currently facing a political crisis the government may be incapable of resolving, as the traditional elite, located in the white, eastern areas of the country, refuse to submit to the progressive policies of the Morales government. In the rural areas, indigenous communities used more direct means to preserve their

---

92 Oscar Olivera, *Cochabamba! Water War in Bolivia*, Cambridge: South End Press, 2004.

autonomy. They continued blockading highways, and sabotaged attempts of government control of their villages through daily acts of resistance. On no fewer than a dozen occasions when a particular mayor or other government official proved especially intrusive or abusive, he would be lynched by the villagers.

Decentralized resistance can defeat the government in an armed standoff—it can also overthrow governments. In 1997, government corruption and an economic collapse sparked a massive insurrection in Albania. In a matter of months, people armed themselves and forced the government and secret police to flee the country. They did not set up a new government or unite under a political party. Rather, they pushed out the state to create autonomous areas where they could organize their own lives. The rebellion spread spontaneously; without central leadership or even coordination. People across the country identified the state as their oppressor and attacked. Prisons were opened and police stations and government buildings burned to the ground. People sought to meet their needs at the local level within pre-existing social networks. Unfortunately, they lacked a consciously anarchist or anti-authoritarian movement. Rejecting political solutions intuitively but not explicitly, they lacked an analysis that could identify all political parties as enemies by their nature. Consequently the opposition Socialist party was able to install itself in power, though it took an occupation by thousands of European Union troops to pacify Albania completely.

Even in the wealthiest countries of the world, anarchists and other rebels can defeat the state within a limited area, creating an autonomous zone in which new social relations can flourish. In January 1981, the Socialist mayor of Berlin resigned after a combination of scandals relating to construction companies and urban renewal planning, and a series of major street battles sparked by the attempted evictions of squats. Hundreds and thousands of people fought in the streets in defense of autonomous spaces and against capitalist housing practices, and they defeated the government's attempt to crush the squatters' movement by force. The squatters occupied abandoned buildings as a struggle against gentrification and urban decay, or simply to provide themselves with free housing. Many squatters, known as autonomen, identified with an anti-capitalist, anti-authoritarian movement that saw these squats as bubbles of freedom in which to create the beginnings of a new society. In Berlin, the struggle was fiercest in the Kreuzberg neighborhood. In some areas, the majority of the residents were autonomen, dropouts, and immigrants—it was in many aspects an autonomous zone. Using the full might of the police, the city attempted to evict the squats and crush the movement, but the autonomen fought back. They defended their neighborhood with barricades, rocks, and molotov cocktails and outmaneuvered the police in street fighting. They counterattacked by wreaking havoc in the financial and commercial districts of the city. The ruling party gave up in disgrace. After elections to the Berlin Senate in the summer of 1981, the new government employed a legalization strategy in an attempt to undermine the movement's autonomy, since they were unable to forcibly evict them. Meanwhile, the autonomen in Kreuzberg took measures to protect the neighborhood from drug pushers, with a "fists against needles" campaign. They also fought against gentrification, smashing up bourgeois restaurants and bars.

In Hamburg, in 1986 and 1987, the police were stopped by the barricades of the autonomen when they attempted to evict the squats of Hafenstrasse. After losing several major street battles and suffering counterattacks, such as a coordinated arson attack against thirteen department stores causing $10 million in damage, the mayor legalized the squats, which still stand and continue to be centers of cultural and political resistance as of this writing.

In Copenhagen, Denmark, the autonomous youth movement went on the attack in 1986. At a time of militant squatting actions and sabotage attacks on Shell Oil stations and other targets of anti-imperialist struggle, several hundred people rerouted their protest march by surprise and occupied Ryesgade, a street in the neighborhood of Osterbro. They built barricades, and won neighborhood support and brought groceries to elderly neighbors blocked in by the barricades. For nine days, the autonomen held the streets, defeating the police in several major battles. Free radio stations throughout Denmark helped mobilize support, including food and supplies. Finally, the government announced it would bring in the military to clear the barricades. The youth at the barricades announced a press conference, but when the appointed morning came, they had all disappeared. Two city negotiators wondered:

> Where did the BZers [Occupation Brigaders] go when they left? What did the town hall learn? It seems the act can start all over again, anywhere, at any time. Even bigger. With the same participants.[93]

In 2002, Barcelona police attempted to evict Can Masdeu, a large squatted social center on a mountainside just outside the city. Can Masdeu was connected to the squatters' movement, the environmental movement, and the local tradition of resistance. The surrounding hillside was covered in gardens, many of them used by older neighbors who remembered the dictatorship and the struggle against it, and understood that this struggle still continued in the present day despite the veneer of democracy. Accordingly, the center received support from many corners of society. When the police came, the residents barricaded and locked down, and for days eleven people hung in harnesses on the outside of the building, dangling over the hillside, high above the ground. Supporters streamed in and challenged the police; others took action throughout the city, blocking traffic and attacking banks, real estate offices, a McDonalds, and other stores. Police tried to starve out the ones hanging from the building and used psychological torture tactics against them, but ultimately failed. The resistance defeated the eviction attempt and the autonomous zone survives to this day, with active community gardens and a social center.

On December 6, 2008, Greek police shot to death the fifteen-year-old anarchist Alexis Grigoropoulos in the middle of Exarchia,

---

93 George Katsiaficas, *The Subversion of Politics: European Autonomous Social Movements and the Decolonization of Everyday Life.* Oakland: AK Press, 2006, p. 123

the anarchist and autonomous stronghold in downtown Athens. Within minutes, anarchist affinity groups communicating by internet and cell phone sprang into action across the country. These affinity groups, in their hundreds, had developed relationships of trust and security and the capacity for taking offensive action over the previous years as they organized and carried out numerous small-scale attacks on state and capital. These attacks included simple graffiti actions, popular expropriations from supermarkets, molotov attacks on police, police cars, and commissaries, and bomb attacks against the vehicles and offices of political parties, institutions, and corporations that had led the reaction against social movements, immigrants, workers, prisoners, and others. The continuity of actions created a background of fierce resistance that could come to the fore when Greek society was ready.

Their rage over the murder of Alexis provided a rallying point for the anarchists, and they began attacking police all over the country, before the police in many cities even knew what was happening. The force of the attack broke the illusion of social peace, and in subsequent days hundreds of thousands of other people came out into the streets to vent the rage they too harbored against the system. Immigrants, students, high school kids, workers, revolutionaries from the previous generation, old folks—all of Greek society came out and participated in a diversity of actions. They fought against the police and won, winning the power to transform their cities. Luxury shops and government buildings were smashed and burned to the ground. Schools, radio stations, theaters, and other buildings were occupied. Their mourning turned into celebration as people set fires and commemorated the burning away of the old world with parties in the streets. The police responded in force, injuring and arresting hundreds of people and filling the air with tear gas. The people defended themselves with more fires, burning down everything they hated and producing thick clouds of black smoke that neutralized the tear gas.

On the days when people started to go home, perhaps to return to normality, the anarchists kept the riots going, so that there could be no doubt that the streets belonged to the people and a new world was within their reach. Amidst all the graffiti that appeared on the walls was the promise: "We are an image from the future." The riots went on for two weeks straight. The police had long lost all semblance of control, and had run out of tear gas. In the end people went home out of sheer physical exhaustion, but they did not stop. Attacks continued, and huge parts of Greek society began participating in creative actions as well. Greek society had been transformed. All the symbols of capitalism and government were proven to provoke the scorn of the masses. The state had lost its legitimacy and the media was reduced to repeating the transparent lie, *these rioters simply don't know what they want.* The anarchist movement won respect throughout the country, and inspired the new generation. The riots subsided, but the actions continued. As of this writing, people throughout Greece continue occupying buildings, starting social centers, protesting, attacking, evaluating their strategies, and holding massive assemblies to determine the direction of their struggle.

Democratic states still entertain the option of calling in the military when their police forces cannot maintain order, and occasionally do so in even the most progressive countries. But this choice opens dangerous possibilities, as well. The dissidents may also take up arms; if the struggle continues to gain popularity, more and more people will see the government as an occupying force; in an extreme case, the military may mutiny and the struggle spread. In Greece, soldiers were circulating letters promising that if they were called in to crush the revolt, they would give their arms to the people and open fire on the cops. Military intervention is an unavoidable stage of any struggle to overthrow the state; but if social movements can demonstrate the courage and organizational capacity to defeat the police, they may be able to defeat the military or win them over. Thanks to the rhetoric of democratic governments, soldiers today are much less prepared psychologically to repress local uprisings as brutally as they would in a foreign country.

Because of the globally integrated nature of the system, states and other institutions of power are mutually reinforcing, and thus stronger up to a certain point. But beyond that point, they are all weaker, and vulnerable to collapse on a global scale like never before in history. Political crisis in China could destroy the US economy, and send other dominoes falling as well. We have not yet reached the point at which we can overthrow the global power structure, but it is significant that in specific contests the state is often unable to crush us, and bubbles of autonomy exist alongside the system that purports to be universal and without alternatives. Governments are overthrown every year. The system has still not been abolished because the victors of such struggles have always been co-opted and reincorporated into global capitalism. But if explicitly anti-authoritarian movements can take the initiative in popular resistance, this is a hopeful sign for the future.

How do we know revolutionaries won't become new authorities?

IT IS NOT INEVITABLE FOR REVOLUTIONARIES TO BECOME THE NEW dictators, especially if their primary goal is the abolition of all coercive authority. Revolutions throughout the 20th century created new totalitarian systems, but all of these were led or hijacked by political parties, none of which denounced authoritarianism; on the contrary, a great many of them promised to create a "dictatorship of the proletariat" or a nationalist government.

Political parties, after all, are inherently authoritarian institutions. Even in the rare case that they legitimately come from dispempowered constituencies and build internally democratic structures, they still must negotiate with existing authorities to gain influence, and their ultimate objective is to gain control over a centralized power structure. For political parties to gain power through the parliamentary process, they must set aside whatever egalitarian principles and revolutionary goals they might have had and cooperate with pre-existing arrangements of power—the needs of capitalists, imperialist wars, and so on. This sad process was demonstrated by social democratic parties around the world from Labour in the UK to the Communist Party in Italy, and more recently by the Green Party in Germany or the Workers' Party in Brazil. On the other hand, when political parties—such as the Bolsheviks, the Khmer Rouge, and the Cuban communists—seek to impose change by taking control in a coup d'etat or civil war, their authoritarianism is even more immediately visible.

However, expressly anti-authoritarian revolutionaries have a history of destroying power rather than taking it. None of their uprisings have been perfect, but they do provide hope for the future and lessons on how an anarchist revolution could be achieved. While authoritarianism is always a danger, it is not an inevitable outcome of struggle.

In 2001, following years of discrimination and brutality, the Amazigh (Berber) inhabitants of Kabylia, a region of Algeria, rose up against the predominantly Arab government. The trigger to the uprising came on the 18th of April when the gendarmerie killed a local youth and later subjected a number of students to arbitrary arrest, though the resulting movement clearly demonstrated itself to be much broader than a reaction against police brutality. Starting April 21, people fought with the gendarmerie, burned down police stations, government buildings, and offices of opposition political parties. Noting that the offices of government social services were not spared, domestic intellectuals and journalists as well as leftists in France paternalistically admonished that the misguided rioters were destroying their own neighborhoods—omitting out of hypocrisy or ignorance the fact that social services in poor regions serve the same function as the police, only that they perform the softer part of the job.

The riots generalized into insurrection, and the people of Kabylia soon achieved one of their main demands—the removal of the gendarmerie from the region. Many police stations that were not burnt down outright were besieged and had their supply lines cut off so that the gendarmerie had to go out in force on raiding missions just to supply themselves. In the first months, police killed over a hundred people, and wounded thousands, but the insurgents did not back down. Due to the fierceness of the resistance rather than the generosity of the government, Kabylia was still off limits to the gendarmerie as of 2006.

The movement was soon organizing the liberated region along traditional and anti-authoritarian lines. The communities resurrected the Amazigh tradition of the *aarch* (or *aaruch* in plural), a popular assembly for self-organization. Kabylia benefited from a deep-rooted anti-authoritarian culture. During the French colonization, the region was the home to frequent uprisings, and daily resistance to government administration.

> In 1948, a village assembly, for example, formally prohibited communication with the government about community affairs: "Passing information to any authority, be it about the morality of another citizen, be it about tax figures, will be sanctioned with a fine of ten thousand francs. It is the most grave type of fine that exists. The mayor and the rural guard are not excluded"[...] And when the current movement began to organize committees of neighborhoods and villages, one delegate (from the aarch of Ait Djennad) declared, to demonstrate that at least the memory of this tradition had not been lost: "Before, when the *tajmat* took charge of the resolution of a conflict between people, they punished the thief or the fraudster, it wasn't necessary to go to the tribunal. In fact it was shameful."[94]

Starting from April 20, 2001, delegates from 43 cities in the sub-prefecture of Beni Duala, in Kabylia, were coordinating the call for a general strike, as people in many villages and neighborhoods organized assemblies and coordinations. On the 10th of May, delegates from the different assemblies and coordinations throughout Beni Duala met to formulate demands and organize the movement. The press, demonstrating the role they would play throughout the insurrection, published a false announcement saying the meeting was cancelled, but still a large number of delegates came together, predominantly from the *wilaya,* or district, of Tizi Uzu. They kicked out a mayor who tried to participate in the meetings. "Here we don't need a mayor or any other representative of the state," said one delegate.

---

94 Jaime Semprun, *Apología por la Insurrección Argelina,* Bilbao: Muturreko Burutazioak, 2002, p. 34 (translated from French to Spanish by Javier Rodriguez Hidalgo; the translation to English is my own). The quotes in the next paragraphs are from p. 18 and p. 20.

Delegates from the *aaruch* kept meeting and created an inter-wilaya coordination. On the 11th of June they met in El Kseur:

> We, representatives of the wilayas of Sétis, Bordj-Bu-Arreridj, Buira, Bumerdes, Bejaia, Tizi Uzu, Algiers, as well as the Collective Committee of Universities of Algiers, meeting today Monday the 11th of June 2001, in the Youth House "Mouloud Feraoun" in El Kseur (Bejaia), have adopted the following table of demands:

For the State to urgently take responsibility for all the injured victims and the families of the martyrs of the repression during these events.

For the trial by civil tribunal of the the authors, instigators and accomplices of these crimes and their expulsion from the security forces and from public office.

For a martyr status for every dignified victim during these events and the protection of all witnesses to the drama.

For the immediate withdrawal of the brigades of the gendarmerie and the reinforcements from the URS.

For the annulment of judicial processes against all the protestors as well the liberation of those who have already been sentenced during these events.

Immediate abandonment of the punitive expeditions, the intimidations, and the provocations against the population.

Dissolution of the investigation commissions initiated by the power.

Satisfaction of the Amazigh claims, in all their dimensions (of identity, civilization, language, and culture) without referendum and without conditions, and the declaration of Tamazight as a national and official language.

For a state that guarantees all socio-economic rights and all democratic liberties.

Against the policies of underdevelopment, pauperization, and miserablization of the Algerian people.

Placing all the executive functions of the State including the security forces under the effective authority of

> democratically elected bodies.
> For an urgent socio-economic plan for all of Kabylia.
> Against the Tamheqranit [roughly, the arbitrariness of power] and all forms of injustice and exclusion.
> For a case by case reconsideration of the regional exams for all students who did not pass them.
> Installment of unemployment benefits for everyone who makes less than 50% of the minimum wage.
>
> We demand an official, urgent, and public reply to this table of demands.
>
> Ulac Smah Ulac [the struggle continues][95]

On June 14, hundreds of thousands went to march on Algiers to present these demands but they were preemptively waylaid and dispersed through heavy police action. Although the movement was always strongest in Kabylia, it never limited itself to national/cultural boundaries and enjoyed support throughout the country; nonetheless opposition political parties tried to water down the movement by reducing it to simple demands for measures against police brutality and the official recognition of the Berber language. But the defeat of the march in Algiers did effectively demonstrate the movement's weakness outside of Kabylia. Said one resident of Algiers, regarding the difficulty of resistance in the capital in contrast to the Berber regions: "They're lucky. In Kabylia they're never alone. They have all their culture, their structures. We live in between snitches and Rambo posters."

In July and August, the movement set itself the task of reflecting strategically on their structure: they adopted a system of coordination between the *aaruch*, dairas and communes within a wilaya, and the election of delegates within towns and neighborhoods; these delegates would form a municipal coordination that enjoyed full autonomy of action. A coordination for the whole wilaya

---

95 Jaime Semprun, *Apología por la Insurrección Argelina*, Bilbao: Muturreko Burutazioak, 2002, pp.73–74 (translated from French to Spanish by Javier Rodriguez Hidalgo; the translation to English is my own).

would be composed of two delegates from each of the municipal coordinations. In a typical case in Bejaia, the coordination kicked out the trade unionists and leftists that had infiltrated it, and launched a general strike on their own initiative. At the culmination of this process of reflection, the movement identified as one of its major weaknesses the relative lack of participation by women within the coordinations (although women played a large role in the insurrection and other parts of the movement). The delegates resolved to encourage more participation by women.

Throughout this process some delegates kept secretly trying to dialogue with the government while the press shifted between demonizing the movement and suggesting that their more civic demands could be adopted by the government, while ignoring their more radical demands. On August 20, the movement demonstrated its power within Kabylia with a major protest march, followed by a round of interwilaya meetings. The country's elite hoped that these meetings would demonstrate the "maturity" of the movement and result in dialogue but the coordinations continued to reject secret negotiations and reaffirmed the agreements of El Kseur. Commentators remarked that if the movement continued to reject dialogue while pushing for their demands and successfully defending their autonomy, they effectively made government impossible and the result could be the collapse of state power, at least within Kabylia.

On October 10, 2002, after having survived over a year of violence and pressure to play politics, the movement launched a boycott of the elections. Much to the frustration of the political parties, the elections were blocked in Kabylia, and in the rest of Algeria participation was remarkably low.

From the very beginning, the political parties were threatened by the self-organization of the uprising, and tried their hardest to bring the movement within the political system. It was not so easy, however. Early on the movement adopted a code of honor that all the coordination delegates had to swear to. The code stated:

The delegates of the movement promise to

> Respect the terms enunciated in the chapter of Directing Principles of the coordinations of *aaruch*, dairas, and communes.
> Honor the blood of the martyrs following the struggle until the completion of its objectives and not using their memory for lucrative or partisan ends.
> Respect the resolutely peaceful spirit of the movement.
> Not take any action leading to establishing direct or indirect connections with power.
> Not use the movement for partisan ends or drag it into electoral competitions or attempts to take power.
> Publicly resign from the movement before seeking any elected office.
> Not accept any political office (nomination by decree) in the institutions of power.
> Show civic-mindedness and respect to others.
> Give the movement a national dimension.
> Not circumvent the appropriate structure in matters of communication.
> Give effective solidarity to any person who has suffered any injury due to activity as a delegate of the movement.
>
>> Note: Any delegate who violates this Code of Honor will be publicly denounced.[96]

And in fact, delegates who broke this pledge were ostracized and even attacked.

The pressure of recuperation continued. Anonymous committees and councils began issuing press releases denouncing the "spiral of violence" of the youth and the "poor political calculations" of "those who continue loudly parasitizing the public debate" and

---

96 Ditto, p. 80. Regarding the fourth point, in contrast to Western society and its various forms of pacifism, the peacefulness of the movement in Algeria does not preclude self-defense or even armed uprising, as evidenced by the preceding point regarding the martyrs. Rather, peacefulness indicates a preference for peaceful and consensual outcomes over coercion and arbitrary authority.

silencing the "good citizens." Later this particular council clarified that these good citizens were "all the scientific and political personages of the municipality capable of giving sense and consistency to the movement."[97]

In the following years, the weakening of the movement's anti-authoritarian character has demonstrated a major obstacle to libertarian insurrections that win a bubble of autonomy: not an inevitable, creeping authoritarianism, but constant international pressure on the movement to institutionalize. In Kabylia, much of that pressure came from European NGOs and international agencies who claimed to work for peace. They demanded that the aarch coordinations adopt peaceful tactics, give up their boycott of politics, and field candidates for election. Since then, the movement has split. Many aarch delegates and elders who appointed themselves leaders have entered the political arena, where their main objective is to rewrite the Algerian constitution to institute democratic reforms and end the present dictatorship. Meanwhile, the Movement for Autonomy in Kabylia (MAK) has continued to insist that power should be decentralized and the region should win independence.

Kabylia did not receive significant support and solidarity from anti-authoritarian movements across the globe, which might have helped offset the pressure to institutionalize. Part of this is due to the isolation and eurocentrism of many of these movements. At the same time, the movement itself restricted its scope to State boundaries and lacked an explicitly revolutionary ideology. Taken on its own, the civic-mindedness and emphasis of autonomy found within Amazigh culture is clearly anti-authoritarian, but in a contest with the State it gives rise to a number of ambiguities. The movement demands, if fully realized, would have made government impractical and thus they were revolutionary; however they did not explicitly call for the destruction of "the power," and thus left plenty of room for the state to reinsert itself in the movement. Even though the Code of Honor exhaustively prohibited collaboration with political parties, the movement's civic ideology

97 Ditto, p. 26.

made such collaboration inevitable by demanding good government, which is of course impossible, a code word for self-deception and betrayal.

An ideology or analysis that was revolutionary as well as anti-authoritarian might have prevented recuperation and facilitated solidarity with movements in other countries. At the same time, movements in other countries might have been positioned to give solidarity had they developed a broader understanding of struggle. For example, due to a host of historical and cultural reasons it is not at all likely that the insurrection in Algeria would ever have identified itself as "anarchist," yet it was one of the most inspiring examples of anarchy to appear in those years. Most self-identified anarchists were prevented from realizing this and initiating relationships of solidarity due to a cultural bias against struggles that do not adopt the aesthetics and cultural inheritance prevalent among Euro/American revolutionaries.

The historic experiments in collectivization and anarchist communism that took place in Spain in 1936 and 1937 could only happen because anarchists had been preparing themselves to defeat the military in an armed insurrection, and when the fascists launched their coup they were able to defeat them militarily throughout much of the country. To protect the new world they were building, they organized themselves to hold back the better equipped fascists with trench warfare, declaring "No pasarán!" *They shall not pass!*

Though they had plenty to keep them busy on the homefront, setting up schools, collectivizing land and factories, reorganizing social life, the anarchists raised and trained volunteer militias to fight on the front. Early in the war, the anarchist Durruti Column pushed back the fascists on the Aragon front, and in November it played an important role in defeating the fascist offensive on Madrid. There were many criticisms of the volunteer militias, mostly from bourgeois journalists and the Stalinists who wanted to crush the militias in favor of a professional military fully under their control. George Orwell, who fought in a Trotskyist militia, sets the record straight:

> Everyone from general to private drew the same pay, ate the same food, wore the same clothes, and mingled on terms of complete equality. If you wanted to slap the general commanding the division on the back and ask him for a cigarette, you could do so, and no one thought it curious. In theory at any rate each militia was a democracy and not a hierarchy... They had attempted to produce within the militias a sort of temporary working model of the classless society. Of course there was not perfect equality, but there was a nearer approach to it than I had ever seen or than I would have thought conceivable in time of war...
>
> ...Later it became the fashion to decry the militias, and therefore to pretend that the faults which were due to lack of training and weapons were the result of the equalitarian system. Actually, a newly raised draft of militia was an undisciplined mob not because the officers called the privates 'Comrade' but because raw troops are *always* an undisciplined mob... The journalists who sneered at the militia-system seldom remembered that the militias had to hold the line while the Popular Army was training in the rear. And it is a tribute to the strength of 'revolutionary' discipline that the militias stayed in the field at all. For until about June 1937 there was nothing to keep them there, except class loyalty... A conscript army in the same circumstances—with its battle-police removed—would have melted away... At the beginning the apparent chaos, the general lack of training, the fact that you often had to argue for five minutes before you could get an order obeyed, appalled and infuriated me. I had British Army ideas, and certainly the Spanish militias were very unlike the British Army. But considering the circumstances they were better troops than one had any right to expect.[98]

Orwell revealed that the militias were being deliberately starved of the weaponry they needed for victory by a political apparatus determined to crush them. Notwithstanding, in October, 1936, the anarchist and socialist militias pushed the fascists back on the Aragon front, and for the next eight months they

---

98 George Orwell, *Homage to Catalonia,* London: Martin Secker & Warburg Ltd., 1938, pp.26–28.

held the line, until they were forcefully replaced by the government army.

The conflict was long and bloody, full of grave dangers, unprecedented opportunities, and difficult choices. Throughout it the anarchists had to prove the feasibility of their ideal of a truly anti-authoritarian revolution. They experienced a number of successes and failures, which, taken together, show what is possible and what dangers revolutionaries must avoid to resist becoming new authorities.

Behind the lines, anarchists and socialists seized the opportunity to put their ideals in practice. In the Spanish countryside, peasants expropriated land and abolished capitalist relations. There was no uniform policy governing how the peasants established anarchist communism; they employed a range of methods for overthrowing their masters and creating a new society. In some places, the peasants killed clergy and landlords, though this was often in direct retaliation against those who had collaborated with the fascists or the earlier regime by giving names of radicals to be arrested and executed. In several uprisings in Spain between 1932 and 1934, revolutionaries had shown little predisposition to assassinate their political enemies. For example, when peasants in the Andalucian village of Casas Viejas had unfurled the red and black flag, their only violence was directed against land titles, which they burned. Neither political bosses nor landlords were attacked; they were simply informed that they no longer held power or property. The fact that these peaceful peasants were subsequently massacred by the military, at the behest of those bosses and landlords, may help explain their more aggressive conduct in 1936. And the Church in Spain was very much a pro-fascist institution. The priests had long been the purveyors of abusive forms of education and the defenders of patriotism, patriarchy, and the divine rights of the landlords. When Franco launched his coup, many priests acted as fascist paramilitaries.

There had been a long-running debate in anarchist circles about whether fighting capitalism as a system necessitated attacking specific individuals in power, apart from situations of self-defense. The fact that those in power, when shown mercy, turned right around and gave names to the firing squads to punish the rebels and discourage future uprisings underscored the argument that elites are not just innocently playing a role within an impersonal system, but that they specifically involve themselves in waging war against the oppressed. Thus, the killings carried out by the Spanish anarchists and peasants were not signs of an authoritarianism inherent in revolutionary struggle so much as an intentional strategy within a dangerous conflict. The contemporaneous behavior of the Stalinists, who established a secret police force to torture and execute their erstwhile comrades, demonstrates how low people can sink when they think they're fighting for a just cause; but the contrasting example offered by anarchists and other socialists proves that such behavior is not inevitable.

A demonstration of the absence of authoritarianism among the anarchists can be seen in the fact that those same peasants who liberated themselves violently did not force individualistic peasants to collectivize their lands along with the rest of the community. In most of the villages surveyed in anarchist areas, collectives and individual holdings existed side by side. In the worst scenario, where an anti-collective peasant held territory dividing peasants who did want to join their lands, the majority sometimes asked the individualist peasant to trade his land for land elsewhere, so the other peasants could pool their efforts to form a collective. In one documented example, the collectivizing peasants offered the individual landholder land of better quality in order to ensure a consensual resolution.

In the cities and within the structures of the CNT, the anarchist labor union with over a million members, the situation was more complicated. After defense groups prepared by the CNT and FAI (the Iberian Anarchist Federation) defeated the fascist uprising in Catalunya and seized weapons from the armory, the CNT rank and file spontaneously organized factory councils, neighborhood assemblies, and other organizations capable of coordinating economic life; what's more, they did so in a nonpartisan way, working with other workers of all political persuasions. Even though the anarchists were the strongest force in Catalunya, they demonstrated little desire to repress other groups—in stark contrast to the Communist Party, the Trotskyists, and the Catalan nationalists. The problem came from the CNT delegates. The union had failed to structure itself in a way that prevented its becoming institutionalized. Delegates to the Regional and National Committees could not be recalled if they failed to perform as desired, there was no custom to prevent the same people from maintaining constant positions on these higher committees, and negotiations or decisions made by higher committees did not always have to be ratified by the entire membership. Furthermore, principled anarchist militants consistently refused the top positions in the Confederation, while intellectuals focused on abstract theories and economic planning gravitated to these central committees. Thus, at the time of the revolution in July, 1936, the CNT had an established leadership, and this leadership was isolated from the actual movement.

Anarchists such as Stuart Christie and veterans of the libertarian youth group that went on to participate in the guerrilla struggle against the fascists during the following decades have argued that these dynamics separated the de facto leadership of the CNT from the rank and file, and brought them closer to the professional politicians. Thus, in Catalunya, when they were invited to participate in an antifascist Popular Front along with the authoritarian socialist and republican parties, they obliged. To them, this was a gesture of pluralism and solidarity, as well as a means of self-defense against the threat posed by fascism.

Their estrangement from the base prevented them from realizing that the power was no longer in the government buildings; it was already in the street and wherever workers were spontaneously taking over their factories. Ignorant of this, they actually impeded social revolution, discouraging the armed masses from pursuing the full realization of anarchist communism for fear of upsetting their new allies.[99] In any case, anarchists in this period faced extremely

---

99 There were 40,000 armed anarchist militants in Barcelona and the surrounding region alone. The Catalan government would have been effectively abolished had the CNT simply ignored it, rather than entering into negotiations. Stuart Christie, We, the Anarchists! A study of the Iberian

difficult decisions. The representatives were caught between advancing fascism and treacherous allies, while those in the streets had to choose between accepting the dubious decisions of a self-appointed leadership or splitting the movement by being overly critical.

But despite the sudden power gained by the CNT—they were the dominant organized political force in Catalunya and a major force in other provinces—both the leadership and the base acted in a cooperative rather than a power-hungry manner. For example, in the antifascist committees proposed by the Catalan government, they allowed themselves to be put on an equal footing with the comparatively weak socialist labor union and the Catalan nationalist party. One of the chief reasons the CNT leadership gave for collaborating with the authoritarian parties was that abolishing the government in Catalunya would be tantamount to imposing an anarchist dictatorship. But their assumption that getting rid of the government—or, more accurately, allowing a spontaneous popular movement to do so—meant replacing it with the CNT showed their own blinding self-importance. They failed to grasp that the working class was developing new organizational forms, such as factory councils, that might flourish best by transcending pre-existing institutions—whether the CNT or the government—rather than being absorbed into them. The CNT leadership "failed to realise how powerful the popular movement was and that their role as union spokesmen was now inimical to the course of the revolution."[100]

Rather than painting a rosy picture of history, we should recognize that these examples show that navigating the tension between effectiveness and authoritarianism is not easy, but it is possible.

How will communities decide to organize themselves at first?

ALL PEOPLE ARE CAPABLE OF SELF-ORGANIZATION, WHETHER OR not they are experienced in political work. Of course, taking control

---

Anarchist Federation (FAI) 1927–1937, Hastings, UK: The Meltzer Press, 2000, p. 106.

100 Ditto, p. 101

of our lives won't be easy at first, but it is imminently possible. In most cases, people take the obvious approach, spontaneously holding large, open meetings with their neighbors, co-workers, or comrades on the barricades to figure out what needs to be done. In some cases, society is organized through pre-existing revolutionary organizations.

The 2001 popular rebellion in Argentina saw people take an unprecedented level of control over their lives. They formed neighborhood assemblies, took over factories and abandoned land, created barter networks, blockaded highways to compel the government to grant relief to the unemployed, held the streets against lethal police repression, and forced four presidents and multiple vice presidents and economic ministers to resign in quick succession. Through it all, they did not appoint leadership, and most of the neighborhood assemblies rejected political parties and trade unions trying to co-opt these spontaneous institutions. Within the assemblies, factory occupations, and other organizations, they practiced consensus and encouraged horizontal organizing. In the words of one activist involved in establishing alternative social structures in his neighborhood, where unemployment reached 80%: "We are building power, not taking it."[101]

People formed over 200 neighborhood assemblies in Buenos Aires alone, involving thousands of people; according to one poll, one in three residents of the capital had attended an assembly. People began by meeting in their neighborhoods, often over a common meal, or *olla popular*. Next they would occupy a space to serve as a social center—in many cases, an abandoned bank. Soon the neighborhood assembly would be holding weekly meetings "on community issues but also on topics such as the external debt, war, and free trade" as well as "how they could work together and how they saw the future." Many social centers would eventually offer:

> an info space and perhaps computers, books, and various workshops on yoga, self defence, languages, and basic

101   John Jordan and Jennifer Whitney, *Que Se Vayan Todos: Argentina's Popular Rebellion*, Montreal: Kersplebedeb, 2003, p. 56.

skills. Many also have community gardens, run after school kids' clubs and adult education classes, put on social and cultural events, cook food collectively, and mobilise politically for themselves and in support of the *piqueteros* and reclaimed factories.[102]

The assemblies set up working groups, such as healthcare and alternative media committees, that held additional meetings involving the people most interested in those projects. According to visiting independent journalists:

> Some assemblies have as many as 200 people participating, others are much smaller. One of the assemblies we attended had about 40 people present, ranging from two mothers sitting on the sidewalk while breast feeding, to a lawyer in a suit, to a skinny hippie in batik flares, to an elderly taxi driver, to a dreadlocked bike messenger, to a nursing student. It was a whole slice of Argentinean society standing in a circle on a street corner under the orange glow of sodium lights, passing around a brand new megaphone and discussing how to take back control of their lives. Every now and then a car would pass by and beep its horn in support, and this was all happening between 8 pm and midnight on a Wednesday evening![103]

Soon the neighborhood assemblies were coordinating at a citywide level. Once a week the assemblies sent spokespeople to the interbarrio plenary, which brought together thousands of people from across the city to propose joint projects and protest plans. At the interbarrio, decisions were made with a majority vote, but the structure was non-coercive so the decisions were not binding—they were only carried out if people had the enthusiasm to

---

102   Natasha Gordon and Paul Chatterton, *Taking Back Control: A Journey through Argentina's Popular Uprising*, Leeds (UK): University of Leeds, 2004.

103   John Jordan and Jennifer Whitney, *Que Se Vayan Todos: Argentina's Popular Rebellion*, Montreal: Kersplebedeb, 2003, p. 9.

carry them out. Accordingly, if a large number of people at the interbarrio voted to abstain on a specific proposal, the proposal was reworked so it would receive more support.

The assembly structure quickly expanded to the provincial and national levels. Within two months of the beginning of the uprising, the national "Assembly of Assemblies" was calling for the government to be replaced by the assemblies. That did not occur, but in the end the government of Argentina was forced to make popular concessions—it announced it would default on its international debt, an unprecedented occurrence. The International Monetary Fund was so scared by the popular rebellion and its worldwide support in the anti-globalization movement, and so embarrassed by the collapse of its poster child, that it had to accept this stunning loss. The movement in Argentina played a pivotal role in accomplishing one of the major goals of the anti-globalization movement, which was the defeat of the IMF and World Bank. As of this writing, these institutions are discredited and facing bankruptcy. Meanwhile, the Argentine economy has stabilized and much of the popular outrage has subsided. Still, some of the assemblies that made a vital niche in the uprising continue to operate seven years later. The next time the conflict comes to the surface, these assemblies will remain in the collective memory as the seeds of a future society.

The city of Gwangju (or Kwangju), in South Korea, liberated itself for six days in May, 1980, after student and worker protests against the military dictatorship escalated in response to declarations of martial law. Protestors burned down the government television station and seized weapons, quickly organizing a "Citizen Army" that forced out the police and military. As in other urban rebellions, including those in Paris in 1848 and 1968, in Budapest in 1919, and in Beijing in 1989, students and workers in Gwangju quickly formed open assemblies to organize life in the city and communicate with the outside world. Participants in the uprising tell of a complex organizational system developed spontaneously in a short period of time—and without the leaders of the main student groups and protest organizations, who had already been arrested. Their system included a Citizen's Army, a Situation

Center, a Citizen-Student Committee, a Planning Board, and departments for local defense, investigation, information, public services, burial of the dead, and other services.104 It took a full-scale invasion by special units of the Korean military with US support to crush the rebellion and prevent it from spreading. Several hundred people were killed in the process. Even its enemies described the armed resistance as "fierce and well-organized." The combination of spontaneous organization, open assemblies, and committees with a specific organizational focus left a deep impression, showing how quickly a society can change itself once it breaks with the habit of obedience to the government.

In the Hungarian Revolution of 1956, state power collapsed after masses of student protestors armed themselves; much of the country fell into the hands of the people, who had to reorganize the economy and quickly form militias to repel Soviet invasion. Initially, each city organized itself spontaneously, but the forms of organization that arose were very similar, perhaps because they developed in the same cultural and political context. Hungarian anarchists were influential in the new Revolutionary Councils, which federated to coordinate defense, and they took part in the workers' councils that took over the factories and mines. In Budapest old politicians formed a new government and tried to harness these autonomous councils into a multiparty democracy, but the influence of the government did not extend beyond the capital city in the days before the second Soviet invasion succeeded in crushing the uprising. Hungary did not have a large anarchist movement at the time, but the popularity of the various councils shows how contagious anarchistic ideas are once people decide to organize themselves. And their ability to keep the country running and defeat the first invasion of the Red Army shows the effectiveness of these organizational forms. There was no need

---

104 George Katsiaficas, "Comparing the Paris Commune and the Kwangju Uprising," www.eroseffect.com. That the resistance was "well-organized" comes from a report from the conservative Heritage Foundation, Daryl M. Plunk's "South Korea's Kwangju Incident Revisited," *The Heritage Foundation*, No. 35, September 16, 1985.

for a complex institutional blueprint to be in place before people left their authoritarian government behind. All they needed was the determination to come together in open meetings to decide their futures, and the trust in themselves that they could make it work, even if at first it was unclear how.

How will reparations for past oppressions be worked out?

IF GOVERNMENT AND CAPITALISM DISAPPEARED OVERNIGHT, people would still be divided. Legacies of oppression generally determine where we live; our access to land, water, a clean environment, and necessary infrastructure; and the level of violence and trauma in our communities. People are accorded vastly differing degrees of social privilege according to skin color, gender, citizenship, economic class, and other factors. Once the exploited of the earth rise up to seize the wealth of our society, what exactly will they inherit? Healthy land, clean water, and hospitals, or depleted soil, garbage dumps, and lead pipes? It depends largely on their skin color and nationality.

An essential part of an anarchist revolution is global solidarity. Solidarity is the polar opposite of charity. It does not depend on an inequality between giver and receiver. Like all good things in life, solidarity is shared, thus it destroys the categories of giver and receiver and neither ignores nor validates whatever unequal power dynamics may exist between the two. There can be no true solidarity between a revolutionary in Illinois and a revolutionary in Mato Grosso if they must ignore that the one's house is built with wood stolen from the lands of the other, ruining the soil and leaving him and his entire community with fewer possibilities for the future.

Anarchy must make itself wholly incompatible with colonialism, either a colonialism that continues to the present day in new forms, or a historical legacy which we try to ignore. Thus an anarchist revolution must also base itself in the struggles against colonialism. These include people in the Global South who are trying to reverse neoliberalism, indigenous nations struggling to regain their land, and black communities still fighting to survive the legacies of slavery. Those who have been privileged by colonialism—white people and everyone living in Europe or a European settler state (the US, Canada, Australia)—should support these other struggles politically, culturally, and materially. Because anti-authoritarian rebellions have been limited in scope thus far, and meaningful reparations would have to be global in scale because of the globalization of oppression, there are no examples that fully demonstrate what reparations would look like. However, some small-scale examples show that the willingness to make reparations exists, and that the anarchist principles of mutual aid and direct action can accomplish reparations more effectively than democratic governments—with their refusal to acknowledge the extent of past crimes and their embarrassing half measures. The same goes for revolutionary governments, which typically inherit and cover up oppression within the states they take over—as exemplified by how callously the governments of the USSR and China took their places at the heads of racial empires while claiming to be anti-imperialist.

In the state of Chiapas, in southern Mexico, the Zapatistas rose up in 1994 and won autonomy for dozens of indigenous communities. Named after Mexican peasant revolutionary Zapata and espousing a mix of indigenous, Marxist, and anarchist ideas, the Zapatistas formed an army guided by popular "encuentros," or gatherings, to fight back against neoliberal capitalism and the continuing forms of exploitation and genocide inflicted by the Mexican state. To lift these communities up out of poverty following generations of colonialism, and to help counter the effects of military blockades and harassment, the Zapatistas called for support. Thousands of volunteers and people with technical experience came from around the world to help Zapatista communities build up their infrastructure, and thousands of others continue to support the Zapatistas by sending donations of money and equipment or buying fair-trade goods[105] produced in the autonomous territory. This assistance is given in a spirit of solidarity; most importantly, it is on the Zapatista's own terms. This contrasts

---

105 Goods produced in environmentally friendly ways, by workers who receive a living wage in healthier labor conditions.

starkly with the model of Christian charity, in which the goals of the privileged giver are imposed on the impoverished receiver, who is expected to be grateful.

Peasants in Spain had been oppressed throughout centuries of feudalism. The partial revolution in 1936 enabled them to reclaim the privilege and wealth their oppressors had derived from their labors. Peasant assemblies in liberated villages met to decide how to redistribute territory seized from large landowners, so those who had labored as virtual serfs could finally have access to land. Unlike the farcical Reconciliation Commissions arranged in South Africa, Guatemala, and elsewhere, which protect oppressors from any real consequences and above all preserve the unequal distribution of power and privilege that is the direct result of past oppressions, these assemblies empowered the Spanish peasants to decide for themselves how to recover their dignity and equality. Aside from redistributing land, they also took over pro-fascist churches and luxury villas to be used as community centers, storehouses, schools, and clinics. In five years of state-instituted agrarian reform, Spain's Republican government redistributed only 876,327 hectares of land; in just a few weeks of revolution, the peasants seized 5,692,202 hectares of land for themselves.106 This figure is even more significant considering that this redistribution was opposed by Republicans and Socialists, and could only take place in the part of the country not controlled by the fascists.

How will a common, anti-authoritarian, ecological ethos come about?

IN THE LONG RUN, AN ANARCHIST SOCIETY WILL WORK BEST IF IT develops a culture that values cooperation, autonomy, and environmentally sustainable behaviors. The way a society is structured can encourage or hinder such an ethos, just as our current society rewards competitive, oppressive, and polluting behaviors and discourages anti-authoritarian ones. In a non-coercive society, social

---

106 Sam Dolgoff, *The Anarchist Collectives*, New York: Free Life Editions, 1974, p. 71.

structures cannot force people to live in accordance with anarchist values: people have to want to do so, and personally identify with such values themselves. Fortunately, the act of rebelling against an authoritarian, capitalist culture can itself popularize anti-authoritarian values.

Anarchist anthropologist David Graeber writes of the Tsimihety in Madagascar, who rebelled and removed themselves from the Maroansetra dynasty in the 19th century. Even over a century after this rebellion, the Tsimihety "are marked by resolutely egalitarian social organization and practices," to such an extent that it defines their very identity.[107] The new name the tribe chose for themselves, Tsimihety, means "those who do not cut their hair," in reference to the custom of subjects of the Maroansetra to cut their hair as a sign of submission.

During the Spanish Civil War in 1936, a number of cultural changes took place. In the countryside, politically active youth played a leading role in challenging conservative customs and pushing their villages to adopt an anarchist-communist culture. The position of women in particular began to change rapidly. Women organized the anarcha-feminist group Mujeres Libres to help accomplish the goals of the revolution and ensure that women enjoyed a place at the forefront of the struggle. Women fought on the front, literally, joining the anarchist militias to hold the line against the fascists. Mujeres Libres organized firearms courses, schools, childcare programs, and women-only social groups to help women gain the skills they needed to participate in the struggle as equals. Members of Mujeres Libres argued with their male comrades, emphasizing the importance of women's liberation as a necessary part of any revolutionary struggle. It was not a minor concern to be dealt with after the defeat of fascism.

In the cities of Catalunya, social restrictions on women lessened considerably. For the first time in Spain, women could walk alone on the streets without a chaperon—not to mention that many were walking down the streets wearing militia uniforms and

---

107 David Graeber, *Fragments of an Anarchist Anthropology*, Chicago: Prickly Paradigm Press, 2004, pp. 54–55.

carrying guns. Anarchist women like Lucia Sanchez Saornil wrote about how empowering it was for them to change the culture that had oppressed them. Male observers from George Orwell to Franz Borkenau remarked on the changed conditions of women in Spain.

In the uprising spurred by Argentina's economic collapse in 2001, participation in the popular assemblies helped formerly apolitical people build an anti-authoritarian culture. Another form of popular resistance, the *piquetero* movement, exerted a great influence on the lives and culture of many of the unemployed. The *piquetero*s were unemployed people who masked their faces and set up pickets, shutting down the highways to cut off trade and gain leverage for demands such as food from supermarkets or unemployment subsidies. Aside from these activities, the *piquetero*s also self-organized an anti-capitalist economy, including schools, media groups, clothing give-away shops, bakeries, clinics, and groups to fix up people's houses and build infrastructure such as sewage systems. Many of the *piquetero* groups were affiliated with the Movement of Unemployed Workers (MTD). Their movement had already developed considerably before the December 2001 run on the banks by the middle class, and in many ways they were at the forefront of the struggle in Argentina.

Two Indymedia volunteers who traveled to Argentina from the US and Britain to document the rebellion for English-speaking countries spent time with a group in the Admiralte Brown neighborhood south of Buenos Aires.[108] The members of this particular group, similar to many of the *piquetero*s in the MTD, had been driven to activism only recently, by unemployment. But their motivations were not purely material; for example, they frequently held cultural and educational events. The two Indymedia activists recounted a workshop held in an MTD bakery, in which the collective members discussed the differences between a capitalist bakery and an anti-capitalist one. "We produce for our neighbors… and to teach ourselves to do new things, to learn to produce for

---

108 John Jordan and Jennifer Whitney, *Que Se Vayan Todos: Argentina's Popular Rebellion,* Montreal: Kersplebedeb, 2003, pp. 42–52.

ourselves," explained a woman in her fifties. A young man in an Iron Maiden sweatshirt added, "We produce so that everyone can live better."[109] The same group operated a *Ropero*, a clothing shop, and many other projects as well. It was run by volunteers and depended on donations, even though everyone in the area was poor. Despite these challenges, it opened twice a month to give out free clothes to people who could not afford them. The rest of the time, the volunteers mended old clothes that were dropped off. In the absence of the motives that drive the capitalist system, the people there clearly took pride in their work, showing off to visitors how well restored the clothes were despite the scarcity of materials.

The shared ideal among the *piquetero*s included a firm commitment to non-hierarchical forms of organization and participation by all members, young and old, in their discussions and activities. Women were often the first to go to the picket lines, and came to hold considerable power within the *piquetero* movement. Within these autonomous organizations, many women gained the opportunity to participate in large-scale decision-making or take on other male-dominated roles for the first time in their lives. At the particular bakery holding the workshop described above, a young woman was in charge of security, another traditionally male role.

Throughout the 2006 rebellion in Oaxaca, Mexico, as well as before and after, indigenous culture was a wellspring of resistance. However much they exemplified cooperative, anti-authoritarian, and ecologically sustainable behaviors before colonialism, indigenous peoples in the Oaxacan resistance came to cherish and emphasize the parts of their culture that contrasted with the system that values property over life, encourages competition and domination, and exploits the environment into extinction. Their ability to practice an anti-authoritarian and ecological culture—working together in a spirit of solidarity and nourishing themselves on the small amount of land they had—increased the potency of their resistance, and thus their very chances for survival. Thus, resistance to capitalism and the state is both a means of protecting indigenous cultures and a crucible that forges a

109 Ditto, pp. 43–44.

stronger anti-authoritarian ethos. Many of the people who participated in the rebellion were not themselves indigenous, but they were influenced and inspired by indigenous culture. Thus, the act of rebellion itself allowed people to choose social values and shape their own identities.

Before the rebellion, the impoverished state of Oaxaca sold its indigenous culture as a commodity to entice tourists and bring in business. The Guelaguetza, an important gathering in native cultures, had become a state-sponsored tourist attraction. But during the rebellion in 2006, the state and tourism were pushed to the margins, and in July the social movements organized a People's Guelaguetza—not to sell to the tourists, but to enjoy for themselves. After successfully blocking the commercial event set up for the tourists, hundreds of students from Oaxaca City and people from villages across the state began organizing their own event. They made costumes and practiced dances and songs from all seven regions of Oaxaca. In the end the People's Guelaguetza was a huge success. Everyone attended for free and the venue was packed. There were more traditional dances than there had ever been in the commerical Guelaguetzas. While the event had previously been performed for money, most of which was pocketed by the sponsors and government, it became a day of sharing, as it had been traditionally. At the heart of an anti-capitalist, largely indigenous movement was a festival, a celebration of the values that hold the movement together, and a revival of indigenous cultures that were being wiped out or pared down to a marketable exoticism.

While the Guelaguetza was reclaimed as a part of indigenous culture in support of an anti-capitalist rebellion and the liberatory society it sought to create, another traditional celebration was modified to serve the movement. In 2006 the Day of the Dead, a Mexican holiday that syncretizes indigenous spirituality with Catholic influences, coincided with a violent government assault upon the movement. Just before the 1st of November, police forces and paramilitaries killed about a dozen people, so the dead were fresh in everybody's minds. Graffiti artists had long played an important role in the movement in Oaxaca, covering the walls with messages well before the people had seized radio stations to give themselves a voice. When the Day of the Dead and the heavy government repression coincided in November, these artists took the lead in adapting the holiday to commemorate the dead and honor the struggle. They covered the streets with the traditional *tapetes*—colorful murals made from sand, chalk, and flowers—but this time the *tapetes* contained messages of resistance and hope, or portrayed the names and faces of all the people killed. People also made skeleton sculptures and altars for each person murdered by police and paramilitaries. One graffiti artist, Yescka, described it:

> This year on Day of the Dead, the traditional festivities took on new meaning. The intimidating presence of the Federal Police troops filled the air—an atmosphere of sadness and chaos hung over the city. But we managed to overcome our fear and our loss. People wanted to carry on with the traditions, not only for their ancestors, but also for all those fallen in the movement in recent months.
>
> Although it sounds a bit contradictory, Day of the Dead is when there is the most life in Oaxaca. There are carnivals, and people dress up in different costumes, such as devils or skeletons full of colorful feathers. They parade through the streets dancing or creating theatrical performances of comical daily happenings—this year with a socio-political twist.
>
> We didn't let the Federal Police forces standing guard stop our celebrating or our mourning. The whole tourist pathway in the center of the city, Macedonio Alcalá, was full of life. Protest music was playing and people danced and watched the creation of our famous sand murals, called *tapetes*. We dedicated them to all the people killed in the movement. Anyone who wanted to could join in to add to the mosaics. The mixed colors expressed our mixed feelings of repression and freedom; joy and sadness; hatred and love. The artwork and the chants permeating the street created an unforgettable scene that ultimately transformed our sadness into joy.[110]

While artwork and traditional festivals played a role in the

110   Diana Denham and C.A.S.A. Collective (eds.), *Teaching Rebellion:*

development of a liberating culture, the struggle itself, specifically the barricades, provided a meeting point where alienation was shed and neighbors built new relationships. One woman described her experience:

> You found all kinds of people at the barricades. A lot of people tell us they met at the barricades. Even though they were neighbors, they didn't know each other before. They'll even say, "I didn't ever talk to my neighbor before because I didn't think I liked him, but now that we're at the barricade together, he's a *compañero.*"
>
> So the barricades weren't just traffic barriers, but became spaces where neighbors could chat and communities could meet. Barricades became a way that communities empowered themselves.[111]

Throughout Europe, dozens of autonomous villages have built a life outside capitalism. Especially in Italy, France, and Spain, these villages exist outside regular state control and with little influence from the logic of the market. Sometimes buying cheap land, often squatting abandoned villages, these new autonomous communities create the infrastructure for a libertarian, communal life and the culture that goes with it. These new cultures replace the nuclear family with a much broader, more inclusive and flexible family united by affinity and consensual love rather than bloodlines and proprietary love; they destroy the division of labor by gender, weaken age segregation and hierarchy, and create communal and ecological values and relationships.

A particularly remarkable network of autonomous villages can be found in the mountains around Itoiz, in Navarra, part of the Basque country. The oldest of these, Lakabe, has been occupied for twenty-eight years as of this writing, and is home to about thirty people. A project of love, Lakabe challenges and changes the traditional aesthetic of rural poverty. The floors and walkways

Stories from the Grassroots Mobilization in Oaxaca, Oakland: PM Press, 2008, interview with Yescka.
111 Ditto, interview with Leyla.

are beautiful mosaics of stone and tile, and the newest house to be built there could pass for the luxury retreat of a millionaire—except that it was built by the people who live there, and designed in harmony with the environment, to catch the sun and keep out the cold. Lakabe houses a communal bakery and a communal dining room, which on a normal day hosts delicious feasts that the whole village eats together.

Another of the villages around Itoiz, Aritzkuren, exemplifies a certain aesthetic that represents another idea of history. Thirteen years ago, a handful of people occupied the village, which had been abandoned for over fifty years before that. Since then, they have constructed all their dwellings within the ruins of the old hamlet. Half of Aritzkuren is still ruins, slowly decomposing into forest on a mountainside an hour's drive from the nearest paved road. The ruins are a reminder of the origin and foundation of the living parts of the village, and they serve as storage spaces for building materials that will be used to renovate the rest of it. The new sense of history that lives amidst these piled stones is neither linear nor amnesiac, but organic—in that the past is the shell of the present and compost of the future. It is also post-capitalist, suggesting a return to the land and the creation of a new society in the ruins of the old.

Uli, another of the abandoned and reoccupied villages, disbanded after more than a decade of autonomous existence; but the success rate of all the villages together is encouraging, with five out of six still going strong. The "failure" of Uli demonstrates another advantage of anarchist organizing: a collective can dissolve itself rather than remaining stuck in a mistake forever or suppressing individual needs to perpetuate an artificial collectivity. These villages in their prior incarnations, a century earlier, were only dissolved by the economic catastrophe of industrializing capitalism. Otherwise, their members were held fast by a conservative kinship system rigidly enforced by the church.

At Aritzkuren as at other autonomous villages throughout the world, life is both laborious and relaxed. The residents must build all their infrastructure themselves and create most of the things they need with their own hands, so there is plenty of work to do.

People get up in the morning and work on their own projects, or else everyone comes together for a collective effort decided on at a previous meeting. Following a huge lunch which one person cooks for everyone on a rotating basis, people have the whole afternoon to relax, read, go into town, work in the garden, or fix up a building. Some days, nobody works at all; if one person decides to skip a day, there are no recriminations, because there are meetings at which to make sure responsibilities are evenly distributed. In this context, characterized by a close connection to nature, inviolable individual freedom mixed with a collective social life, and the blurring of work and pleasure, the people of Aritzkuren have created not only a new lifestyle, but an ethos compatible with living in an anarchist society.

The school they are building at Aritzkuren is a powerful symbol of this. A number of children live at Aritzkuren and the other villages. Their environment already provides a wealth of learning opportunities, but there is much desire for a formal educational setting and a chance to employ alternative teaching methods in a project that can be accessible to children from the entire region.

As the school indicates, the autonomous villages violate the stereotype of the hippy commune as an escapist attempt to create a utopia in microcosm rather than change the existing world. Despite their physical isolation, these villages are very much involved in the outside world and in social movements struggling to change it. The residents share their experiences in creating sustainable collectives with other anarchist and autonomous collectives throughout the country. Many people divide each year between the village and the city, balancing a more utopian existence with participation in ongoing struggles. The villages also serve as a refuge for activists taking a break from stressful city life. Many of the villages carry on projects that keep them involved in social struggles; for example, one autonomous village in Italy provides a peaceful setting for a group that translates radical texts. Likewise, the villages around Itoiz have been a major part of the twenty-year-running resistance to the hydroelectric dam there.

For about ten years, starting with the occupation of Rala, near Aritzkuren, the autonomous villages around Itoiz have created a network, sharing tools, materials, expertise, food, seeds, and other resources. They meet periodically to discuss mutual aid and common projects; residents of one village will drop by another to eat lunch, talk, and, perhaps, deliver a dozen extra raspberry plants. They also participate in annual gatherings that bring together autonomous communities from all over Spain to discuss the process of building sustainable collectives. At these, each group presents a problem it has been unable to resolve, such as sharing responsibilities or putting consensus decisions into practice. Then they each offer to mediate while another collective discusses their problem—preferably a problem the mediating group has experience resolving.

The Itoiz villages are remarkable, but not unique. To the east, in the Pyrenees of Aragon, the mountains of La Solana contain nearly twenty abandoned villages. As of this writing, seven of these villages have been reoccupied. The network between them is still in an informal stage, and many of the villages are only inhabited by a few people at an early point in the process of renovating them; but more people are moving there every year, and before long it could be a larger constellation of rural occupations than Itoiz. Many in these villages maintain strong connections to the squatters' movement in Barcelona, and there is an open invitation for people to visit, help out, or even move there.

Under certain circumstances, a community can also gain the autonomy it needs to build a new form of living by buying land, rather than occupying it; however though it may be more secure this method creates added pressures to produce and make money in order to survive, but these pressures are not fatal. Longo Maï is a network of cooperatives and autonomous villages that started in Basel, Switzerland, in 1972. The name is Provençal for "long may it last," and so far they have lived up to their eponym. The first Longo Maï cooperative are the farms Le Pigeonnier, Grange neuve, and St. Hippolyte, located near the village Limans in Provence. Here 80 adults and many children live on 300 hectares of land, where they practice agriculture, gardening, and shepherding. They keep 400 sheep, poultry, rabbits, bees, and draft horses; they run a garage, a metal workshop, a carpentry workshop, and a textile studio. The alternative station Radio Zinzine has been broadcasting from the cooperative for 25 years, as of 2007. Hundreds of youth pass through and help out at the cooperative, learning new skills and often gaining their first contact with communal living or non-industrial agriculture and crafting.

Since 1976 Longo Maï has been running a cooperative spinning-mill at Chantemerle, in the French Alps. Using natural dyes and the wool from 10,000 sheep, mostly local, they make sweaters, shirts, sheets, and cloth for direct sale. The cooperative established the union ATELIER, a network of stock-breeders and wool-workers. The mill produces its own electricity with smallscale hydropower.

Also in France, near Arles, the cooperative Mas de Granier sits on 20 hectares of land. They grow fields of hay and olive trees, on good years producing enough olive oil to provide for other Longo Maï cooperatives as well as themselves. Three hectares are devoted to organic vegetables, delivered weekly to subscribers in the broader community. Some of the vegetables are canned as preserves in the cooperative's own factory. They also grow grain for bread, pasta, and animal feed.

In the Transkarpaty region of Ukraine, Zeleniy Hai, a small Longo Maï group, started up after the fall of the Soviet Union. Here they have created a language school, a carpentry workshop, a cattle ranch, and a dairy factory. They also have a traditional music group. The Longo Maï network used their resources to help form a cooperative in Costa Rica in 1978 that provided land to 400 landless peasants fleeing the civil war in Nicaragua, allowing them to create a new community and provide for themselves. There are also Longo Maï cooperatives in Germany, Austria, and Switzerland, producing wine, building buildings with local, ecological materials, running schools, and more. In the city of Basel they maintain an office building that serves as a coordinating point, an information hub, and a visitors' center.

The call-out for the cooperative network, drafted in Basel in 1972, reads in part:

> What do you expect from us? That we, in order not to be excluded, submit to the injustice and the insane compulsions of this world, without hope or expectations?
>
> We refuse to continue this unwinnable battle. We refuse to play a game that has already been lost, a game whose only outcome is our criminalization. This industrial society goes doubtlessly to its own downfall and we don't want to participate.
>
> We prefer to seek a way to build our own lives, to create our own spaces, something for which there is no place within this cynical, capitalist world. We can find enough space in the economically and socially depressed areas, where the youth depart in growing numbers, and only those stay behind who have no other choice.[112]

As capitalist agriculture becomes increasingly incapable of feeding the world in the wake of catastrophes related to climate and pollution, it seems almost inevitable that a large number of people must move back to the land to create sustainable and localized forms of agriculture. At the same time, city dwellers need to cultivate consciousness of where their food and water come from, and one way they can do this is by visiting and helping out in the villages.

A revolution that is many revolutions

MANY PEOPLE THINK THAT REVOLUTIONS ALWAYS FOLLOW A TRAGIC course from hope to betrayal. The ultimate result of revolutions in Russia, China, Algeria, Cuba, Vietnam, and elsewhere was the establishment of new authoritarian regimes—some worse than their predecessors, others hardly different. But the major revolutions of the 20th century were carried out by authoritarians who intended to create new governments, not abolish them. It is now obvious, if it wasn't before, that governments always uphold oppressive social orders.

But history is full of evidence that people can overthrow their oppressors without replacing them. To do so, they need reference to an egalitarian culture, or explicitly anti-authoritarian aims,

---

112 "Longo Maï," *Buiten de Orde,* Summer 2008, p. 38. My own translation.

structures, and means, and an egalitarian ethos. A revolutionary movement must reject all possible governments and reforms, so as not to be recuperated like many of the rebels in Kabylia and Albania. It must organize in flexible and horizontal ways, ensuring that power is not permanently delegated to leaders or anchored down in a formal organization, as happened with the CNT in Spain. Finally, it must take into account that all insurrections involve diverse strategies and participants. This multitude will benefit from communication and coordination, but it should not be homogenized or controlled from a central point. Such standardization and centralization are neither desirable nor necessary; decentralized struggles such as those waged by the Lakota or the squatters in Berlin and Hamburg have proven capable of defeating the slower-moving forces of the state.

A new ethos can come about in the process of resisting, as we find common cause with strangers and discover our own powers. It can also be nourished by the environments we build for ourselves. A truly liberating ethos is not just a new set of values, but a new approach to the relationship between the individual and her culture; it requires that people shift from being passive recipients of culture to participants in its creation and reinterpretation. In this sense, the revolutionary struggle against hierarchy never ends, but continues from one generation to the next.

To be successful, revolution must occur on many fronts at once. It won't work to abolish capitalism while leaving the state or patriarchy untouched. A successful revolution must be composed of many revolutions, accomplished by different people using different strategies, respecting each another's autonomy and building solidarity. This will not happen overnight, but in the course of a series of conflicts that build on each other.

Unsuccessful revolutions are not failures unless people give up hope. In their book on the popular rebellion in Argentina, two UK activists close with the words of a *piquetero* from Solano:

> I don't think December 2001 was a lost opportunity for revolution nor was it a failed revolution. It was and is part of the ongoing revolutionary process here. We have learnt

many lessons about collective organizing and strength, and the barriers to self-management. For many people it opened their eyes to what we can do together, and that taking control of our lives and acting collectively whether it's as part of a piquete, a communal bakery or an afterschool club dramatically improves the quality of our lives. If the struggle stays autonomous and with the people the next uprising will have strong foundations to build upon...[113]

Recommended Reading:

- Dee Brown, *Bury My Heart at Wounded Knee,* New York: Holt, Rinehart & Winston, 1970.
- David Dixon, *Never Come to Peace Again: Pontiac's Uprising and the Fate of the British Empire in North America.* Norman: University of Oklahoma Press, 2005.
- Diana Denham and C.A.S.A. Collective (eds.), *Teaching Rebellion: Stories from the Grassroots Mobilization in Oaxaca,* Oakland: PM Press, 2008.
- Alexandre Skirda, *Nestor Makhno, Anarchy's Cossack: The Struggle for Free Soviets in the Ukraine 1917–1921,* London: AK Press, 2005.
- Alfredo Bonanno, *From Riot to Insurrection: analysis for an anarchist perspective against post industrial capitalism.* London: Elephant Editions, 1988.
- John Jordan and Jennifer Whitney, *Que Se Vayan Todos: Argentina's Popular Rebellion,* Montreal: Kersplebedeb, 2003.
- Jaime Semprun, *Apologie pour l'Insurrection Algérienne,* Paris: Editions de L'Encyclopédie des Nuisances, 2001.[114]
- George Orwell, *Homage to Catalonia,* London: Martin

---

[113] Natasha Gordon and Paul Chatterton, *Taking Back Control: A Journey through Argentina's Popular Uprising,* Leeds (UK): University of Leeds, 2004.

[114] For those who cannot read French or Spanish, in 2004 Firestarter Press put out a good zine about this insurrection, called *"You Cannot Kill Us, We Are Already Dead." Algeria's Ongoing Popular Uprising.*

Secker & Warburg Ltd., 1938.
- George Katsiaficas, *The Subversion of Politics: European Autonomous Social Movements and the Decolonization of Everyday Life*. Oakland: AK Press, 2006.
- A.G. Grauwacke, *Autonome in Bewegung*, Berlin: Assoziation A, 2008.
- Leanne Simpson, ed. *Lighting the Eighth Fire: The Liberation, Resurgence, and Protection of Indigenous Nations,* Winnipeg: Arbeiter Ring, 2008.
- A.G. Schwarz, Tasos Sagris, and Void Network, eds. *We Are an Image from the Future: The Greek Revolts of December 2008*. Oakland: AK Press, 2010.

7. NEIGHBORING SOCIETIES

BECAUSE ANARCHISM OPPOSES DOMINATION AND ENFORCED conformity, an anarchist revolution would not create a completely anarchist world. Anarchist societies would need to find peaceful ways of coexisting with neighboring societies, defending themselves from authoritarian neighbors, and supporting liberation in societies with oppressive internal dynamics.

Could an anarchist society defend itself from an authoritarian neighbor?

SOME PEOPLE WORRY THAT AN ANARCHIST REVOLUTION WOULD BE a pointless venture because an anti-authoritarian society would quickly be conquered by an authoritarian neighbor. Of course, an anarchist revolution is not a strictly national affair limiting itself to the borders of the government it is overthrowing. The idea is not to create a small pocket of freedom where we can hide or retire, but to abolish systems of slavery and domination on a worldwide scale. Because some areas might liberate themselves before others, the question remains whether an anarchist society could be safe from an authoritarian neighbor.

Actually, the answer is no. States and capitalism are imperialist by nature, and they will always try to conquer neighbors and universalize their rule: the elite class of hierarchical societies are already at war with their own lower classes, and they extend this logic to their relations with the rest of the world, which becomes nothing but a pool of resources for them to exploit so as to win more advantages in their unending war. Anarchist societies, meanwhile, encourage revolution in authoritarian societies both through intentional solidarity with rebels in those societies and by providing a subversive example of freedom, showing the subjects of the state that they do not need to live in fear and submission. So in fact, neither of these societies would be safe from the other. But an anarchist society would by no means be defenseless.

The anarchist society of southern Ukraine at the end of the First World War was a major threat to the German and Austrian empires, the White Army, the short-lived nationalist Ukrainian state, and the Soviet Union. The volunteer militias of the Makhnovists inspired major desertions from the ranks of the authoritarian Red Army, forced out the Austro-Germans and the nationalists who tried to lay claim to their lands, and aided the defeat of the White Army. This is especially remarkable considering that they were armed almost entirely with weapons and ammunition seized from the enemy. Coordinating forces of up to tens of thousands, the anarchists regularly fought on multiple fronts and shifted between frontal and guerrilla warfare with a fluidity conventional armies are incapable of. Despite always being vastly outnumbered, they defended their land for several years. At two decisive battles, Peregonovka and the Perekop isthmus, the Makhnovist militias smashed the larger White Army, which was supplied by Western governments.

> Extraordinary mobility and a bag of clever tricks constituted Makhno's chief tactical devices. Traveling on horseback and in light peasant carts (*tatchanki*) on which machine guns were mounted, his men [ed: and women] moved

> swiftly back and forth across the open steppe between the Dnieper and the Sea of Azov, swelling into a small army as they went, and inspiring terror in the hearts of their adversaries. Hitherto independent guerrilla bands accepted Makhno's command and rallied behind his black banner. Villagers willingly provided food and fresh horses, enabling the *Makhnovtsy* to travel 40 or 50 miles a day with little difficulty. They would turn up quite suddenly where least expected, attack the gentry and military garrisons, then vanish as quickly as they had come[...] When cornered, the *Makhnovtsy* would bury their weapons, make their way singly back to their villages, and take up work in the fields, awaiting the next signal to unearth a new cache of arms and spring up again in an unexpected quarter. Makhno's insurgents, in the words of Victor Serge, revealed "a truly epic capacity for organization and combat."[115]

After their supposed allies, the Bolsheviks, endeavored to impose bureaucratic control over southern Ukraine while the Makhnovists were fighting at the front, they successfully waged guerrilla warfare against the massive Red Army for two years, aided by popular support. The ultimate defeat of the Ukrainian anarchists demonstrates the need for greater international solidarity. If other uprisings against the Bolsheviks had been better coordinated, they might not have been able to concentrate so much of their might on smashing the anarchists in Ukraine—likewise if libertarian socialists in other countries had spread news of the Bolshevik repression rather than all rallying behind Lenin. An anti-authoritarian rebellion in one corner of the world might even be able to defend itself from the government it is overthrowing and several neighboring governments, but not from all the governments of the entire world. Global repression must be met with global resistance. Fortunately, as capital globalizes, popular networks do as well; our ability to form worldwide movements and act quickly in solidarity with a struggle on the other side of the planet is greater than ever before.

115 Paul Avrich, *The Russian Anarchists*, Oakland: AK Press, p. 212–213.

In parts of pre-colonial Africa, anarchic societies were able to exist side-by-side with "predatory states" for centuries because the terrain and available technology favored "defensive warfare with bows and arrows—the 'democratic' weapon of warfare since anyone can have one."[116] The Seminole tribe of Florida provide an inspiring example of a stateless, anarchistic society persisting despite the best efforts of an extremely powerful, technologically advanced neighboring state with a population thousands of times larger. The Seminole, whose name originally means "runaways," formed out of several indigenous nations, principally the Western Creek, fleeing genocide through the southeastern part of what white people had decided was the United States. The Seminole also included a significant number of escaped African slaves and even a few white Europeans who had run away from the oppressive society of the United States.

The inclusivity of the Seminole demonstrates how indigenous Americans viewed tribe and nation as matters of voluntary association and acceptance within a community, rather than the restrictive ethnic/hereditary categories they are assumed to be in Western civilization. The Seminole call themselves the "unconquered people" because they never signed a peace treaty with the colonizers. They survived a series of wars waged against them by the United States and managed to kill 1,500 US soldiers and an unknown number of militiamen. During the Second Seminole War, from 1835 to 1842, the one thousand Seminole warriors in the Everglades employed guerrilla tactics to devastating effect, even though they faced 9,000 professional, well-equipped soldiers. The war cost the US government $20 million, a huge sum at the time. By the end of the war, the US government had managed to force most of the Seminole into exile in Oklahoma, but gave up on conquering the remaining group, who never surrendered and continued to live free of government control for decades.

The Mapuche are a large indigenous group living on land now occupied by the states of Chile and Argentina. Traditionally they

---

116   Harold Barclay, *People Without Government: An Anthropology of Anarchy*, London: Kahn and Averill, 1982, p. 57.

made decisions with consensus and a minimum of hierarchy. Lacking any kind of state apparatus did not prevent them from defending themselves. Before the European invasion, they successfully defended themselves from their hierarchical neighbors, the Inca, who were, by European standards, far more advanced. During the Spanish conquest, the Inca fell quickly, but the Mapuche lands became known as the "Spanish Cemetery." After the Mapuche defeated the conquistadors in a series of wars spanning a hundred years, Spain signed the treaty of Killin, admitting its failure to conquer the Mapuche and recognizing them as a sovereign nation. Mapuche sovereignty was further recognized in 28 subsequent treaties.

In their wars against the Spanish, Mapuche groups unified under elected war leaders (*Taqui* or "axe carriers"). Unlike troops in a military, the groups maintained their autonomy and fought freely rather than under coercion. This lack of hierarchy and coercion proved to be a military advantage for the Mapuche. Throughout the Americas, hierarchical indigenous groups like the Inca and Aztecs were defeated quickly by the invaders, as they often surrendered after the loss of the leader or capital. They were also weakened by revenge attacks from the enemies they had made by conquering neighboring groups before the Europeans arrived. The anarchistic indigenous groups were often the ones most capable of waging guerrilla warfare against the occupiers.

From 1860–65, the Mapuche were invaded and "pacified" by the Chilean and Argentinian states, a genocide that claimed hundreds of thousands of lives. The invaders began a process of suppressing the Mapuche language and Christianizing the conquered people. But Mapuche resistance continues, and thanks to this a number of Mapuche communities still enjoy a relative degree of autonomy. Their resistance remains a threat to the security of the Chilean state; as of this writing, several Mapuche are imprisoned under Pinochet-era anti-terrorism laws for attacks against forestry plantations and copper mines that were destroying the land.

Fierce indigenous resistance was not the only major barrier to colonialism. As resources were forcibly transferred from the Americas to Europe, a phenomenon arose from the long and proud tradition of banditry to strike fear into the hearts of merchants trafficking gold and slaves. Writers from Daniel Defoe to Peter Lamborn Wilson have portrayed piracy as a struggle against Christendom, capitalism and its predecessor mercantilism, and government. Pirate havens were a constant threat to established order—disruptors of globalized plunder under colonialism, instigators of slave rebellions, refuges where lower class runaways could retreat and join in the war against their former masters. The pirate republic of Salé, near what is now the capital of Morocco, pioneered forms of representative democracy a century before the French revolution. In the Caribbean, many of the runaways joined the remnants of indigenous societies and adopted their egalitarian structures. This pirate social class also contained many proto-anarchist social revolutionaries, such as Levellers, Diggers and Ranters, banished to English penal colonies in the New World. Many pirate captains were elected and immediately recallable.

> The authorities were often shocked by their libertarian tendencies; the Dutch Governor of Mauritius met a pirate crew and commented: "Every man had as much say as the captain and each man carried his own weapons in his blanket." This was profoundly threatening to the order of European society, where firearms were restricted to the upper classes, and provided a stark contrast to merchant ships where anything that could be used as a weapon was kept under lock and key, and to the navy where the primary purpose of the marines stationed on naval vessels was to keep the sailors in their place.[117]

Pirate societies cultivated greater gender equality as well, and a number of pirate captains were women. Many pirates thought of themselves as Robin Hoods, and few considered themselves subjects of any state. While numerous other pirates engaged in mercantilism, selling their stolen goods to the highest bidders, or even participated in the slave trade, another current in piracy constituted an early force for abolitionism, aiding slave rebellions and

117 "Pirate Utopias," *Do or Die*, No. 8, 1999, pp. 63–78.

involving many ex-slaves. Authorities in North American colonies like Virginia were concerned about connections between piracy and slave insurrections. Fear of slaves running away to join the pirates and rob their former masters, and of racially mixed uprisings, encouraged the development of laws in the colonies to punish racial mixing. These were some of the first juridical attempts to institutionalize segregation and generalize racism among the white lower class.

Throughout the Caribbean and other parts of the world, liberated pirate enclaves thrived for years, though they are shrouded in mystery. The fact that these pirate societies were a widespread and long-lasting problem for the imperial powers, and that many of them were shockingly libertarian, is documented, but other information is lacking, given that they existed at war with the writers of history. It is telling that the best described pirate utopia, Libertalia or alternately Libertatia, is heavily disputed. Many parts of its history are generally recognized to be fictitious, but some sources allege that Libertatia in its entirety never existed while others maintain that its legendary founder, Captain James Misson, was just a literary invention but the pirate settlement itself did exist.

The expanding navies of Great Britain and the United States finally crushed piracy in the 19th century, but in the 17th and 18th centuries pirates constituted a powerful stateless society that waged war against imperialism and government, and enabled thousands of people to liberate themselves at a time when the oppressiveness of Western civilization surpassed all the previous barbarities in world history.

What will we do about societies that remain patriarchal or racist?

ANARCHISM EMPHASIZES AUTONOMY AND LOCAL ACTION, BUT IT IS not an isolationist or provincial tendency. Anarchist movements have always concerned themselves with global issues and distant struggles. While governments also profess concern about problems in other parts of the world, anarchism is distinguished by its refusal to impose solutions. Statist propaganda claims we need world government to liberate the peoples of oppressive societies, even as the UN, NATO, the US, and other institutions continue to foster oppression and engage in warfare to uphold the hierachical world order.[118]

Anarchist approaches are both local and global, premised on autonomy and solidarity. If a neighboring society were patriarchal or racist or oppressive in some other way, an anarchist culture would offer a range of possible responses beyond apathy and "liberation" by force. In all oppressive societies, one can find people fighting for their own freedom. It is much more realistic and effective to support such people, letting them lead their own struggles, rather than trying to deliver liberation the way a missionary delivers "good news."

When Emma Goldman, Alexander Berkman, Mollie Steimer, and other anarchists were deported from the US to Russia and discovered the oppressive state created by the Bolsheviks, they spread information internationally to encourage protests against the Bolsheviks and support for the many anarchist and other political prisoners. They worked with the Anarchist Black Cross, a political prisoner support organization with chapters internationally, that supported political prisoners in Russia and elsewhere. On several occasions, the international support and solidarity they organized pressured Lenin to temporarily suspend the repression he was levying against his political opponents and to release political prisoners.

The Anarchist Black Cross, originally called the Anarchist Red Cross, formed in Russia during the failed revolution of 1905 to aid those persecuted in the government reaction. In 1907, international chapters formed in London and New York. The international

---

118 To name just one example, "humanitarian" UN missions have been caught repeatedly setting up sex trafficking rings in the countries where they are stationed for peacekeeping. "But the problem goes beyond Kosovo and sex trafficking. Wherever the UN has established operations in recent years, various violations of women seem to follow." Michael J. Jordan, "Sex Charges haunt UN forces," *Christian Science Monitor*, 26 November 2004. What the mainstream press cannot go so far as to admit is that this reality is universal to militaries, whether they wear blue helmets or not.

solidarity they mobilized helped keep anarchist prisoners alive, and enabled others to escape. The result was that in 1917, the revolutionary movement in Russia was stronger, enjoyed more international connections, and was better equipped to overthrow the tsarist government.

The Revolutionary Association of Women of Afghanistan, founded in Kabul in 1977, has struggled for women's liberation against the violence of Islamic fundamentalists as well as against occupation by regimes like the USSR, which was responsible for assassinating the founder of RAWA in Pakistan in 1987. After fighting the Soviet occupation and the Taliban, they went on to oppose the Northern Alliance that came into power with US backing. Through a series of desperate situations, they remained steadfast in their conviction that liberation can only come from within. Even amidst the oppression of the Taliban, they opposed the US invasion in 2001, arguing that if Westerners really wanted to help liberate Afghanistan they had to support Afghan groups fighting to liberate themselves. Their predictions have proved sound, as Afghan women faced many of the same oppressions under the US occupation as they did under the Taliban. According to RAWA: "RAWA believes that freedom and democracy can't be donated; it is the duty of the people of a country to fight and achieve these values."[119]

What will prevent constant warfare and feuding?

IN STATIST SOCIETY, THE CRISIS OF WARFARE HAS LED TO A PURSUIT of unified government at higher and higher levels, ultimately towards world government. This effort has clearly been unsuccessful—after all, war is the health of the state—but success within this model is not even desirable. It is global occupation, not global peace, that a world government strives for. To take the example of Palestine, because it is here that the technologies and methods of control are developed that are later adopted by the US military and governments around the world, the occupation only flares

---

119 "About RAWA," http://www.rawa.org/rawa.html Viewed June 22, 2007

up into visible war once every few years, but the occupiers are constantly fighting an invisible war to preserve and extend their control, with the use of the media, the schools, the criminal justice system, traffic systems, advertisements, minute policies, surveillance, and covert operations. It is only when the Palestinians fight back and a war that cannot be ignored breaks out that the United Nations and the humanitarian organizations jump into action, not to right past and ongoing wrongs but to return to the prior illusion of peace and ensure that these wrongs can never be questioned. Though with less intensity, the same invisible war is fought against indigenous nations, immigrants, ethnic minorities, poor people, workers; everyone who has been colonized or exploited.

In the stateless, small-scale societies of the past, warfare was common but it was not universal, and in many of its manifestations it was not particularly bloody. Some stateless societies never participated in warfare. Peace is a choice, and they chose it by valuing cooperative reconciliation of conflicts and nurturing behaviors. Other stateless societies that did engage in warfare often practiced a harmless, ritualized variety thereof. In some cases, the line between sporting event and warfare is unclear. As described in some anthropological accounts, teams or war parties from two different communities would meet at a prearranged place to fight. The purpose was not to annihilate the other side, or even necessarily to kill anyone. Someone on one side would throw a spear or shoot an arrow, and they would all watch to see if it hit anyone before throwing the next spear. They would often go home after one person got hurt, or even earlier.[120] In warfare as practiced by the Lakota and other Plains Indians of North America, it was more highly valued to touch an enemy with a stick—"counting coup"—than to kill him. Other forms of war were simply raiding—vandalizing or stealing from neighboring communities and often trying to get away before a fight broke out. If these sorts of chaotic fighting were the warfare of an anarchist society, how preferable that would be to the cold, mechanical bloodbaths of the state!

---

[120] See the citation of van der Dennen and Rappaport in Chapter 1.

But societies that do not want to war with their neighbors can structure themselves to prevent it. Not having borders is an important first step. Often we can arrive at the truth by simply reversing the rationalizations of the state, and the line about borders keeping us safe can easily be decoded: borders endanger us. If there is a social conflict, violence is much more likely to break out if there is an "us" and a "them." Clear social divisions and borders prevent reconciliation and mutual understanding and encourage competition and polarization.

Anarchist anthropologist Harold Barclay describes some societies in which each individual is connected to others through multiple, overlapping networks, arising from kinship, marriage, clan affiliations, and so on:

> We do have examples of anarchic polities among peoples[…] numbering in the hundreds of thousands and with fairly dense populations, often over 100 people to the square mile. Such social orders may be achieved through a segmentary lineage system which as we have seen already has certain parallels to the anarchist notion of federalism. Or, as among the Tonga and some East African pastoralists, large populations may be integrated by a more complex arrangement which affiliates the individual with a number of cross cutting and bisecting groups so as to extend his or her social ties over a wide area. In other words, individuals and groups constitute a multitude of interconnected loci, which produces the integration of a large social entity, but without any actual centralised co-ordination.[121]

In addition to this self-balancing property of cooperative societies, some stateless peoples have developed other mechanisms to prevent feuds. The Mardu aborigines of western Australia traditionally lived in small bands, but these periodically came together to hold mass meetings, where disputes between individuals or between different groups would be resolved under the eyes of the whole

---

121 Harold Barclay, *People Without Government: An Anthropology of Anarchy*, London: Kahn and Averill, 1982, p. 122.

society. In this way, protracted, unaccountable feuding could be avoided, and everyone was on hand to help resolve the conflict. The Konkomba and the Nuer of Africa recognized bilateral kinship relationships and overlapping economic relationships. Insofar as everyone was related to everyone else, there was no clear axis of conflict that might support warfare. A commonly upheld cultural taboo against feuding also encouraged people to resolve disputes peacefully. Anthropologist E.E. Evans Pritchard described Nuer society as "ordered anarchy."

The anarchist movement today continues to fight against the borders that divide a capitalist world. The anti-authoritarian No Border Network, formed in western Europe in 1999, has since become active throughout Europe and in Turkey, North America, and Australia. No Border efforts include support for illegal immigrants, education about the racism encouraged by government immigration policies, protests against government officials, actions against airlines to halt deportations, and No Border camps spanning the borders of two countries. In the course of the campaign, participants have forcibly opened border crossings between Spain and Morocco, broken into a children's detention facility in the Netherlands to bring aid and open up communication, partially destroyed a detention facility and sabotaged the companies involved in deportations in Italy, shut down a detention facility in Greece, and freed dozens of immigrants from a detention facility in Australia. No Border camps bring people from many countries together to develop strategies and carry out actions. They often take place on the periphery of expanding "First World" zones—for example, in Ukraine, between Greece and Bulgaria, or between the US and Mexico. Common slogans at No Borders protests include: "No Border, No Nation, Stop Deportations!" "Freedom of Movement, Freedom of Residence: Right to Come, Right to Go, Right to Stay!"

Anarchist societies encourage the free creation of overlapping networks between neighbors, communities, and societies. These networks may include material exchange, cultural communication, friendships, family relationships, and solidarity. There is no clear delineation of where one society ends and another begins, or what the sides would be in a conflict. When there is a feud, the feuding parties are likely to have many social relationships in common, and many third parties will be caught in the middle. In a culture that emphasizes competition and conquest, they may still take sides and offset the possibility of reconciliation. But if their culture values cooperation, consensus, and social connectedness, and their economic relationships reinforce these values, they are more likely to encourage mediation and peace between the feuding parties. They might do so out of a personal desire for peace, because of a concern for the well-being of the people involved in the fight, or out of self-interest, as they also depend on the health of the social networks in question. In such a society, self-interest, community interests, and ideals enjoy a greater confluence than in our own society.

In larger areas or more diverse populations, in which a commonly held cultural ethos and spontaneous conflict resolution may not suffice to protect against serious conflicts, multiple societies can create intentional federations or peace pacts. One example of an anti-authoritarian peace pact with greater longevity than most treaties between states is the confederation enacted among the Haudennosaunne, often referred to as the Iroquois League. The Haudennosaunne are comprised of five nations that all speak similar languages, in the northeastern part of the territory appropriated by the United States and the southern parts of what are now considered to be the Canadian provinces of Ontario and Quebec.

The confederation was formed around August 31, 1142.[122] It covered a geographically huge area, considering that the only options for transportation were by canoe and on foot. The

---

122 Haudennosaunne oral traditions always maintained this early date, but racist white anthropologists discounted this claim and estimated the league began in the 1500s. Some even hypothesized that the Five Nations constitution was written with European help. But recent archaeological evidence and the record of a coinciding solar eclipse backed up the oral histories, proving that the federation was their own invention. Wikipedia, "The Iroquois League," http://en.wikipedia.org/wiki/Iroquois_League Viewed 22 June 2007

Haudennosaunne were sedentary agriculturalists who lived with the highest population densities, averaging 200 people per acre, of any inhabitants of the Northeast until the 19th century.123 Communal farming lands surrounded walled towns. The five nations involved—Seneca, Cayuga, Onondaga, Oneida, and Mohawk—had a long history of infighting, including wars spurred by competition for resources. The confederation was hugely successful in ending this. By all accounts the five nations—and later a sixth, the Tuscarora, who fled English colonization of the Carolinas—lived in peace for over five hundred years, even throughout the genocidal European expansion and trading of guns and alcohol for animal pelts that caused so many other nations to split or war with their neighbors. The confederation finally fractured—only temporarily—during the American revolution, due to differing strategies about which side to support to mitigate the effects of colonization.

The communal economic life of the five nations played an important role in their ability to live in peace; a metaphor often used for the federation was bringing everyone to live together in the same longhouse and eat from the same bowl. All the groups of the federation sent delegates to meet together and provide a structure for communication, conflict resolution, and discussing relationships with neighboring societies. Decisions were made using consensus, subject to approval by the entire society.

The anarcho-syndicalist movement originating in Europe has a history of creating international federations to share information and coordinate struggles against capitalism. These federations could be a direct precedent to global structures that facilitate living in peace and preventing warfare. The International Workers Association (IWA, or AIT in Spanish) contains anarcho-syndicalist unions from about 15 countries on 4 continents, and it periodically holds international congresses, each time in a different country. The IWA was formed in 1922, and initially contained

---

123 Stephen Arthur, "Where License Reigns With All Impunity:" An Anarchist Study of the Rotinonshón:ni Polity," *Northeastern Anarchist* No. 12, Winter 2007 http://nefac.net/anarchiststudyofiroquois#greatpeace

millions of members. Although nearly all of its member unions were forced underground or into exile during World War II, it has since regenerated and continues to meet.

Networks not borders

As nation-states evolved in Europe over several hundred years, governments worked hard to fabricate a sense of community on the basis of shared language, shared culture, and shared history, all of which were conflated with shared government. This fictive community serves to foster identification with and thus allegiance to the central authorities, to obscure the conflict of interests between lower classes and the elite by framing them as being on the same team, and to confuse the good fortune or glory of the rulers with a good fortune shared by all; it also makes it easier for poor people in one country to kill poor people in another country by creating psychological distance between them.

On inspection, this notion that nation-states are based on shared culture and history is a fraud. For example, Spain created itself by expelling the Arabs and the Jews. Even apart from this, without the central gravity produced by the state, Spain would not exist. There isn't a single Spanish language, but at least five: Catalan, Euskera, Gallego, Castillian, and the dialect of Arabic developed in Morocco and Andalucia. If any of these languages were subject to careful scrutiny, more fractures would appear. The Valencians might say, not without reason, that their language is not the same as Catalan, but if you put the seat of government in Barcelona you would get the same suppression of Valenciano that the Spanish government employed against Catalan.

Without the enforced homogenization of nation-stations, there would be even more variety, as languages and cultures evolve and blend with each other. Borders hinder this cultural diffusion, and thus promote conflict by formalizing similarities and differences. Borders don't protect people; they are a means by which governments protect their assets, which include us. When the borders shift in a war, the victorious state has advanced, staking its claim to new territory, new resources, and new subjects. We are plunder—potential cannon fodder, taxpayers, and laborers—and borders are the walls of our prison.

Even without borders, there may occasionally be clear differences in the ways societies organize—for example, one may attempt to conquer a neighbor or maintain the oppression of women. But decentralized, borderless societies can still defend themselves from aggression. A community with a clear sense of its autonomy does not need to see an invader cross an imaginary line in order to notice aggression. People fighting for their freedom and their own homes fight fiercely and are capable of organizing spontaneously. If there were no governments to fund military complexes, those fighting defensive campaigns would usually enjoy the advantage, so it wouldn't pay to go on the offensive. When European states conquered the rest of the world, they enjoyed certain decisive advantages, including unprecedented population density and technologies their victims had never seen before. These advantages existed at a certain historical moment, and they are no longer pertinent. Communication is now global, population density and resistance to disease are more evenly distributed, and the popular weapons necessary for waging effective defensive warfare against the most technologically advanced of armies—assault rifles and explosives—are available in most parts of the world and can be manufactured at home. In a future without government, aggressive societies would be disadvantaged.

Anarchists are breaking down borders today by creating worldwide networks, undermining nationalism, and fighting in solidarity with immigrants who are upsetting the homogeneity of nation-states. People on the borders can help abolish them by aiding illegal border crossings or supporting people who cross illegally, learning the language spoken on the other side, and building communities that span the border. People farther inland can assist by ending their allegiance to centralized, homogenized culture and developing local culture, by welcoming migrants into their communities, and by spreading awareness and acting in solidarity with struggles in other parts of the world.

Recommended Reading:

- Harold Barclay, *People Without Government: An Anthropology of Anarchy*, London: Kahn and Averill, 1982.
- Starhawk, *The Fifth Sacred Thing*. New York, Bantam, 1993.
- Stephen Arthur, " "Where License Reigns With All Impunity:" An Anarchist Study of the Rotinonshón:ni Polity," *Northeastern Anarchist* No. 12, Winter 2007 http://nefac.net/anarchiststudyofiroquois#greatpeace

8. THE FUTURE

WE ARE FIGHTING FOR OUR OWN LIVES, BUT ALSO FOR A WORLD we might never get to see.

Won't the state just reemerge over time?

MOST OF THE EXAMPLES CITED IN THIS BOOK NO LONGER EXIST, and some only lasted a few years. The stateless societies and social experiments were mostly conquered by imperialist powers or repressed by states. But history has also shown that revolution is possible, and that revolutionary struggle does not inevitably lead to authoritarianism. Authoritarian revolutionary ideas such as social democracy or Marxist-Leninism have been discredited the world over. While socialist political parties continue to be parasites sucking at the vital energies of social movements, predictably selling out their constituencies every time they come to power, a diverse mix of horizontalism, indigenism, autonomism, and anarchism have come to the foreground in all the exciting social rebellions of the last decade—the popular uprisings in Algeria, Argentina, Bolivia, and Mexico, the autonomen in Italy, Germany, and Denmark, the students and insurgents in Greece, the farmers' struggle in Korea, and the antiglobalization movement that united countries around

259

the world. These movements have a chance of abolishing the state and capitalism amidst the crises of the coming years.

But some people fear that even if a global revolution did abolish the state and capitalism, these would inevitably reemerge over time. This is understandable, because statist education has indoctrinated us to believe the myths of progress and unilineal history—the idea that there is only one global narrative and it led inexorably to the ascendancy of Western civilization. In fact, no one knows exactly how the state developed, but it is certain that it was neither an inevitable nor irreversible process. Most societies never voluntarily developed states, and perhaps as many societies developed states and then abandoned them as have kept them. From the perspective of these societies, the state may appear to be a choice or an imposition rather than a natural development. The timeline we use also affects our perspective. For tens of thousands of years humanity had no use for states, and after there are no more states it will be clear that they were an aberration originating in a few parts of the world that temporarily controlled the destiny of everyone on the planet before being cast off again.

Another misconception is that stateless societies are vulnerable to being hijacked by aggressive alpha males who appoint themselves leaders. On the contrary, it seems that the "Big Man" model of a society has never led to a state or even to a chiefdom. Societies that do allow a bossy, more talented or stronger man to have more influence typically ignore him or kill him if he becomes too authoritarian, and the Big Man is unable to extend his influence very far, geographically or temporally. The physical characteristics on which his leadership is based are ephemeral, and he soon fades out or is replaced.[124]

It seems that states developed gradually out of culturally accepted kinship systems that coupled gerontocracy with patriarchy—over a period of generations, older men were accorded more respect and given greater exclusivity as the mediators of disputes

---

124 See, for example, Dmitri M. Bondarenko and Andrey V. Korotayev, *Civilizational Models of Politogenesis*, Moscow: Russian Academy of Sciences, 2000.

and the dispensers of gifts. Not until very late in this process did they possess anything resembling a power to enforce their will. We must remember that as people gradually surrendered more of their responsibilities and afforded certain members of the community more respect, they had no way of knowing the outcomes of their actions—no way of knowing just how bad hierarchical society could become. Once social elites obtained coercive powers, a new dialectic of social development emerged, and at this point the creation of the state was likely, though still not inevitable because the majority remained a social force with the power to dispossess the elite or stop the process.

Modern societies with the collective memory of bureaucratic techniques could redevelop a state much more quickly, but we have the advantage of knowing where that path leads and being aware of the warning signs. After having fought hard to win their freedom people would have plenty of motivation to stop the reemergence of the state if it were occurring anywhere near them.

Fortunately, an anarchist society is its own reward. Many stateless societies, after colonial contact, have had the opportunity to join a hierarchical society and yet continue to resist, such as !Kung who continue to live in the Kalihari desert despite the efforts of the Botswana government to "settle" them.

There are also examples of long-lasting anti-authoritarian social experiments that thrive within statist society. In Gloucestershire, England, Tolstoyan anarchists founded the Whiteway Colony on 40 acres of land in 1898. After they bought the land, they burned the property deed on the end of a pitchfork. Accordingly, they had to build all their houses themselves since they could not obtain mortgages. Over a hundred years later, this pacifist-anarchist commune still exists, and some of the current inhabitants are descendants of the founders. They make decisions in a general assembly and share a number of communal facilities. At times, Whiteway has housed refugees and conscientious objectors. It has also housed a number of cooperative ventures such as a bakery and a handicrafts guild. Despite the external pressures of capitalism and the hierarchical relationships reproduced by statist society, Whiteway remains egalitarian and anti-authoritarian.

Across the North Sea, in Appelscha, Friesland, an anarchist camp celebrated its 75th year in 2008. Currently composed of caravans, campers, and a few permanent buildings, the Appelscha site has been active in the anarchist and anti-militarist movements since the priest Domela Nieuwenhuis left the church and began preaching atheism and anarchism. A group of workers began gathering there and soon acquired land, on which they have held yearly anarchist gatherings every Pentecost. Hearkening back to the socialist temperance movement, which recognized alcohol as a crippling plague on workers and a form of bondage to employers who sold liquor from company stores, the camp is still alcohol free. In 2008, 500 people from all over the Netherlands as well as Germany and Belgium attended the yearly anarchist gathering at Appelscha. They joined the anarchists who live there year-round for a weekend of workshops and discussions on subjects including pacifism, animal liberation, the anti-fascist struggle, sexism within the movement, mental health, and the campaign that kept the Olympics out of Amsterdam in 1992. There were children's programs, presentations on the long history of the camp, communal meals, and enough enthusiasm in the air to promise another generation of anarchism in the region.

Other anarchist projects can also survive a hundred years. Specific societies, communities, and organizations need not be set in stone—anarchists do not need to enact restrictive measures to preserve institutions at the expense of their participants. Sometimes the best thing a community or organization can do for its participants is permit them to move on. There are no hereditary privileges or Constitutions that must be handed down or imposed on the future. In allowing more fluidity and change, anarchist societies can last much longer.

The majority of societies throughout human history have been communal and stateless, and many of them lasted for millennia until they were destroyed or conquered by Western civilization. The growth and power of Western civilization were not inevitable but rather the result of specific historic processes arguably dependent on geographic coincidence.[125] The military successes of our civilization

---

125 The argument that certain societies were able to take over the world

might seem to prove its superiority, but even in the absence of resistance, problems endemic to our civilization such as deforestation and climate change may well bring about its demise, revealing it to be an utter failure in terms of sustainability. Other examples of unsustainable hierarchical societies, from Sumer to Easter Island, show how swiftly a society apparently at its pinnacle can collapse.

The idea that the state will inevitably reemerge over time is another of these hopelessly eurocentric fantasies in which Western culture indoctrinates people. Dozens of indigenous societies around the world never developed states, they thrived for thousands of years, they have never surrendered, and when they finally triumph against colonialism they will cast off the impositions of white culture, which includes the state and capitalism, and revitalize their traditional cultures, which they still carry with them. Many indigenous groups have experience going back hundreds or even thousands of years of contact with the state, and at no point have they voluntarily surrendered to state authority. Western anarchists have much to learn from this persistence, and all people from Western society should take the hint: the state is not an inevitable adaptation, it is an imposition, and once we learn how to defeat it for good, we will not let it come back.

What about other problems we can't foresee?

ANARCHIST SOCIETIES WILL FACE PROBLEMS WE CANNOT POSSIBLY forsee now, just as they will encounter difficulties we might predict but be unable to solve without the historical laboratory revolution provides. But one of the many errors of the state is the neurotic supposition that society is perfectible, that it is possible to craft blueprints that provide for all problems before they occur. Favoring laws over case-by-case evaluation and common sense, maintaining a standing army, granting the police emergency powers on a permanent basis— all these stem from the paranoia of statism.

---

because of geographic conditions rather than any inherent superiority is skillfully presented by Jared Diamond in *Guns, Germs, and Steel: The Fates of Human Societies*. New York: W.W. Norton, 1997.

We cannot tie down the contingencies of life in a blueprint, nor should we. In an anarchist society, we would have to invent entirely new solutions for wholly unpredictable problems. Should we earn the opportunity, we will do so with joy, getting our hands dirty in the complexities of life, realizing our vast potential and reaching new levels of growth and maturity. We need never again surrender the power to solve our own problems in cooperation with those around us.

Making anarchy work

THERE ARE A MILLION WAYS TO GO ABOUT ATTACKING THE INTERconnected structures of power and oppression, and creating anarchy. Only you can decide which paths to take. It's important not to let your efforts be diverted into any of the channels that are built into the system to recuperate and neutralize resistance, such as requesting change from a political party rather than creating it yourself, or allowing your efforts and creations to become commodities, products, or fashions. To free ourselves, we need to regain control over every aspect of our lives: our culture, our entertainment, our relationships, our housing and education and healthcare, the way we protect our communities and produce food—everything. Without getting isolated in single-issue campaigns, figure out where your own passions and skills lie, what problems concern you and your community, and what you can do yourself. At the same time, stay abreast of what others are doing, so you can build mutually inspiring relationships of solidarity.

There may already be anti-authoritarian groups active in your area. You could also start your own group; one great thing about being an anarchist is you don't need permission. If there's no one you could possibly work with, perhaps you could be the next Robin Hood—that position has been vacant far too long! Or if that's too tall an order, start smaller with something like writing graffiti, putting up stickers and posters, distributing literature, or running a small DIY project until you've built up experience and confidence in your own abilities and met other people who want to work alongside you.

Anarchy thrives in the struggle against domination, and wherever oppression exists, resistance exists also. These struggles do not need to call themselves anarchist to be breeding grounds for subversion and freedom. What is important is that we support them and make them stronger. Capitalism and the state will not be destroyed if we consign ourselves to creating wonderful alternatives. Once upon a time the world was full of wonderful alternatives and the system knows quite well how to conquer and destroy these. Whatever we create, we must be prepared to defend.

No one book is enough to explore all the possibilities of anarchist revolution. Here are several others you might find helpful.

Recommended Reading

- CrimethInc., *Recipes for Disaster: An Anarchist Cookbook*, Olympia: CrimethInc. Workers' Collective, 2005; and
- *Expect Resistance*, Salem: CrimethInc. Workers' Collective 2008.
- Kuwasi Balagoon, *A Soldier's Story: Writings by a Revolutionary New Afrikan Anarchist*, Montreal: Kersplebedeb, 2001.
- Ann Hansen, *Direct Action: Memoirs of an Urban Guerrilla*, Toronto: Between the Lines, 2002.
- Lorenzo Komboa Ervin, *Anarchism and the Black Revolution*, 2nd edition online at Infoshop.org, 1993.
- Emma Goldman, *Living My Life*, New York: Knopf, 1931.
- Richard Kempton, *Provo: Amsterdam's Anarchist Revolt*, Brooklyn: Autonomedia, 2007.
- Bommi Baumann (trans. Helene Ellenbogen & Wayne Parker), *How It All Began: A Personal Account of a West German Urban Guerrilla*, Vancouver: Pulp Press, 1977.
- Trapese Collective, ed. *Do It Yourself: a handbook for changing our world*, London: Pluto Press, 2007.
- Roxanne Dunbar Ortiz, *Outlaw Woman: A Memoir of*

the War Years 1960–1975, San Francisco: City Lights, 2001.
- A.G. Schwarz and Void Network, *We Are an Image from the Future: The Greek Uprising of December 2008*, Oakland: AK Press 2009.
- Isy Morgenmuffel and Paul Sharkey (eds.), *Beating Fascism: Anarchist anti-fascism in theory and practice*, London: Kate Sharpley Library, 2005.
- *Call* (*Appel* in the original French, an anonymous manifesto with no publication information given)
- The article, or zine, or book that you are going to write, to share your experiences with the world and expand our collective toolbox...

IT WORKS WHEN WE MAKE IT WORK

THE MANY PEOPLE WHO CONSPIRED TO COMMIT THESE REBEL STOries to paper and get them into your hands have been thoughtful enough to provide you with one parting example of anarchy: the book itself. Imagine the decentralized network, the harmonious chaos, the confluence of liberated desires, that made it possible. With passion and determination millions of people breathed life into the stories we present, and many of them struggled even past the point of certain defeat in the hopes their utopias might inspire future generations. Hundreds of others documented these worlds and kept them alive in our minds. A dozen more came together to edit, design, and illustrate the book, and even more collaborated to proofread, print, and distribute it. We have no bosses, nor are we getting paid to do this. Our goal in distributing it is not to make money, but *to share it with you.*

Publishing is an enterprise we were supposed to leave to the professionals, and books were something we were supposed to buy and consume, not to make ourselves. But we forged ourselves the permission slip to pursue this project, and we hope to show that you can too. It can be tempting to present such ambitious projects as magically final products, leaving the reader to guess how we did it and reveling in the illusion ourselves; however sometimes it's better to let an inopportune gust of wind blow in, sweep up the curtains, and reveal the machinations backstage. This book, then, proves to be no different from all the other examples illuminated herein, in that its creation was also a matter of constructive conflict. The collection of people immediately responsible for publishing it is not a homogeneous circle, but rather includes editorial groups with distinct modes of operation, and a primary author for whom writing is an individual activity. Because of differing needs and opinions, some people could not see this project through to its end, but as anarchists they were free to leave the group when it was in their interests, and they had already affected the manuscript in good ways. Meanwhile, thanks to a flexibility of organization, the project could go forward.

As the individualist in this group, I learned and developed in ways I would not have had I been working in an authoritarian group. With a traditional publisher, I would be forced to concede whenever a disagreement arose, not because I had been convinced of their point of view but because they controlled more resources and could determine whether the book would make it to print or not. But with our horizontal arrangement, I could receive criticism that I knew was intended to develop the book to its outermost potential, rather than just to make it sell better in a dumbed-down market.

Granted, publishing a book is not the most amazing achievement, and this wee paper thing certainly isn't about to storm the Winter Palace, feisty as it is, but one of our most basic points is that anarchy is much more commonplace than we've been led to believe. And hell, if we can make it work, so can you.

Also like the other stories we've told here, the story of our storytelling contains its own weaknesses. We'd like to be the first to point them out. Unavoidably, a couple things are missing. One is a matter of realism. While making this book we've tried not to romanticize the examples, though clearly these pages do not provide the space for a full analysis of the strengths and weaknesses of each cited revolution or social experiment. However we wanted to give some indication of the abundance of complexities and difficulties lurking beneath the surface of every example of anarchy. But if the book is at all successful, if you readers do not simply say, *Oh, that's nice, anarchy is possible*, and then go back to your lives, but instead you actually arm yourselves with this knowledge to plunge into the creation of an anarchist world, you will quickly discover for yourselves how difficult it is.

The truth is, sometimes anarchy doesn't work. Sometimes people don't learn how to cooperate, or a certain group never finds a way to share responsibilities, or infighting leaves an entire movement flat-footed and unable to survive the grave pressures of the world around it. Even some of the examples described in this book eventually fell apart due to their own internal failings. In other cases a liberated community will be brutally repressed, a squatted social center creating a bubble of freedom from state and capital will be kicked out by the landlord, or the state will find some excuse to lock you up for participating in the struggle to create a new world.

Many people who fought for anarchy ended up dead and defeated, or simply demoralized. And their sacrifices will not be celebrated unless we write that history ourselves, to learn from their failures and be inspired by what they won.

Another failing of this book is that we have not been able to romanticize these examples enough. I'm afraid our meekly attempted objectivity omits how inspiring it *feels* to put anarchy into practice, despite all the difficulties. The stories here are real, on a level deeper than the footnotes, the chronicle of dates and names, can express. Some of these stories I have lived myself, and they are wrapped up in the very writing of the book. The tedious satisfaction of organizing infoshops and learning how to use consensus, in defiance of the stifling psychological terrain of the United States, was my inspiration for starting a book about what an anarchist world would actually look like. Though I still haven't finished that project, it led me to research what anarchy *already had looked like.* On a park bench in Berlin, taking a break from studying the autonomous movement of that city, I sketched an outline for this new book, and a couple weeks later, in Christiania, I saw how an entire neighborhood living in anarchy seems perfectly ordinary.

It occurred to me that I might encounter many more living histories if I looked. Over the next year I went to a seventy-five-year-old anarchist camp in the Netherlands, and waded into a continuity of struggle in which the past does not imprison the present, but fertilizes it. I stood in provincial Ukrainian towns that once overthrew authority and tried to imagine how they looked, I gardened in an anarchist village in the mountains of Italy and felt down to my very bones what the abolition of work means. As I traveled I corresponded with one of my best friends as he went off to Oaxaca for six months and participated in the rebellion there.

Appropriately enough, I finished my writing in a squat in Barcelona, where I was stuck awaiting trial and threatened with prison time after a police frame-up. The park down the street used to be the city jail, but the anarchists tore it down in 1936. In 2007 our social center took it over in protest of our impending eviction, setting up a free store, putting out a selection of books from our library, telling stories to the children. Unexpectedly illegalized, I found my survival tied up with the network of liberated spaces throughout the city, that housed and nourished me. And these spaces, in turn, depended on all of us fighting to create and defend them.

The same is true of all the other histories we've seen: none of them owe their existence to spectators. These stories show that anarchy *can* work. But we have to build it ourselves. The courage and confidence we need to do this cannot be found in any book. They already belong to us. We only have to claim them.

May these stories jump off their pages and into your hearts, and find new life.

Peter Gelderloos
Barcelona, December 2008

Bibliography

Emily Achtenberg, "Community Organizing and Rebellion: Neighborhood Councils in El Alto, Bolivia," *Progressive Planning*, No. 172, Summer 2007.

Ackelsberg, Martha A., *Free Women of Spain: Anarchism and the Struggle for the Emancipation of Women,* Bloomington, IN: Indiana University Press, 1991.

William M. Adams and David M. Anderson, "Irrigation Before Development: Indigenous and Induced Change in Agricultural Water Management in East Africa," *African Affairs*, 1998.

AFL-CIO "Facts About Worker Safety and Health 2007." http://www.aflcio.org/issues/safety/memorial/upload/wmd_safetyfacts.pdf [viewed January 19, 2008]

Gemma Aguilar, "Els Okupes Fan la Feina que Oblida el Districte," *Avui*, Saturday, December 15, 2007.

Michael Albert, *Parecon: Life After Capitalism,* New York: Verso, 2003

Michael Albert, "Argentine Self Management," *ZNet*, November 3, 2005.

Anyonymous, "Longo Maï," *Buiten de Orde,* Summer 2008.

Anonymous, "Pirate Utopias," *Do or Die,* No. 8, 1999.

Anonymous, "The 'Oka Crisis' " Decentralized publication and distribution, no date or other publishing information included.

Anonymous, *"You Cannot Kill Us, We Are Already Dead." Algeria's Ongoing Popular Uprising,* St. Louis: One Thousand Emotions, 2006.

Stephen Arthur, "'Where License Reigns With All Impunity:' An Anarchist Study of the Rotinonshón:ni Polity," *Northeastern Anarchist*, No.12, Winter 2007.

Paul Avrich, *The Russian Anarchists*, Oakland: AK Press, 2005.

Paul Avrich, *The Modern School Movement: Anarchism and Education in the United States*, Oakland: AK Press, 2005.

Roland H. Bainton, "Thomas Müntzer, Revolutionary Firebrand of the Reformation." *The Sixteenth Century Journal* 13.2 (1982): 3–16

Jan Martin Bang, *Ecovillages: A Practical Guide to Sustainable Communities*. Edinburgh: Floris Books, 2005.

Harold Barclay, *People Without Government: An Anthropology of Anarchy*, London: Kahn and Averill, 1982.

David Barstow, "U.S. Rarely Seeks Charges for Deaths in Workplace," *New York Times*, December 22, 2003.

Eliezer Ben-Rafael, *Crisis and Transformation: The Kibbutz at Century's End*, Albany: State University of New York Press, 1997.

Jamie Bissonette, *When the Prisoners Ran Walpole: A True Story in the Movement for Prison Abolition*, Cambridge: South End Press, 2008.

Christopher Boehm, "Egalitarian Behavior and Reverse Dominance Hierarchy," *Current Anthropology*, Vol. 34, No. 3, June 1993.

Dmitri M. Bondarenko and Andrey V. Korotayev, *Civilizational Models of Politogenesis*, Moscow: Russian Academy of Sciences, 2000.

Franz Borkenau, *The Spanish Cockpit*, London: Faber and Faber, 1937.

Thomas A. Brady, Jr. & H.C. Erik Midelfort, *The Revolution of 1525: The German Peasants' War From a New Perspective*. Baltimore: The Johns Hopkins University Press, 1981.

Jeremy Brecher, *Strike!* Revised Edition. Boston: South End Press, 1997.

Stuart Christie, *We, the Anarchists! A study of the Iberian Anarchist Federation (FAI) 1927–1937*, Hastings, UK: The Meltzer Press, 2000.

CIPO-RFM website, "Our Story," http://www.nodo50.org/cipo/ourstory.htm [viewed November 6, 2006]

Eddie Conlon, *The Spanish Civil War: Anarchism in Action*, Workers' Solidarity Movement of Ireland, 2nd edition, 1993.

CrimethInc., "The Really Really Free Market: Instituting the Gift Economy," *Rolling Thunder*, No. 4, Spring 2007.

The Curious George Brigade, *Anarchy In the Age of Dinosaurs*, CrimethInc. 2003.

Diana Denham and C.A.S.A. Collective (eds.), *Teaching Rebellion: Stories from the Grassroots Mobilization in Oaxaca*, Oakland: PM Press, 2008.

Robert K. Dentan, *The Semai: A Nonviolent People of Malaya*. New York: Holt, Rinehart and Winston, 1979.

Jared Diamond, *Collapse: How Societies Choose to Fail or Succeed*, New York, Viking, 2005.

Dissent! Network "The VAAAG: A Collective Experience of

Self-Organization," http://www.daysofdissent.org.uk/evian.htm

Sam Dolgoff, *The Anarchist Collectives*, New York: Free Life Editions, 1974.

George R. Edison, MD, "The Drug Laws: Are They Effective and Safe?" *The Journal of the American Medial Association*. Vol. 239 No.24, June 16, 1978.

Martyn Everett, *War and Revolution: The Hungarian Anarchist Movement in World War I and the Budapest Commune (1919)*, London: Kate Sharpley Library, 2006.

Patrick Fleuret, "The Social Organization of Water Control in the Taita Hills, Kenya," *American Ethnologist*, Vol. 12, 1985.

Heather C. Flores, *Food Not Lawns: How To Turn Your Yard Into A Garden And Your Neighborhood Into A Community*, Chelsea Green, 2006.

The Freecycle Network, "About Freecycle," http://www.freecycle.org/ [viewed January 19 2008].

Peter Gelderloos, *Consensus: A New Handbook for Grassroots Social, Political, and Environmental Groups*, Tucson: See Sharp Press, 2006.

Peter Gelderloos and Patrick Lincoln, *World Behind Bars: The Expansion of the American Prison Sell*, Harrisonburg, Virginia: Signalfire Press, 2005.

Malcolm Gladwell, *The Tipping Point: How Little Things Can Make a Big Difference.* New York: Little, Brown, and Company, 2002.

Amy Goodman, "Louisiana Official: Federal Gov't Abandoned New Orleans," *Democracy Now!*, September 7, 2005.

Amy Goodman, "Lakota Indians Declare Sovereignty from US Government," *Democracy Now!*, December 26, 2007.

Natasha Gordon and Paul Chatterton, *Taking Back Control: A Journey through Argentina's Popular Uprising*, Leeds (UK): University of Leeds, 2004.

Uri Gordon, *Anarchy Alive! Anti-authoritarian Politics from Practice to Theory*, London: Pluto Press, 2008.

David Graeber, *Fragments of an Anarchist Anthropology*, Chicago: Prickly Paradigm Press, 2004.

David Graeber, "The Shock of Victory," *Rolling Thunder* no. 5, Spring 2008.

Evan Henshaw-Plath, "The People's Assemblies in Argentina," *ZNet*, March 8, 2002.

Neille Ilel, "A Healthy Dose of Anarchy: After Katrina, nontraditional, decentralized relief steps in where big government and big charity failed," *Reason Magazine*, December 2006.

Inter-Press Service, "Cuba: Rise of Urban Agriculture," February 13, 2005.

Interview with Marcello, "Criticisms of the MST," February 17, 2009, Barcelona.

Derrick Jensen, *A Language Older Than Words*, White River Junction, Vermont: Chelsea Green Publishing Company, 2000.

John Jordan and Jennifer Whitney, *Que Se Vayan Todos: Argentina's Popular Rebellion*, Montreal: Kersplebedeb, 2003.

Michael J. Jordan, "Sex Charges haunt UN forces," *Christian Science Monitor*, November 26, 2004.

George Katsiaficas, *The Subversion of Politics: European Autonomous Social Movements and the Decolonization of Everyday Life*. Oakland: AK Press, 2006.

George Katsiaficas, "Comparing the Paris Commune and the Kwangju Uprising," www.eroseffect.com [viewed May 8, 2008]

Lawrence H. Keeley, *War Before Civilization*. Oxford: Oxford University Press, 1996.

Roger M. Keesing, Andrew J. Strathern, *Cultural Anthropology: A Contemporary Perspective*, 3rd Edition, New York: Harcourt Brace & Company, 1998.

Graham Kemp and Douglas P. Fry (eds.), *Keeping the Peace: Conflict Resolution and Peaceful Societies around the World*, New York: Routledge, 2004.

Elli King, ed., *Listen: The Story of the People at Taku Wakan Tipi and the Reroute of Highway 55, or, The Minnehaha Free State*, Tucson, AZ: Feral Press, 1996.

Aaron Kinney, "Hurricane Horror Stories," Salon.com October 24, 2005.

Peter Kropotkin, *Fields, Factories and Workshops Tomorrow*, London: Freedom Press, 1974.

Wolfi Landstreicher, "Autonomous Self-Organization and Anarchist Intervention," *Anarchy: a Journal of Desire Armed*. No. 58 (Fall/Winter 2004–5), p. 56

Gaston Leval, *Collectives in the Spanish Revolution*, London: Freedom Press, 1975 (translated from the French by Vernon Richards).

A.W. MacLeod, *Recidivism: a Deficiency Disease*, Philadelphia:

University of Pennsylvania Press, 1965.

Alan MacSimoin, "The Korean Anarchist Movement," a talk in Dublin, September 1991.

Sam Mbah and I.E. Igariway, *African Anarchism: The History of a Movement,* Tucson: See Sharp Press, 1997.

The Middle East Media Research Institute, "Algerian Berber Dissidents Promote Programs for Secularism and Democracy in Algeria," Special Dispatch Series No. 1308, October 6, 2006.

George Mikes, *The Hungarian Revolution*, London: Andre Deutsch, 1957.

Cahal Milmo, "On the Barricades: Trouble in a Hippie Paradise," *The Independent,* May 31, 2007.

Bonnie Anna Nardi, "Modes of Explanation in Anthropological Population Theory: Biological Determinism vs. Self-Regulation in Studies of Population Growth in Third World Countries," *American Anthropologist,* vol. 83, 1981.

Nathaniel C. Nash, "Oil Companies Face Boycott Over Sinking of Rig," *The New York Times,* June 17, 1995.

Oscar Olivera, *Cochabamba! Water Rebellion in Bolivia,* Cambridge: South End Press, 2004.

George Orwell, *Homage to Catalonia,* London: Martin Secker & Warburg Ltd., 1938.

Oxfam America, "Havana's Green Revelation," http://www.oxfamamerica.org/whatwedo/where_we_work/camexca/news_publications/art6080.html [viewed December 5, 2005]

Philly's Pissed, http://www.phillyspissed.net/

Daryl M. Plunk, "South Korea's Kwangju Incident Revisited," *The Heritage Foundation*, No. 35, September 16, 1985.

Rappaport, R.A. (1968), *Pigs for the Ancestors: Ritual in the Ecology of a New Guinea People*. New Haven: Yale University Press.

RARA, *Revolutionaire Anti-Racistische Actie Communiqués van 1990–1993*. Gent: 2004.

Revolutionary Association of Women of Afghanistan "About RAWA," http://www.rawa.org/rawa.html Viewed June 22, 2007

James C. Scott, *Seeing Like a State: How Certain Schemes to Improve the Human Condition Have Failed*, New Haven: Yale University Press, 1998.

James C. Scott, "Civilizations Can't Climb Hills: A Political History of Statelessness in Southeast Asia," lecture at Brown University, Providence, Rhode Island, February 2, 2005.

Jaime Semprun, *Apología por la Insurrección Argelina*, Bilbao: Muturreko Burutazioak, 2002 (translated from French to Spanish by Javier Rodriguez Hidalgo).

Nirmal Sengupta, *Managing Common Property: Irrigation in India and The Philippines*, New Delhi: Sage, 1991.

Carmen Sirianni, "Workers Control in the Era of World War I: A Comparative Analysis of the European Experience," *Theory and Society*, Vol. 9, 1980.

Alexandre Skirda, *Nestor Makhno, Anarchy's Cossack: The Struggle for Free Soviets in the Ukraine 1917–1921*, London: AK Press, 2005.

Eric Alden Smith, Mark Wishnie, "Conservation and Subsistence in Small-Scale Societies," *Annual Review of Anthropology*, Vol. 29,

2000, pp. 493–524.

"Solidarity with the Communities of CIPO-RFM in Oaxaca," Presentation at the Montreal Anarchist Bookfair, Montreal, May 21, 2006.

Georges Sossenko, "Return to the Spanish Civil War," Presentation at the Montreal Anarchist Bookfair, Montreal, May 21, 2006.

Jac Smit, Annu Ratta and Joe Nasr, *Urban Agriculture: Food, Jobs and Sustainable Cities,* UNDP, Habitat II Series, 1996.

Melford E. Spiro, *Kibbutz: Venture in Utopia,* New York: Schocken Books, 1963.

"The Stonehenge Free Festivals, 1972–1985." http://www.ukrockfestivals.com/henge-menu.html [viewed May 8, 2008].

Dennis Sullivan and Larry Tifft, *Restorative Justice: Healing the Foundations of Our Everyday Lives,* Monsey, NY: Willow Tree Press, 2001.

Joy Thacker, *Whiteway Colony: The Social History of a Tolstoyan Community,* Whiteway, 1993.

Colin Turnbull, *The Mbuti Pygmies: Change and Adaptation.* Philadelphia: Harcourt Brace College Publishers, 1983.

Marcele Valente, "The Rise and Fall of the Great Bartering Network in Argentina." Inter-Press Service, November 6, 2002.

Judith Van Allen " 'Sitting On a Man': Colonialism and the Lost Political Institutions of Igbo Women." *Canadian Journal of African Studies*. Vol. ii, 1972. 211–219.

Johan M.G. van der Dennen, "Ritualized 'Primitive' Warfare and Rituals in War: Phenocopy, Homology, or...?"

H. Van Der Linden, "Een nieuwe overheidsinstelling: het waterschap circa 1100–1400" in D.P. Blok, *Algemene Geschiednis der Nederlanden, deel III.* Haarlem: Fibula van Dishoeck, 1982, pp. 60–76

Wikipedia, "Asamblea Popular de los Pueblos de Oaxaca," http://en.wikipedia.org/wiki/APPO [viewed November 6, 2006]

Wikipedia, "The Freecycle Network," http://en.wikipedia.org/wiki/Freecycle_Network [viewed January 19, 2008]

Wikipedia, "Gwangju massacre," http://en.wikipedia.org/wiki/Gwangju_massacre [viewed November 3, 2006]

Wikipedia, "The Iroquois League," http://en.wikipedia.org/wiki/Iroquois_League [viewed June 22, 2007]

William Foote Whyte and Kathleen King Whyte, *Making Mondragon: The Growth and Dynamics of the Worker Cooperative Complex*, Ithaca, New York: ILR Press, 1988.

Kristian Williams, *Our Enemies in Blue.* Brooklyn: Soft Skull Press, 2004.

Peter Lamborn Wilson, *Pirate Utopias,* Brooklyn: Autonomedia, 2003.

Daria Zelenova, "Anti-Eviction Struggle of the Squatters Communities in Contemporary South Africa," paper presented at the conference "Hierarchy and Power in the History of Civilizations," at the Russian Academy of Sciences, Moscow, June 2009.

Howard Zinn, *A People's History of the United States.* New York: Perrenial Classics Edition, 1999.